WOMEN EMPOWERMENT IN THE 21ST CENTURY

Editor-in chief

Dr. H. S. Cheema

Editors

Er. Sai Kiran Khanna **Prof. Seema Jha**

Himalaya Publishing House

MUMBAI • NEW DELHI • NAGPUR • BENGALURU • HYDERABAD • CHENNAI • PUNE • LUCKNOW • AHMEDABAD • ERNAKULAM • BHUBANESWAR • INDOR • KOLKATA

FIRST EDITION : 2011

Published by	: Mrs. Meena Pandey for **Himalaya Publishing House Pvt. Ltd.,** "Ramdoot", Dr. Bhalerao Marg, Girgaon, **Mumbai - 400 004.** Phone: 2386 01 70/2386 38 63, Fax: 022-2387 71 78 **Email: himpub@vsnl.com Website: www.himpub.com**
Branch Offices	
New Delhi	: "Pooja Apartments", 4-B, Murari Lal Street, Ansari Road, Darya Ganj, **New Delhi - 110 002.** Phone: 23270392, 23278631 Fax: 011-23256286
Nagpur	: Kundanlal Chandak Industrial Estate, Ghat Road, **Nagpur - 440 018.** Phone: 2738731, 3296733 Telefax : 0712-2721215
Bengaluru	: No. 16/1 (Old 12/1), 1st Floor, Next to Hotel Highlands, Madhava Nagar, Race Course Road, **Bengaluru - 560 001.** Phone : 22281541, 22385461, Telefax: 080-22286611
Hyderabad	: No. 3-4-184, Lingampally, Besides Raghavendra Swamy Matham, Kachiguda, **Hyderabad - 500 027.** Phone: 040-27560041, 27550139, Mobile: 09848130433
Chennai	: No. 85/50, Bazullah Road, T. Nagar, **Chennai - 600 017.** Phone: 044-28144004/28144005
Pune	: First Floor, "Laksha" Apartment, No. 527, Mehunpura, Shaniwarpeth (Near Prabhat Theatre), **Pune - 411 030.** Phone: 020-24496323/24496333
Lucknow	: Jai Baba Bhavan, Church Road, Near Manas Complex and Dr. Awasthi Clinic, Aliganj, **Lucknow - 226 024.** Phone: 0522-2339329, 4068914, Mobile: 9305302158, 9415349385, 9389593752
Ahmedabad	: 114, "SHAIL", 1st Floor, Opp. Madhu Sudan House, C.G.Road, Navrang Pura, **Ahmedabad– 380 009.** Phone: 079-26560126, Mobile: 09327324149,09314679413
Ernakulam	: 39/104 A, Lakshmi Apartment, Karikkamuri Cross Rd., Ernakulam, **Cochin – 622011**, Kerala. Phone: 0484-2378012, 2378016, Mob.: 09344199799
Bhubaneswar	: 5 Station Square, **Bhubaneswar (Orissa) - 751 001.** Mobile: 9861046007
Indore	: Kesardeep Avenue Extension, 73, Narayan Bagh, Flat No. 302, IIIrd Floor, Near Humpty Dumpty School, Narayan Bagh, **Indore 452 007 (M.P.)** Mobile: 09301386468
Kolkata	: 108/4, Beliaghata Main Road, Near ID Hospital, Opp. SBI Bank, **Kolkata** - 700 010, Mobile: 09910440956 .
Typeset by	: Athurva Graphics, Mumbai - 400 002.
Printed by	: Esquire Press, Mumbai.

FOREWORD

Women empowerment has been one of the most sensitive, critical and hotly debated issues for many centuries in the past and it rightly reminds us of the brave fight women have to put up against male-dominated society right from the post-vedic period to the modern times. Though much ground has been covered so far in regard to women's empowerment, still a lot remains to be done for women empowerment. I think **"Women Empowerment in the 21st century,"** ably edited by Dr. H. S. Cheema, the editor-in-chief, and his associate team is a fitting tribute to the epic struggle of women for their rights. I congratulate Dr. Cheema and his team of associate editors on bringing out this book on one of the most relevant topics today.

The book makes an interesting reading as it covers a kaleidoscopic range of current issues in the present context and it also refers to the position of women in the vedic period that treated women equally and respectfully to the subsequent deterioration in her position in the post-vedic period. Even today, in some segments of the world, women are suffering from age-old maladies. However, it is very comforting to see women surging ahead in every field of human activity. As a member of the same class, I feel legitimately proud about the women who have left an indelible imprint on human history for their invaluable contribution and even today many of them occupy very crucial position in different areas of our society.

The books such as the present one go a long way in creating awareness about the critical issues related to women's empowerment and their solutions. The scholarly essays refer to the role of women right from the vedic period to the modern times. Part A covers the challenging role of Indian women from vedic to modern times and make us aware of her changing position throughout this period. In the present context, Self Help Groups have been playing a very constructive role in the empowerment of women, especially women from the underprivileged class of the society. It presents a comprehensive picture of women's role in SHG. The most interesting part of the book is 'Women and Corporate Era' as this period has metamorphosed women into a great force to reckon with and as a result, we see a band of able women such as Indira Nooyi, Chanda Cohar, Kiran Bedi and host of others ruling the world. This part takes into account different aspects of the women's role, her position and challenges she faces in the corporate era of today. And the last section of the book is justifying the main purpose of the book, i.e., women empowerment through case studies and it is amazing to know how women in the different parts of our country are trying to uplift themselves through various schemes and measures.

I wish this thought-provoking book all the success and its relevance in the present scenario is ably justified by the scholarly essay.

Mrs. Swati Salunkhe
Managing Director
Growth Centre (i) Pvt. Ltd.

PREFACE

Of all the sections of the society, it's women who have undergone a lot of humiliation and degradation in a male-dominated society but despite this fact, it's soothing to know that they have been successful, to some extent, in eradicating the discriminative treatment through the epic battle they have fought for ages for their rights to prove to the world that they are equal to their male counterparts in every respect. It's exactly for this reason I am feeling an immense amount of pride and pleasure in presenting the first edition of the book *'Women Empowerment in the 21st Century.'*

This present collection of scholarly essays on women empowerment covers a wide spectrum of issues related to the position of women right, from the vedic period to the present-day women who are rapidly making their marks in all the fields of our society. The introduction part of the book looks at the issue of women empowerment and its progress in the 21st century as well as the pivotal role of education is playing in the empowerment of women. The part A of this books makes a very interesting reading as this part aptly shows the enviable position of women during the vedic period where she commanded great respect in the society of that time and the following deterioration in her position in the post-vedic period and the following ages is really very disturbing. As we pass through this part, we see how women brought a change in their position through their patient struggle for their rights. Parts B and C deal with the most current and critical issues in our times. All this progress women have achieved so far has made inroads into the lives of many underprivileged women who are still leading miserable lives throughout the world and so the movement of the Self Help Groups is also playing a very crucial role in the empowerment of women in our country in particular and in some parts of the world in general. All these scholarly essays discuss the different aspects of this important movement.

In the present era of globalisation, women are playing a very constructive role in the corporate world. Some of them are occupying key positions and are respected the world over for their valuable contribution. So, the role of women in the corporate era becomes one of the most relevant aspects of this book. It deals with their role, the challenges and problems they face while working in the new scenario. Part D of the book is a very apt concluding part as it appropriately deals with case studies in the present era of women empowerment and one can derive great comfort from the fact women are gradually acquiring empowerment though various measures in the different parts of our country. The sample studies show that women in other parts of the country must also be gradually emerging out of the age-old shackles of male dominance and the whole journey is praiseworthy.

Dr. H.S.Cheema
Director
Institute for Future Education Entrepreneurship and Leadership
Karla, Lonavala

CONTENTS

Introduction

1 Introduction : Women Enpowerment in the 21st CENTURY"

India's economy has undergone a substantial transformation since the country's independence in 1947. Today India's economy is the third largest in the world, in terms of purchasing power, which is going to touch new heights in the coming years. As predicted by Goldman Sachs, the global investment bank, by 2035 India would be the third largest economy of the world just after the US and China, it will grow to 60 percent of size of the US economy.

However, the 21st century has begun with new challenges, the world today is witnessing economic integration and India is not an exception to the general trend in the so called global village, women world over are increasingly becoming the driving force of many economies including India. PTI reports that three Indian's – Congress President Sonia Gandhi, ICICI Bank head Chanda Kochhar and PepsiCo chief executive Indra Nooyi – have been named among Asia'a top power women by American broadcaster CNN. PTI further reports that Kathryn Bigelow became the first woman in the 82 history of the Academy Awards to win the best director Oscar as her gritty Iraq War movie The Hurt Locker.

As rightly said by Pandit Jawaharlal Nehru "In order to awaken the people, it is the woman who has to be awakened. Once she is on the move, the household moves, the villages moves, the country moves and thus we build the India of tomorrow". Women are an integral part of human society, in the Vedic period, women had some status and rights, it tells us that women held an important place in ancient culture but this status and rights were devalued in smrithik period.

India's commitment to the objective of economic growth with social justice can be fulfilled only if women are brought in to the mainstream of economic activity through a favorable atmosphere in the socio-economic environment in the country. In most of the developing countries today, more and more emphasis is laid on the need for development of women and their active participation in the main stream of development process.

One of the biggest indicators of society's progress is the empowerment of women, and although women are still treated as a sub-species in most of the country. There is no doubt that India is in the midst of a great revolution in the history of women. The evidence is everywhere; the voice of women is increasingly heard in parliament, courts and in streets. One of the significant developments in the recent times in India is the initiative taken in development of entrepreneurship process among women. Empowerment of any section of society is a myth until they are conferred equality before law.

Let's understand What's Empowerment? Empowerment is the process which enables one to gain authority, power, knowledge, skills and attitude needed to cope with the changing world and the circumstances in which one lives. In short, women empowerment is the ability of the women to exercise full control over one's actions. Hence, developing the culture of women entrepreneurship in India is essential. The status of women has undergone a sea change in the past two decades from a mere home maker to multi-tasker.

However, there are several issues in this endeavor which are to be addressed, like at the corporate level she is a victim of the harsh effects of glass ceiling, pay inequity and discriminatory practices, and at personal levels, she faces the orthodox beliefs and rigid stereotype perception of the society. The different perspective of women empowerment should be brought to light through a process of meaningful discussion and debate. With this objective in view Excelssior Education Society's had conducted Two days Seminar on "Challenges to Women Empowerment in the 21st Century" on 22nd & 23rd January'2010.

OBJECTIVES OF THE SEMINAR

(1) To discuss the challenges to Women in the 21st Century

(2) To highlight the harsh tribulation and trial undergone by women since time immemorial.

(3) To reveal various domains which need comprehensive study and open new areas of research?

(4) To address the theme from multidisciplinary perspective.

TECHNICAL PAPERS

The efforts were made to invite technical papers / research papers from colleges / practitioners / research institutions. We have received papers on different aspects of women empowerment in India, The papers included in these proceedings and presented at the conference address the theme from multidisciplinary perspective. We are pleased to accomplish our goal by bringing together a community of researchers and practitioners from different parts of the country to share their research findings and thoughts. The papers presented in the seminar are the views of the respective authors.

ISSUES DEBATED

The panel discussions were held on the second day and important and relevant issues have been taken up for discussion. The experts from the industry and academia and the authors of the papers had a constructive discussion and answered the questions addressed.

The complex issues like discriminatory practices, glass ceilings, legal hurdles in growth and development of women, and the challenges to women empowerment in the 21st century and so on have been debated. The panelists and the observers in the seminar intervened in the discussion and offered valuable comments on the issues.

In the present stage of economic development, the issues identified for detailed discussion need urgent focus of planners/ policy makers, academicians, education institutions to make concentrated efforts on the task of developing entrepreneurship culture among women. The book is divided into four parts as follows:-

PART A Role of Women – Vedic to Modern times

PART B Self Help Group – Woman Empowerment

PART C Women and Corporate Era

PART D Case Study

The broad consensus and concluding observations of the debate on the challenges to women in the 21st century are as under:-

(1) To eliminate prevailing erroneous and cultural assumptions and practices that lead to inhuman treatment of women, one needs a general plan of action for both governmental and civil social institutions.

(2) To increase the sustainability of benefits of Self Help Group to the society the mechanism of NGOs and Government policy should be appropriate to support function.

(3) Though the intuition of the individual is important, yet motivation through communication and leadership skills should be given more importance for real empowerment.

(4) To gain a competitive edge, corporate should successfully address theses challenges and tackle the issues of diversity to attract and retain talented women professionals.

☆ ☆ ☆

2 The Role of Education in the Empowerment of Women

ABSTRACT

Developed and developing countries alike have recognized the importance of girls' education, the worldwide surge in girls' primary school enrolment over the past two decades is testament to their commitment. The growth in girls' schooling also coincides with the global trend toward mass education that took off after the end of World War II and accelerated in the postcolonial period. Over the past 60 years, most countries have adopted mass education and have accelerated school expansion to accommodate the growing demand for education. Particular attention has been given to girls' schooling, not only because of its importance in reaching universal education but also because of its demonstrated social benefits.

India's recent economic growth rates have generated much optimism about its general social and economic development. But has there been accompanying progress in indicators of girl's educational outcomes even when all the resources are provided?

In an exhaustive survey, this paper tries to unearth the status of women, attitude towards girls? education in society, problems hindering the education of women, the importance of marriage in women's life affecting education as well as the empowerment of women for harassment. The article also highlights that educated and economically empowered women have said a firm "no? to the prevalent malice of the dowry, thus directly bearing the fruit of economic empowerment in society. Finally some recommendations have been made to eradicate the practice of intra-household and social discrimination of girl child and women.

Key Words: Social change, rural education, caste discrimination, dowry

INTRODUCTION

The empowerment of women in India has been obstructed for centuries owing to various reasons amongst which the initial blow was in the form of depriving women from basic educational facilities. Beginning with the Rig Vedic period (Singh, 2004) Indian women were denied political powers. The denial of many basic rights continued to plunge downward during the later Vedic period, with further plummeting through forthcoming centuries. During the eighteenth century women suffered from several handicaps like female infanticide, sati, purdah, child marriage, illiteracy and subsequently forced child widowhood in the19th century. Women were treated no better than domestic animals. Moved by this extreme plight, great social reformers like Raja Rammohan Roy, Iswarchandra Vidyasagar, Sri Ramakrishna Paramhansa, Swami Vivekananda, Swami Dayananda Saraswati, M.G. Ranade, D.K.Karve and Mahatma Gandhi were in the forefront, fighting against social atrocities toward women (Jha and Pujari, 1998).

Women discovered their own potential and played an equal part in India?s struggle for freedom (Barua, 2003). Many women came to be accepted as great patriots in their own rights. The freedom struggle of India was the platform where women again proved themselves. Women?s participation in the revolutionary movement (Mehta, 2004) was significant even when they were deprived of basic human rights in men?s world. The list of women in India who contributed to the movement for equality is enormous. To name just a few, Sarojini Naidu, Kamaladevi Chattopadhyay, Vijaylaxmi Pundit, Aruna Asaf Ali, and Rajkumari Amrit Kaur took up the fight on several fronts. (Jha and poojary, 1998)

RURAL EDUCATION IN INDIA

Following independence, India viewed education as an effective tool for bringing social change through community development. The administrative control was effectively initiated in the 1950s, when, in 1952, the government grouped villages under a Community Development Block, an authority under national programme which could control education in up to 100 villages. A Block Development Officer oversaw a geographical area of 150 square miles which could contain a population of as many as 70000 people. The further division was into *individual-based*, *community based*, or the *Individual-cum-community-based*, in which microscopic levels of development are overseen at village level by an appointed worker:

Despite some setbacks the rural education programmes continued throughout the 1950s, with support from private institutions. A sizable network of rural education had been established by the time the Gandhigram Rural Institute was established and 5,200 Community Development Blocks were established in India. Nursery schools, elementary schools, secondary school, and schools for adult education for women were set up. The government continued to view rural education as an agenda that could be relatively free from bureaucratic backlog and general stagnation. However, in some cases lack of financing balanced the gains made by rural education institutes of India. Some ideas failed to find acceptability among India's poor and investments made by the government sometimes yielded little results. Today, government rural schools remain poorly funded and understaffed. Several foundations, such as the Rural Development Foundation (Hyderabad), actively build high-quality rural schools, but the number of students served is small.

LITERACY AMONG WOMEN

In independent India, illiteracy is the second most important problem following poverty. Female literacy rates are very low nationally. A look at the statistics relating to female literacy reveals a grim picture. Though the female literacy rate has progressively increased from 8.86% in 1951 to 15.34% in 1961 to 21.97% in 1971 to 29.75% in 1981 to 39.42% in 1991, it is still below the desired level (Maitr and Sinha, 1993). Comparing these rates to male literacy is 63.68%, it is clear that female literacy is neglected. This gap ultimately contributes to the subordination of women and greater dowry4 demand in the marriage market. Among the literate women only a handful of women obtain their education in order to acquire economic independence; for the majority, literate women receive an education only to become more eligible in for marriage (Johnson and Johnson, 2001). The link between female literacy rates and development is obvious and has received much attention in the development literature. For example, Rajasthan, which has a very low female literacy rate, is still burdened with widespread practices like „sati?, female foeticide and child-marriage. On the other hand, Kerala, which has a high female literacy rate, is almost devoid of all these practices except the practice of dowry. Although the government has undertaken many programmes for the development of women, and in spite of the equality of status guaranteed under the Indian Constitution, double standards prevail in every sector of society and in the crucial sectors of health, education and social development. Moreover, the social isolation of women contributes to the deterioration of their condition. In spite of the Indian Government's effort to secure justice for women through laws against crimes, the result is far from satisfactory. Without proper education, legal literacy and social awareness it is impossible to elevate the status of women.

LITERATURE REVIEW

Women discovered their own potential and played an equal part in India's struggle for freedom. Many women came to be accepted as great patriots in their own rights. The freedom struggle of India was the platform where women again proved themselves (Bajpai, Nirupam and Jeffrey Sachs, 2000).

Among the literate women only a handful of women obtain their education in order to acquire economic independence; for the majority, literate women receive an education only to become more eligible in for marriage (Hirway Indira and Darshini Mahadevia,2005).

Even though, after independence, considerable developments have taken place in the lives of women, there remains a bleak picture. A majority of women are still underprivileged in a tradition bound society like ours, where there is a distinction between lawful legitimacy and general practice. "In spite of women's contribution towards family income, their position in the family hierarchy mostly remains subordinate" (Drèze, Jean and Aparajita Goyal,2003).

METHODOLOGY

Personal interviews were conducted to find out the role of education in empowering women. Questionnaire method was also used to collect the data, which was then tabulated in excel. Thus, survey and case study method is used.

DEMOGRAPHICS OF RESPONDENTS

Information from both the rural and urban areas of Baramati district was collected. There were 26% semi- urban and 74% rural respondents. Respondents of this survey were from different economic strata as well as representing different educational levels. Some women who never had been to school and had no scope of education were also interviewed and constitute

6% of the interviewees. Among the women, 26% has primary schooling up to secondary education; 20% studied up to higher secondary levels. Undergraduates and graduates represent 27% of total respondents. Post graduates represents 11% while another 11% of respondents educational qualification is higher than post graduation. In addition, 26% were employed and 74% were unemployed. Among the employed women 70% were employed by the government, 20% were employed with NGOs and 10% were employed in small private enterprises.

The age at marriage of the respondents is also a very important factor, which indicates the status of women in society and their place in their family. In this survey it is revealed that a considerable number of women (32%) from lower economic strata (income Rs 3000/ per month) with very little education got married at an early age, on average of 14/15 years. The percentage of respondents married below 18 years are as follows 2.9% at 10 years, 2.9% at 12 years, 5.9% at 13 years, 5.9% at 14 years, 29.4% at 15 years, 41.2% at 16 years and 11.8% at 17 years. Marriage below 18 years is illegal and this practice of early marriage overburdens women with early motherhood spoiling their opportunity to get an education

The economic distribution of the economic condition of respondents is as follows: the majority of the women (44.5%) are from the household earning up to Rs 3000/, 18.8% up to Rs 6000/, 12% up to Rs 9000/, 12% up to Rs 12,000/, 4.2% up to Rs 15,000/, 3.7% up to Rs 18,000/, 1.0% up to Rs 21,000/, and 4.2% up to Rs 30,000/.

SURVEY RESULTS

(1) Priorities in general education: In Baramati district there is preference for boys in education and parents are accustomed to take their studies with more seriousness. The reason for this preference, as narrated by the respondents, is that it is the societal norm that boys must become economically independent. Families place the most importance on the marriage of their girls. When asked, some of the women the reasons for their illiteracy, they responded that it was because of their parents negligence that they never had been to school. The same parents have, however taken many pains to send their sons to school. According to these respondents, their parents never felt the need for their girls to get educated. These women, a victim of their parental negligence, told that they feel very ashamed when they are unable to help their small children in their present educational pursuits. It is noteworthy, however, that a majority of the women (62%) expressed a keen interest in educating their daughters. So, there is a very positive change at least among women in Baramati district who are much more concerned about their daughters education, when compared to their previous generation, as seen and felt during the survey.

(2) Problems affecting women's education: The findings of the survey show that even at the primary level of education poverty is the most significant factor shaping opportunities for women's education. Two of the elderly respondents mentioned that they worked as domestics to obtain their primary education. She and her sister faced severe economic problems as well as parental negligence in their childhood which deterred them from getting an education. Today they are extremely interested in educating their granddaughters.

Other problems which deterred women from getting an education, as cited by the respondents, are parental negligence and early marriage (Fig.1). Responsibilities for the family or the death of mother or father also emerged as reasons for the compulsory dropout from school at an early age as girl children had to take care of their younger siblings Many poor, uneducated villagers do not attribute much importance to the education of girls. Early marriage is another common feature leading parents to withdraw their girls from school, and once they are gone, very few girls return to school, according to a senior teacher. In a hurry to get them married, some girls fell into the wrong hand. As a result they have to suffer a broken marriage at a very immature age. Thus, economic problems are the main hindrance deterring women from getting an education, coupled with early marriage and parental negligence playing an important part in the ultimately deteriorating status of women.

Fig 1

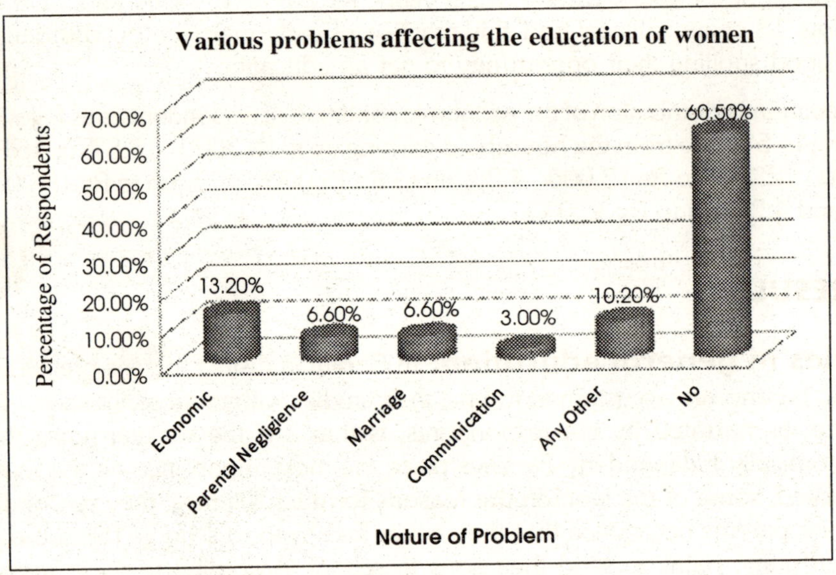

(3) Education influencing the practice of dowry: As the results of the survey indicate there are few factors which can increase or decrease the demand of a dowry. One such factor is the economic empowerment of women. In the lowest educational strata, incidents of a dowry are highest and here the average age of marriage is only 16 years. Respondents who were educated up to the secondary level married at the average age of 18; and those who had achieved higher secondary education married at the average age of 21. In all cases, incidents of dowry were also very high. **(Fig.2)**. However, when the average age of marriage was 24, cases of a dowry came down considerably and the majority of women were married without a demand for a dowry. It is important to mention that graduated women who had economic independence constituted the group saying a strict "no" to dowry. So, it is revealed that economic empowerment enabled by proper education has a sizeable impact in the downfall of the dowry system in the society of Baramati district.

Women educated up to post-graduation and beyond were inevitably found to be employed.It was observed that almost all of them were very confident and in control of their lives, reflected in part by a very high percentage of women refusing a dowry as a condition for marriage.

Fig 2

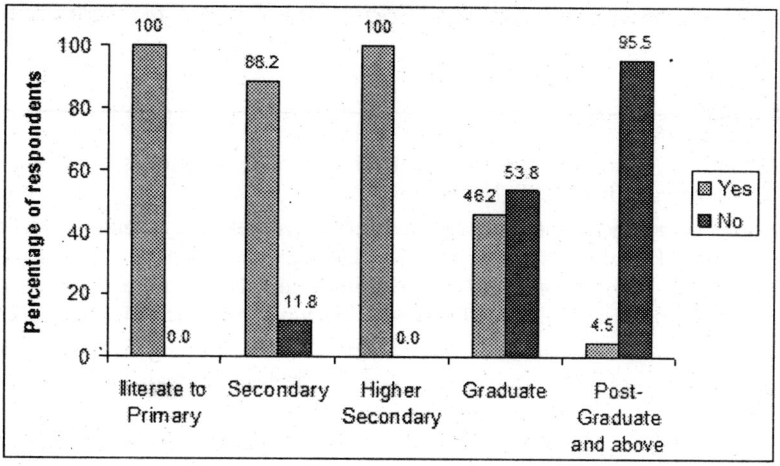

Role of Education in refusal of system of dowry in women

CONCLUSION

Overall this study confirms that women's status is inferior to men in Baramati district. Women face discrimination within families as well as in society, where society maintains double standards in the case of education, marriage, spousal relationships, domestic violence, laws of patriarchal society, property laws, dowry system, sexual morality, sexual harassment as well as discriminatory social stigma and also less recognition and respect for women's work.

Managerial Implications: The survey indicates that prevailing intra-household discrimination in educational matters for girls and women persists. Therefore, a strong message needs to be conveyed in support of education and economic empowerment as equally important for both the sexes. Education emerges as the single most important parameter empowering women. Education builds the way for economic empowerment and uplifts the status of women. Reducing the gender gap in secondary and higher education should be the focus area.

Marriage only at mature, legal age is also crucial. Women should get married only after receiving an education or after acquiring some skill, which can make her economically independent. The survey suggests that there should be more importance placed on the economic empowerment of women. As women rise in economic status, they will gain greater social standing in the household and the society granting greater voice in important issues. Not only does economic empowerment fortify the position of women, it serves as a deterrent to dowries. The parental property should be distributed to sons and daughters on an equal footing so the responsibility of looking after parents falls to all offspring. As women?s economic power grows, it will be easier for them to take care of their parents, to become a respectable member of their natal family, and to overcome the tradition of "son preference."

Given these circumstances, the commitment to education of the village of Baramati and those like it is truly remarkable. Families say they believe education will help their daughters "stand on her own two feet" and "have a bright future" and for these reasons they have made innumerable sacrifices. But due to the social differences, the families are not able to deliver the right value to the girl child.

Government gives grants, supports financially the girl's education, but it is the villagers themselves who will have to work towards this "Social Taboo" of "caste discrimination", to enhance quality education.

BIBLIOGRAPHY

- Aggarwal, Yash (1999), 'Trends in Access and Retention: A Study of Primary Schools in DPEP Districts,' Educational Consultants of India Ltd., New Delhi.
- Bajpai, Nirupam, Jeffrey Sachs and Nicole Volavka. (2005). 'India's Challenge to Meet the Millennium Development Goals', Background paper for the United Nations Millennium Project Task Force on Poverty and Economic Development, *UN Millennium Project*, New York and *Center on Globalization and Sustainable Development*, Columbia University, Working Paper No. 24, New York.
- Bajpai, Nirupam, Ravindra Dholakia and Jeffrey Sachs. (2005a). 'Scaling up Primary Health Services in Rural India: Case Studies of Uttar Pradesh and Madhya Pradesh', Mimeo, *Center on Globalization and Sustainable Development*, Columbia University, New York.
- Bajpai, Nirupam and Sangeeta Goyal. (2004) 'Primary Education in India: Quality and Coverage Issues,' Background paper for the United Nations Millennium Project Task Force on Poverty and Economic Development, *UN Millennium Project*, New York and *Center on Globalization and Sustainable Development*, Columbia University, Working Paper No. 11, New York.
- Bajpai, Nirupam and Jeffrey Sachs (2000), 'India's Decade of Development,' Working Paper 46, *Center for International Development*, Kennedy School of Government, Harvard University.
- Banerji, Rukmini (2003), 'Making the Grade: Teach Children the Joy of Learning.' *Times of India*, July 14, New Delhi.
- Burns, B, A Mingat and R Rakotomalala. (2003), 'Achieving Primary Education by 2015: A Chance for Every Child', World Bank, Washington, D.C.
- Drèze, Jean and Aparajita Goyal, (2003), 'Future of Mid-Day Meals,' *Economic and Political Weekly*, November 1.
- Drèze, Jean and Amartya Sen (2002), 'India Development and Participation,' *Oxford University Press*, New Delhi.
- Drèze, Jean and Geetha Gandhi Kingdon (2001), 'School Participation in Rural India,' *Review of Development Studies* 5.
- Drèze, Jean and H. Gazdar (1997) 'Uttar Pradesh: The Burden of Inertia', in Drèze, J. and A. Sen eds. (1997) Indian Development: Selected Regional Perspectives, *Clarendon Press, Oxford.*
- Filmer, Deon and Lant Pritchett (2001), 'Estimating Wealth Effects without Expenditure Data – or Tears: An Application to Educational Enrollments in States of India, Working Paper, *The World Bank*, Washington D.C.
- Geetha Rani, P, (2003), 'Financing Primary Education and Sarva Shiksha Abhiyan,' *National Institute of Educational Planning and Administration*, New Delhi.
- Government of India, (2004), 'Report of the Twelfth Finance Commission, New Delhi.
- Government of India, (Aug.2004) Indian Public Finance Statistics, 2003-04, Ministry of Finance.
- Government of Uttar Pradesh, (2004). Annual Plan – 2004/05, State Planning Commission, Volume I, Parts I and II.
- Grover, Shuchi and Nishu Harpreet Singh (2002), 'The Quality of Primary Education: A Case Study of Madurai and Villupuram Districts in Tamil Nadu, India,' *Center for International Development*, Harvard University.
- Hirway Indira and Darshini Mahadevia (2005): Gujarat Human Development Report, 2004, Ahmedabad: *Mahatma Gandhi Labour Institute*, June.
- Leclercq, Francois. (2003). 'Education Guarantee Scheme and Primary Schooling in Madhya Pradesh', *Economic and Political Weekly*, Special Articles 05-10.

☆ ☆ ☆

PART - A

ROLE OF WOMEN - VEDIC TO MODERN TIMES

1 Challenges Faced by Women: Vedic to Modern Times

It is a paradox of modern India that women wield power and hold positions at the topmost levels, yet large sections of women are among the most underprivileged. Some women from the upper classes head political parties and command large followings, yet women's representation in the Parliament and state legislatures has not been more than 10 percent.

The Indian women have come a long way from women sages and scholars in the Rig Vedic period to the women of today. They are now in the armed forces, IT sector, politics, industry and other significant areas while balancing their role as a daughter, wife and mother. This journey towards modernization has not been easy. Women have had to fight the traditional Indian male-dominated society to emerge as stronger and independent entities. 'While all these are positive developments, cases of rape, harassment at workplace and dowry deaths are rampant. Illiteracy and ignorance about their rights are still prevalent among a majority of the women. It was in this background that the Committee on the Status of Women in India. The CSWI recommended nearly two decades ago, the setting up of a National Commission for Women to fulfill the surveillance functions to facilitate redressal of grievances and to accelerate the socio-economic development of women. 'The modern Indian legislation has helped in stabilising the position of women and they have become economically independent which helped them to break permanent bondage of dependence on men.

The roots of discrimination against women lie in the religious and cultural practices of India. The status of women in the contemporary context is reflected in the state of their health, education, employment and life in society.

SOCIAL STATUS

Women in Ancient India Rig-Veda 1500-1000B.C.: In ancient India women enjoyed equal status with men in all fields of life. In the early Vedic period women had the right to education, she shared equal rights, practiced liberal attitudes to choose their partners and had the freedom to take part in social and religious activities. Marriage was not compulsory during this period.

Aryans were patriarchal. A widow was permitted to marry younger brother of her deceased husband. Social atmosphere for women in the early vedic period and in the works of Grammarians such as 'Patanjali' & 'Katyayana was liberal.

Scriptures such as Rig Veda and Upanishads mention many women sages and seers, notably Gargi and Maitreyi. There are some kingdoms in ancient India, which had customs such as 'nagarvadhu'. Women, in fact, had superior position than their male counterparts. It is truly in this period that women were treated as Durga and Parvati.

There was a special thread ceremony in which girls were tied threads of honour based on merit. Later this ceremony was replaced by 'child-marriage'. Girls were married when they were infants. They were sent to their husband's house when they attained puberty. Giils were not permitted to gain education. Although many Jam institutions admitted girls but it was of no use as only a few number of girls attended these institutes.

The high status enjoyed by the women in Rig Vedic period, gradually started deteriorating in the late vedic period especially between I000B.c and 500B.C. Women started to be confined to the household because of importance given to the purity and pollution. Women began to be considered impure during certain periods of their life. They were kept away from many religious and social occasions. This is one of the reasons behind the rise in the social and economic status of men and status of women started to decline .The strong belief of these clays was that male child can save his parent from cycle of rebirth. One of the reason behind value of the son was that male child also took responsibility of his parents. And thereby women went on witnessing a steady decline in their status. The daughter was treated as a liability or an unwelcome guest.

Women in Medieval India : The condition of Women in society deteriorated more during the medieval period. At this point of time child-marriage, sati, female infanticide were practised largely. The Muslim seclusion in India introduced the 'purdah' system by and large on Muslim women. These women were also forced to practise 'zenana'. The Rajput women of Rajasthan who are known to place a high premium on honour practised 'jauhar'. Jauhar refers to the practise of the voluntary immolation of all the wives and daughters of defeated warriors, in order to avoid capture and consequent molestation by the enemy. Polygamy i.e. husband marrying more than once was practised by most Hindu Kshatriyas. Devadasi is a religious practice in which women are 'married" to a deity or temple. The ritual was well established by the 10th century AD. In the later period, the illegitimate sexual exploitation of the devdasis became a norm in some parts of India.

At the same time many women excelled in arts, literature, and music. Women were also rulers in the medieval period, Razia Sultan became the only woman monarch to have ever ruled Delhi. The Gond queen Durgavati, Chand Bibi, Nur Jehan, Jahanara and Zebunnissa were well-known poets, and also influenced the ruling administration.

The Bhakti movements tried to restore women's status. Mirabai, a female saint-poet, was one of the most important Bhakti movement figures, Akka Mahadevi, Rami Janabai and Lal Ded. Bhakti sects within Hinduism such as the Mahanubhav, Varkari and many others were principal movements within the Hindu fold to openly advocate social justice and equality between men and women.

Guru Nanak, the first Guru of Sikhs also preached the message of equality between men and women. He advocated that women be allowed to lead religious assemblies; to perform and lead congregational hymn singing called Kirtan or Bhajan; also preached against the discrimination.

Modern: Modern era is divided into two parts;

British period 1800-1947

Period after independence 1947- till date

In the era of 19th century a change began and efforts were made by both British and progressive section of the society. British banned sati in 1829 with the efforts of Raja Rammohan Roy and William Bentfick. Jyotiba Phule and his wife Savitribai Phule dedicated their life to the education of women. An Act of 1929 fixed limitation on the age of marriage for girls at 14 and 21 for boys. Ishwar Chandra Vidhysagar initated widow's remarriage act in 1954 and also promoted education to women inspite of great opposition.

In the pre-independence era of the 20th century, large scale participation of women in the freedom movement under the leadership of Gandhiji changed the attitude of Indian women towards life.

After independence the Constitution of India gave equal rights to the men and women with no discrimination. It also gave some special provisions of equal pay, rights and security.

Education : Education builds awareness. What's the educational scenario in India be it Hindu or Muslim? It's a fact that in human development index 2010 India ranks 134th among 182 countries and 40% of women are illiterate. Let us examine the historical and contemporary reasons.

Women in ancient india : The Vedic period was characterized by equitability treated woman with a fair deal. The status of the woman during the Vedic Period could be judged by the way in which the birth of a girl child received. Rigveda, never considered birth of a girl inauspicious. Woman was allowed to recite vedic verses and perform Yagna. It is said that there were 32 women compilers of Rigveda who expound or expanded vedic literature. In the 6th century BC, Gautam Buddha's teachings had a revolutionary impact on women's status. In fact, two of the very first disciples were women. The deterioration of status of women started from the period of Smritis, that is, to a period when the vast body of law codes such as Manusmritis, commentaries, epics-the Malabharata, and the Ramayana and puranas or the stories of Gods were written. The period was literally called as 'dark age". Girls were not permitted to gain education. Although many Jam institutions admitted girls it was of no use as only a few number of girls attended these institutes.

WOMEN IN MODERN INDIA

Pre independence : With the advent of the British in India, the status of women, had reached its nadir - the lowest pit. At the beginning of the 1880s, the condition of women was very pitiable. For some strange reason, both women and untouchable castes were compared to drums, fit only for being beaten.

Touched by the work done by missionaries and philanthropic Englishmen, several Indians lent their support to the opening of girls schools. Raja Ram Mohan Roy and Ishwar Chandra Vidyasagar actively fought for the emancipation of women. In this regard, the first move was made by Lord Dalhousie, the then Governor-General. He actively supported female education and gave orders that women's education was something that could not be ignored.

Before the British had established themselves in India, the Christian missionaries were quite active in India. Their efforts affected the status of women. They ridiculed the Hindu religion for their merciless activities toward women. They realised they would be able to plant Christian values into Hindu homes and thus fulfill their mission of religious conversion. So women became their prime focus.

Influenced by the western education, many reformists tried to bring out the fact that the scriptures did not support the subjugation of women. Many schools were opened for girls. It was in this period that India saw the floodgates open to social reforms.

Many reformers like Ishwar Chandra Vidyasagar, Jyotiba Phule with his wife Savitribai Phule undertook various measures to eradicate social stigmas from the society. Sir Sayyed Ahmad Khan established the Aligarh Muslim University for the spread of education among the Muslims.

Post independence : In the modern times, Indian women were given liberties and rights such as freedom of expression and equality, as well as the right to get education. But still today, we are fighting for crisis such as dowry, female infanticide, sex selective abortions, health, domestic violence, etc. Women today are educated but illiterate in terms of knowing their rights properly.

In 1951, shortly after Independence, the Census recorded that only 25 per cent of men and 7 per cent of women were literate. By the 1991 Census, female literacy had risen to 39 per cent. Census 2001 figures indicate that 54.16 per cent of women are now able to read and write. Still, 245 million Indian women cannot read or write, comprising the world's largest number of unlettered women.

National averages in literacy conceal wide disparities. For instance, while 87 per cent of women in Mizoram are literate, only 34 per cent of women in Bihar can read and write.

Since the majority of India's unlettered people are female, literacy and education programmes need to focus on girls and women. Yet progressive government programmes like the Mahila Samakhya, that designed a scheme to empower rural women and motivate them to educate themselves, have been distorted in recent years. The District Primary Education Programme focuses on enrolment but not on the retention of girls in schools. In the absence of an enabling and empowering environment, girls are unlikely to stay on in school, say critics of the large World Bank funded programme.

The average Indian female has only 1-2 years of schooling, while the Indian male spends 3-5 years in school. More than 50 per cent girls drop out by the time they are in middle school.

Women's organisations point out that sibling care is a major reason for girls dropping out of school and suggest that creches be attached to schools so that girls are free to attend classes. Midday meals, free books and uniforms, and the provision of toilets are other facilities suggested to bring more girls into the school system, besides more same sex schools and more female teachers.

The women's movement has repeatedly called upon the government to fulfill its pledge to invest 6 per cent of the country's GDP in education set by government as far back as back as 1968 by Kothari Commission. But, in fact, expenditure on education fell from 3.4 per cent of GDP in 1989-90 to 2.8 per cent in 1995-96 and to 4.02 per cent in 2001-02. Further, amounts actually made available and real spending falls far short of budgetary provisions.

The Constitution had promised free education for all Indian children up to the age of 14. This promise was never fulfilled. The government is contemplating passing a law to grant children ages 6-14 the right to education. Child rights and women's activists argue that this right is already enshrined in the Constitution and the Right to Education Bill has been designed to absolve the government of its responsibility towards those less than six years of age.

ECONOMIC STATUS OF WOMEN

Vedic age: The economic status of women in the vedic age was almost equivalent to that of men. Hindu women enjoyed property rights and shared the produce of the common earning. Muslim women also seem to have a similar system with certain exceptions.

After Manu and his opinions about women, the economic status sees a drastic dip with exceptions of Southern India, where because of the matriarchal system, women enjoyed the apex economic status. Still, by and large, the economic status of women was never exactly at par with the men. Subordinate position of women was rooted in the social and economic structure of the society in the ancient period.

There was a complete devaluation of their roles, which were confined to specific areas- the kitchen and the bedroom and to stereotype gender roles. e.g. Bondsrnaids, nurses, domestic helps, cleaning temples and agricultural labour. Opportunities for development were not only denied to women, these were not even within the realm of social consciousness.

Pre independence : The economic status of women in the pre-independence era shows hardly any difference in the pattern of earning though women were in the forefront in education, social-reforms etc. sectors.

Post-independence : Women's empowerment appears to be constrained by socio-economic and cultural factors that give priority to masculine over the feminine in almost all environments, that is to say school, household, labour market and community.

The concept of empowerment is a product of early eighties of the twentieth century; it has its grounding in the changes in development thinking of the mid-1970s.

The Eighth Plan emphasised on organisation and strengthening of women's group at the grass-root level. The National Commission for Women was set up; Indira Mahila Yojana was launched through Self-Help Groups (SHGs).

The Ninth Plan actually committed itself to empower women as agents of social change and development. The Plan also adopted National Policy for Empowerment of Women (2001) in order to create an enabling environment to exercise the rights of women as equal partners along with men and to create large-scale awareness with the active participation of women themselves.

Employment : Invisibility of the women work -

Most of the work that women do, such as collecting fuel, fodder and water, or growing vegetables, or keeping poultry for domestic consumption, goes unrecorded in the Census counts. Many women and girls who work on family land are not recorded as workers. In 1991 women and girls comprised 22.5 per cent of the official workforce. And 2009 data shows women comprise only 19 per cent of the organized sector. Data from the National Sample Surveys records higher work participation than the Census. This can be seen by a report of the National Commission on self employed women and women in the formal sector, director of social welfare in one state said 'There are no women in any unorganized sector in our state." Women employed in family's farm or business is rarely recognized as economically productive.

Women constitute 90 per cent of the total marginal workers of the country. Rural women engaged in agriculture form 78 per cent of all women in regular work. They are a third of all workers on the land. The traditional gender division of labour ensures that these women get an average 30 per cent lower wages than men. The total employment of women in organised sector is only 4 per cent.

Although industrial production increased in the 1980s, jobs in factories and establishments — or non-household jobs — stagnated at eight per cent of the workforce. Increasingly, companies tend to rely on outsourcing, using cheap labour.

It is well known that women and children work in huge numbers in bidi-rolling, agarbatti-rolling, bangle making, weaving, brassware, leather, crafts and other industries. Yet, only 3 per cent of these women are recorded as labourers. They are forced to work for pitiable wages and are denied all social security benefits. A study by SEWA (Self Employed Women's Association) of 14 trades found that 85 per cent of women earned only 50 per cent of the official poverty level income.

BIBLIOGRAPHY

Web sites:

- (See http ://wccl.nic. in!CEDAW4 .htm)
- (See http://infochpngeindia.org/www.sewa.org,)
- UNDP (United Nations Development Program) website
- Ministry of education

Books:

- From Independeice to freedom — edited by Bharati Ray & Aparna Basu — Oxford University Press.
- Encyclopedia of women and development — by Sushma Srivastava — Commonwealth Publishers
- Indian Women Today, Traditional, Modernity & Challenge — Vol. 3 — Edited by Uma Shankar Jha & Preinlata Pujari — Kanishka Publishers.
- Indian Women across generations — by Uma Narula — Atlantis Publishers.

- Modernizing women searching their Identity by Kalinath Jha — Rawat Publications.
- New Cambridge History india — Women's Modern India — by Jeradin Forbes — Cambrige Publications.

Newspapers

Figuring out India's decade - Times of India, 26th December 2009 — complied by Atul Thakur

☆ ☆ ☆

2 Challenging Role of Indian Women from the Vedic to Modern Times

INTRODUCTION

The four Vedas, namely, **Rig, Sama, Yajur** and **Atharva** form the main literary sources for this period. Veda means knowledge. Among the four Vedas the **Rig** is the earliest one. It consists of 1028 songs divided into 10 parts. The Brahmanas, Upanishads, Aranyakas, Puranas, Mahabharata and Ramayana are the other literary sources for this period. There appeared sub-Vedas. They are (1) Ayur Veda (Medicine), (2) Dhanur Veda (War tactics), (3) Gandharva Veda (the art or music), and (4) Shilpa Veda (the art of architecture). The Indian woman's position in the society deteriorated during the medieval period when Sati, child marriages and a ban on widow remarriages became a part of social life in India. Bhakti movements tried to restore women's status and questioned some of the forms of oppression.

We are able to understand from these literary works the political, social, economic, religious and cultural life of the people of the vedic period. The Vedic age is divided into two.

(1) The Early Vedic period from B.C. 2000 to B.C. 1000 and

(2) The Later Vedic period from B.C. 1000 to B.C. 600. We see some differences in the life of the people during these two stages.

During the British Raj, many reformers such as Ram Mohan Roy, Ishwar Chandra Vidyasagar, Jyotirao Phule etc. fought for the upliftment of women. The Eighth Plan (1992-1997) projected paradigm shift, from development to empowerment.

EARLY VEDIC OR RIG VEDIC AGE

Position of Women: Women enjoyed a respectable position in the early Vedic society. They had freedom to choose husbands. The wife was the mistress of the house. They participated in public meetings. There were women scholars like Ghosha, Lopamudra, Sulabha Maitreyi and Gargi .

Lopamudra was created by sage Agasthya and was given as a daughter to the King of Vidarbha. The royal couple gave her the best possible education and brought her up amidst luxury. When she attained a marriageable age, Agasthya, the sage who was under vows of celibacy and poverty, wanted to own her. Lopamudra agreed to marry him, and left her palace for Agasthya's hermitage. After serving her husband faithfully for a long period, Lopa grew tired of his strict practices. She wrote a hymn of two stanzas making an impassioned plea for his attention and love. Soon afterwards, the sage realized his duties towards his wife and performed both his domestic and ascetic life with equal zeal, reaching a wholeness of spiritual and physical powers.

Maitreyi: The *Rig Veda* contains about one thousand hymns, of which about 10 are accredited to Maitreyi, the woman seer and philosopher. She contributed towards the enhancement of her sage-husband Yajnavalkya's personality and the flowering of his spiritual thoughts. Yajnavalkya had two wives, Maitreyi and Katyayani. While Maitreyi was well versed in the Hindu scriptures and was a 'brahmavadini', Katyayani was an ordinary woman. One day the sage decided to make a settlement of his worldly possessions between his two wives and renounce the world by taking up ascetic vows. He asked his wives their wishes. The learned Maitreyi asked her husband if all the wealth in the world would make her immortal. The sage replied that wealth could only make one rich, nothing else. She then asked for the wealth of immortality. Yajnavalkya was happy to hear this, and imparted Maitreyi the doctrine of the soul and his knowledge of attaining immortality.

Gargi: the Vedic prophetess and daughter of sage Vachaknu, composed several hymns that questioned the origin of all existence. When King Janak of Videha organized a 'brahmayajna', a philosophic congress cantered around the fire sacrament, Gargi was one of the eminent participants. She challenged the sage Yajnavalkya with a volley of perturbing questions on the soul or 'atman' that confounded the learned man who had till then silenced many an eminent scholar.

LATER VEDIC PERIOD

The period between B.C. 1000 and B.C. 600 is generally known as Later Vedic period. This age is also called as the Epic Age because the two great epics Ramayana and Mahabharata were written during this period. This study considers three significant women in Mahabharata - **Satyawati, Kunti and Draupadi**.

Satyavati virtually takes Hastinapura by storm and ensures that it is her blood which runs through its rulers. She is the cause of Devavrata turning into Bhishma, and she fulfils her desire of having her children on the throne in a way that Shantanu had never dreamt of while agreeing with indecent enthusiasm to meet her father's conditions for the marriage. Satyavati is not ashamed to own her unmarried motherhood before society.. After the death of her sons Vichitravirya and Chitrangada she called her illegitimate son Vyasa to father children of the widows of her son. After Pandu's death, Satyavati gracefully retires to the forest, unlike the obsessed Bhishma. She accepts Vyasa's advice not to be a witness to the suicide of her race.

Kunti, Satyavati's daughter-in-law Pritha-Kunti is the epic's most remarkable study in leadership and the use of power. Given away in childhood by her father Shura to Kuntibhoja, her adoptive father asked her to serve the eccentric Durvasa who gifts her Mantra by chanting the same she can summon any god to her bed. The adolescent Kunti is curious to test the potency of the mantra and impulsively chants that powerful mantra to the Sun god. The Sun God arrives and refuses to leave without enjoying her. Kunti displays remarkable presence of mind in obtaining two similar boons from the important deity - her virginity will remain unimpaired and the son will resemble his father in glory. Later on, after her marriage to Pandu, Kunti shares the secret of her mantra only after bringing her husband literally to his knees. Thereafter, too, Kunti has the last word where Pandu's desires are concerned. After obtaining three sons, when the greedy Pandu urges Kunti to have more, she bluntly refuses to abuse that rare power for self-indulgence.

Ghatotkacha, was Kunti's first grandchild born to Hidimba, wife of Bhima, during their exile and as the saviour of Arjuna from Karna's infallible weapon in the war at the cost of his own life. It is again Kunti who instructs her first grandchild so as to ensure his loyalty:

"You are one of the Kurus. To me you are like Bhima himself. You are the eldest son of the Pandavas." After staying with a poor Brahmana in Ekachakra, Kunti now puts up in a potter's house in Panchala, further down in the caste hierarchy. The point to note is how she is bringing up her children virtually from the lowest level of society to the status of rulers. In that process, she turns necessity to glorious gain. For, the enforced exile brings her sons into close contact with the common people. In this way Kunti structured the Pandava dynasty slowly but surely into an entity with multi-racial affinities.

Kunti's intention is to obtain the daughter of Drupada as daughter-in-law and thus gain the alliance of the traditional enemy of the Kauravas, so that a firm foundation can be established for the plan to win back her sons' birthright. Kunti is fully aware that Arjuna had won Draupadi, but she also knows that so long their lives have revolved only around her. She can be replaced only by a *single* woman, not five, if their unity is to remain intact.

When her sons are exiled, she decided to stay back in Hastinapura as a silent but constant reminder to the Kauravas of the violated rights of the Pandavas. She will not allow Dhritarashtra to forget conveniently what is due to his nephews just because they are in exile.

The other instance of her outstanding leadership is the last act to secure the safety of her beloved sons, by obtaining promise from Karna that he will not kill any of them except Arjuna. Moreover, she effectively weakens him from within. For, while he knows that he is battling his mother's sons. On the other hand, she keeps Arjuna unaware of this and lets him remain under the impression that he has to kill Karna, the charioteer's son.

Kunti's actions are, indeed, quite unconventional, right from her pre-marital pregnancy. She agrees to shoulder the burden of bringing up five teenagers without resources but for the tacit support of Vidura.

Draupadi: The last of this unique trio of "Virgins" is Draupadi, the one who is able to regain her virginity before changing each husband. She replaces Kunti as the nave of the Pandava-wheel, and also acts as the axle for the Panchala-Pandava-Yadava chariot.

Draupadi shocks her contemporaries by daring to challenge the Kuru elders' very concept of Dharma in a situation where any other woman would have collapsed in hysterics.

Unlike many women in her era, Draupadi's father, Drupada, allowed Draupadi to be educated. King Drupada had engaged learned Brahmanas for the education of his sons. Draupadi also joined them and became an expert in Political Science. Perhaps this is the reason why Draupadi was so confident which was unfamiliar to most women.

She could threaten the Kauravas, Jayadratha and Kichaka for molesting her and was bold enough to argue with the members of the assemblies of the Kurus and also Virata. It is Draupadi's reaction to situations like these that set her apart from her husbands. She is often the first to react to any injustices and is a visibly powerful figure often controlling the Pandavas. She had her own individuality.

COMPARISON OF WOMEN IN EARLY VEDIC PERIOD AND LATER VEDIC PERIOD

- There exists remarkable difference between women in these two periods. Women in the former period were allowed to learn Vedas and hence gained spiritual knowledge i.e. Atma dyan and excelled intellectually. There were many female sages too.
- On the other hand, in the later vedic period women are inclined to acquire power, wealth, they wish to rule and participate in administration and management of their kingdom.
- Females in this era are assertive as well as aggressive too. E.g. Satyawati agreed to marry King Shantanu only when he accepted to fulfil her condition that her son would inherit his throne instead of Devavrata.
- Females of three generation i.e. Satyawati, Kunti and Draupadi seem to have good knowledge of politics, are good diplomats, at the same time effective human resource managers with vision required for expansion of territory.

MEDIEVAL PERIOD

The Indian woman's position in the society deteriorated during the medieval period when Sati, child marriages and a ban on widow remarriages became part of social life in India. The Muslim conquest in the Indian subcontinent brought the purdah practice in the Indian society. Among the Rajputs of Rajasthan, the Jauhar was practised. In some parts of India, the Devadasis or the temple women were sexually exploited. Polygamy was widely practised especially among Hindu Kshatriya rulers. In many Muslim families, women were restricted to the Zenana areas.

Women rulers: In spite of these conditions, some women excelled in the fields of politics, literature, education and religion. Razia Sultana became the only woman monarch to have ever ruled Delhi. The Gond queen Durgavati ruled for fifteen years, before she lost her life in a battle with Mughal emperor Akbar's general Asaf Khan in 1564. Chand Bibi defended Ahmednagar against the mighty Mughal forces of Akbar in 1590s. Jahangir's wife Nur Jehan effectively wielded imperial power and was recognized as the real force behind the Mughal throne. The Mughal princesses Jahanara and Zebunnissa were well-known poets, and also influenced the ruling administration. Shivaji's mother; Jijabai was deputed as queen regent, because of her ability as a warrior and an administrator. In South India, many women administered villages, towns, divisions and heralded social and religious institutions.

The Bhakti movements and women: The Bhakti movements tried to restore women's status and questioned some of the forms of oppression. Mirabai, a female saint-poet, was one of the most important Bhakti movement figures. Some other female saint-poets from this period include Akka Mahadevi, Rami Janabai and Lal Ded. Bhakti sects within Hinduism such as the

Mahanubhav, Varkari and many others were principal movements within the Hindu fold to openly advocate social justice and equality between men and women.

Shortly after the Bhakti movement, Guru Nanak, the first Guru of Sikhs also preached the message of equality between men and women. He advocated that women be allowed to lead religious assemblies; to perform and lead Kirtan or Bhajan and become members of religious management committees; to lead armies on the battlefield; have equality in marriage, and equality in Amrit (Baptism). Other Sikh Gurus also preached against the discrimination against women.

PRE-INDEPENDENCE ERA

Social reformers and women in pre-independence India: During the British Raj, many reformers such as Ram Mohan Roy, Ishwar Chandra Vidyasagar, Jyotirao Phule etc. fought for the upliftment of women. While this list might suggest that there was no positive British contribution during the Raj era, that is not entirely so, since missionaries' wives like Martha Mault née Mead and her daughter Eliza Caldwell née Mault are rightly remembered for pioneering the education and training of girls in south India - a practice that initially met with local resistance, as it flew in the face of tradition. Raja Rammohan Roy's efforts led to the abolition of the Sati practice under Governor-General William Cavendish-Bentinck in 1829. Ishwar Chandra Vidyasagar's crusade for the improvement in condition of widows led to the Widow Remarriage Act of 1856. Many women reformers such as Pandita Ramabai also helped the cause of women upliftment.

Kittur Chennamma, the queen of the princely state Kittur in Karnataka, led an armed rebellion against the British in response to the Doctrine of lapse. Abbakka Rani, the queen of coastal Karnataka led the defense against invading European armies, notably the Portuguese in the 16th century. Rani Lakshmi Bai, the Queen of Jhansi, led the Indian Rebellion of 1857 against the British. She is now widely considered as a nationalist hero. Begum Hazrat Mahal, the co-ruler of Awadh, was another ruler who led the revolt of 1857. She refused the deals with the British and later retreated to Nepal. The Begums of Bhopal were also among the few of the notable female rulers during this period. They did not observe purdah and were trained in martial arts. Chandramukhi Basu, Kadambini Ganguly and Anandi Gopal Joshi were few of the earliest Indian women to obtain educational degrees.

Women in the freedom struggle: Women played an important part in India's independence struggle. Some of the famous freedom fighters include Bhikaiji Cama, Dr. Annie Besant, Pritilata Waddekar, Vijayalakshmi Pandit, Rajkumari Amrit Kaur, Anjali Ammal, Aruna Asaf Ali, Sucheta Kriplani and Kasturba Gandhi. Other notable names include Muthulakshmi Reddy, Durgabai Deshmukh etc. The Rani of Jhansi Regiment of Subhash Chandra Bose's Indian National Army consisted entirely of women including Captain Lakshmi Sahgal. Sarojini Naidu, a poet and a freedom fighter, was the first Indian woman to become the President of the Indian National Congress and the first woman to become the governor of a state in India.

Women in independent india: Women in India now participate in all activities such as education, politics, media, art and culture, service sectors, science and technology, etc.The Constitution of India guarantees to all Indian women equality (Article 14), no discrimination by the State (Article 15(1)), equality of opportunity (Article 16), equal pay for equal work (Article 39(d)). In addition, it allows special provisions to be made by the State in favour of women and children (Article 15(3)), renounces practices derogatory to the dignity of women (Article 51(A)(e)), and also allows for provisions to be made by the State for securing just and humane conditions of work and for maternity relief. (Article 42). The feminist activism in India picked up momentum during later 1970s.

Eminent social activist and trade union leader Ms.Ela Bhatt started and established Self Employed Women's Association (SEWA). It has played a major role in women's rights in India. Padmashree Prematai Purau set up Annapurna Mahila Mandal to support destitute women and making them economically independent through the system of microfinance. Women like Dr. Ms. Kiran Bedi, Ms. Lalita Gupte a banker, Ms. Ritu Beri a fashion designer, Ms.Sania Mirza a sportswoman are certainly the examples of achievers in the 21st century, yet at mass level a large proportion of women are far away from various aspects of development like literacy, health. Income generation, etc.

Women in india's five year plan: trends and need: It was in The Fifth Plan (1974-1978) that a major shift in the approach towards women, from welfare to development was seen remarkably. Later on during the Seventh Plan (1985-1990) the Department of women and child was established within the Ministry of Human Resource development of GoI. The Eighth Plan (1992-1997) projected a paradigm shift, from development to empowerment. The Ninth Plan (1997-2002) stated that Empowerment of women was its strategic objective and adopted 'Women Component Plan' as one of the major strategies.

Though for the first time, a separate section on 'Gender Equity' was included in the Draft Approach Paper to the **11th Five Year Plan**, although the paper has not given enough focus on women's empowerment issues in the country. Over the years there have been efforts made to socially, economically and politically empower women but as a result of the lack of synergy or coordination between these activities, the outcomes could never be completely satisfactory. For example, the increasing induction of women representatives into the PRIs should have meant automatic improvement in the lives of rural women, but if it has not happened, it is because the elected women were not educated or literate or even made aware of their rights.

Challenges of women empowerment in Modern Era

Status of women in terms of sex ratio, work participation rate, women's representation at decision making levels and women in panchayati raj is displayed in the following tables.

Table - 1
Sex Ratio (1981 – 2001)

Census	Sex Ratio
1981	934
1991	927
2001	933

Source: Census of India, 2001

Table 1 sohws that in 1991, sex ratio declined, but in 2001 it improved. This is due to various reasons like increase in literacy rate and general awareness of wrong practice of female foeticide, reduction in MMR and improved health facilities.

Table - 2
Work Participation Rate (1981-2001) in%

Census	Females	Males
1981	19.7	52.6
1991	22.3	51.6
2001	25.7	51.9

Source: Census of India, 1991

Work participation rate as compared to males is very low. There is need to create more income generating opportunities for women. The most important point of concern is that, the rate of female literacy is increasing but WPR is not increasing accordingly. This leads to waste of resources for increasing and overall waste of literate female human resource.

Table - 3
Representation of women in premier services (1987-2000)

Service	1987		1997		2000	
	Women	Total	Women	Total	Women	Total
IAS	339 7.5%	4204	512 10.2%	4991	535 10.4%	5159
IPS	21 0.9%	2418	67 2.2%	3045	110 3.3%	3301
Total	**360** 5.4%	**6622**	**579** 7.2%	**8036**	**645** 7.6%	**8460**

Source: Department of Personnel & Training, GOI,New Delhi.

Table 3 shows the representation of women in premier services particularly like the IAS, which has very high decision making powers in administration is very low. As seen in the earlier part of this research, history shows that women were excellent leaders as well as administrators. Hence there must be a thrust on developing policies to increase women administrators.

Table - 4
Women in Panchayati Raj (1995-2001) (Fig. in Thousand)

Year	Women	Men	Total
1995	318 33.5%	630	948
2001	725 26.6%	1997	2722

Source: Ministry of Rural Development, GOI, New Delhi.

Table 4 shows that in 1995 the criterion of 33% of female representation was followed but in 2001 the same was not followed. This is due to inadequate empowerment of women in rural areas.

CONCLUSIONS AND SUGGESTIONS

(1) Let us develop strategies wherein, we can inculcate in today's women power and capacity to rule, administer state affairs and handle various resources effectively.

(2) Higher %age of women should represent in the government both at rural as well as urban level. Capacity building programs need to be introduced.

(3) There must be a rise in working population of women. They must contribute productively to the economy. This is possible with the help of NGO's and other women's organisations like mahila mandals at the local level.

(4) Increase in literacy programme, participation in higher education, motivation to take up administration and management courses is bound to contribute immensely to the economy.

(5) Colleges and other educational institutions can contribute substantially through their Entrepreneurship Development Program Units. Our college K.B. COLLEGE OF ARTS AND COMMERCE FOR WOMEN has such unit.

BIBLIOGRAPHY

- Women Empowerment, issues, challenges and strategies. By – Hajira Kumar & Jaimon Varghese.
- Ancient Indian warfare with special reference to the Vedic period. By Sarve Daman Singh.
- The danger of gender –caste, class and gender in contemporary Indian women's writing. By Clara Nubile.
- Empowering women: Key to the third world development. By Ranjit Kumar Samantha.
- Research paper on Gender Budgeting in India. By Dr. Vibhuti Patel.
- Leadership & Managing power – insight from Mahabharata. Web Article by Pradeep Bhattachrya – bologi.com
- Vedic period – Wikipedia.
- Crossing Threshold – By Meera Kosambi.
- Women entrepreneurship in India. By R. Vasanthagopal & Santha S.
- Education and Socio-economic perspectives of women development and empowerment. By Aruna Goel.

☆ ☆ ☆

3 Matriarchal System During the Vedic Times

ABSTRACT

This is on behalf of all the women who are suffering in the name of domestic violence and all the women who suffered, divorced and separated and those who in the future are going to suffer. In India there were so many communities which followed matriarchal system in which the women were revered, acknowledged, honored and given prime importance in all the fields of activities and after marriage she was allowed to stay in her matriarchal house where she was never abused or tortured. She had full fledged freedom to lead a peaceful life and bring up her children without any kind of mental as well as physical harassment. The lineage of the family can survive only if the family had a female member and the properties of the parents goes to the female child so there was a demand for female child in the family and this resulted in the increasing the number of females in that particular society. The new rules and regulations changed everything and the atrocities on women have increased at an alarming level in all spheres of life. It starts when the female is still unborn. She is killed at this stage itself. Due to the existing patriarchal system, females are an unwanted member of the society. If, by luck she is born then the discrimination starts in the name of male-female as the parents think it better to save money for her marriage than educating the female child. And even if she is married off with a hefty amount of dowry then again the woman is not happy as she goes through all kinds of domestic violence like mental and physical harassment from the husband and her in laws and an indifference from her own parents and relatives to keep up the reputation of the family which either results in suicide or death or separation or divorce. The women of today are frustrated and depressed and a change in the society at this situation is very important factor to the womankind.

INTRODUCTION

A matriarchy is a tradition i.e. a form of government in which community power lies with the eldest mother of a community. The word matriarchy derives from the Latin words matri meaning mother and arch meaning chief or prime. It refers to the ancient tradition of mother-dominated societies and clans, though it is often confused as meaning woman-dominated.

Matriarchy is distinct from matrilineal, where children are identified in terms of their mother rather than their father, and extended families and tribal alliances form along female blood-lines.

Matriarchy is sometimes extended to refer to "government by women", although this is more technically termed gynocracy.

VEDIC ERA

In the ancient Vedic India, women were nearly full citizens: they were educated; they were eligible to study Brahmanic lore, to be initiated into the Brahmanic mysteries, to conduct sacrifices and to read the sacred texts. Women, like men wore the sacred thread. And—far from being secluded as they were in later times—the early Vedic marriage hymn expressed the hope that the bride would speak composedly and successfully at the public assemblies that governed the people.

"Indus valley civilization which was the first known civilization in India is said to have flourished in the 25th century B.C. During this civilization historical evidence shows that the people worshipped the natural forces and divine references were mostly feminine. Nature was often called mother. Mother goddess was the first worshipped deity for the people of the Indus valley civilization. From these facts we may conclude that Indus community was basically matriarchal. Family was headed by mothers."[1]

A mother goddess is a term used to refer to any goddess associated with motherhood, fertility, creation or the bountiful embodiment of the earth. There have been many different mother goddesses throughout history and in the present day, including such deities as the Hindu Kali Ma, ancient Greek Gaia and ancient Irish Danu. In Hinduism, the Mother of all creation is called "Gayatri", a surprisingly close form of Gaia. In Irish mythology, Danu is the mother goddess. Indeed, the presence of a goddess named Danu in Hindu mythology, associated with water and mother of a race of Asuras called the Danavas, may indicate a very ancient Proto-Indo-European origin. In some forms of Neopaganism, and in the Hindu idea of Shakti, all the many mother goddesses are viewed as being the embodiment of one singular deity.

The Harappan society was matriarchal. The ancient Indus Valley people (Veddoids following the matrilineal system) were the food-producing tribes. "Most of the tribes and individuals mentioned in the vedas take their names from their mothers and not from their fathers.....The fact that in a particular community people are called by their mother's name need not necessarily be indicative of the uncertainty of the real begetter. In most of the matriarchal communities fatherhood is known and recognized but descent is counted through the mother. Therefore, the fact of a man being known by his mother's name should be taken as indicative of the dominance of women in that society rather than the uncertainty of his father."[2]

In the Hindu context, the worship of the Mother entity can be traced back to the early Vedic culture, and perhaps, even before that time. The Rig-Veda calls the divine female power, Mahimata (R.V. 1.164.33), a term which literally means Mother Earth. At places, the Vedic literature alludes to her as Viraj, the universal mother, as Aditi, the mother of gods, and as Ambhrini, the one born of the Primeval Ocean. Durga represents the empowering and protective nature of motherhood. An incarnation of Durga is Kali, who came from her forehead during war

---

1 Kumar H & Varghese J ,Woman's empowerment, issues challenges, and strategies: a source book, p.36-37, 2005, Regency Publication

2 Usha S, Marriage in Indian society : from tradition to modernity, p.31, Mittal Publications, 2005

(as a means of defeating Durga's enemy, Mahishasura). Durga and her incarnations are particularly worshipped in Bengal.

Today, Devi is seen in manifold forms, all representing the creative force in the world, as Maya and prakriti, the force that galvanizes the divine ground of existence into self-projection as the cosmos.

• All of the various Hindu female entities are seen as forming many faces of the same female Divinity. However, mother and nursing child imagery has been found in the Hindu art, namely the depiction of Yashoda and Krishna. In Sanskrit, there is the term Yaganmatri for Mother of the Universe. This form of Hinduism, known as Shaktism, is strongly associated with Vedanta, Samkhya, and Tantra Hindu philosophies and is ultimately monist, although there is a rich tradition of Bhakti yoga associated with it. The feminine energy, Shakti, is considered to be the motive force behind all action and existence in the phenomenal cosmos in Hinduism. The cosmos itself is Brahman, the concept of the unchanging, infinite, immanent, and transcendent reality that is the Divine Ground of all being, the "world soul". Masculine potentiality is actualized by feminine dynamism, embodied in multitudinous goddesses who are ultimately reconciled in one. The keystone text is the Devi Mahatmya which combines earlier Vedic theologies, emergent Upanishadic philosophies and developing tantric cultures in a laudatory exegesis of Shakti religion. Demons of ego, ignorance, and desire bind the soul in maya (illusion) and it is Mother Maya, Shakti, herself, who can free the bonded individual. The immanent Mother, Devi, is for this reason focused on with intensity, love, and self-dissolving concentration in an effort to focus the shakta (as a Shakti worshipper is sometimes known) on the true reality underlying time, space, and causation, thus freeing one from karmic cyclism. "Shaktism has also become a focus of some Western spiritual seekers attempting to construct new Goddess-centered faiths. A powerful motivation behind Western interest is that many central concepts of Shaktism – including aspects of kundalini yoga as well as goddess worship – were once "common to the Hindu, Chaldean, Greek and Roman civilizations," but were largely lost to the West, as well as the Near and Middle East, with the rise of the Abrahamic religions."[3]

ETHIC PERIOD

Sita, wife of Rama was born out of a furrow when king Janak ploughed the land in order to stop draught! This alone links her to earth mother goddess which incidentally swallows Sita at the end of the story. These points to a matrilineal society, a society in which the man has right to a property by the virtue of him marrying the woman to whom the property itself being transmitted through the female line. A large part of India was matriarchal in character at one time. The reason for the Kaikayi's insistence that her own son Bharata should inherit the kingdom after Dasratha is perfectly in line with the matrilineal tradition. Dasratha had made a promise to her, on their marriage, that her son would inherit the kingdom. The fact that Bharata was brought up in his maternal grandparent's home also points to Kaikayi's matrilineal background.

Ancient Hindus gave extreme liberties to women. To make this explicitly clear, it has been enjoined to all performing Hindus that they recite with reverence names of the five great virgins (pancha mahakanya) every morning. You will be interested to know who these pancha-mahakanyas are. They are Draupadi, Kunti, Mandodari, Tara and Ahilya. We need to know about the sexual history of these ladies.

[3] Wikipedia, the free encyclopedia

Draupadi: A well known lady of Mahabharata epic had five husbands simultaneously.

Kunti: Her husband Pandu was not capable of having sex even once with her because of some liver problem (probably Indian Childhood Cirrhosis). Kunti used to visit forest ashramas and return pregnant. By this method she produced three kids, Yudhisthira, Bhima and Arjuna. She gave birth to Karna before her marriage. Madri also adopted same method to give birth to two children, Nakul and Sahadeo.

Mandodari: She was wife of Ravana who after the death of Ravana married his younger brother Vibhishana who had sided with her husband's enemies.

Tara: Tara was the wife of Guru Vrihaspati. In the boarding school (gurukula) run by her husband there was a handsome student Chandrama. She fell in love with him. The secret became open to him when Tara gave birth to Budha out of this extra-marital relationship.

Ahilya: Ahilya was wife of another rishi. Once her husband caught her red handed sleeping with Indra. Ahilya claimed that she could not distinguish between Indra and her husband as Indra had come in disguise of the rishi. All the Hindus look at Ahilya with highest esteem and the name is favorite choice for daughters in the rural India.

Whereas many non-Indian religions ruled that women could not leave home without being accompanied by a male member of the family, ancient Indian literature is full of such instances that the ladies could go out, visit fairs, markets, theatres, alone or with their female or male friends. They could swim in the ponds and rivers for as long as they wanted. All the paintings and sculpture from ancient India depict women bare above waist or wearing minimum cloth. This was a perfect dress suited to a warm climate, and must have been common sight on the roads and streets. Nowhere have they been depicted in veils.

PRESENT ERA

The royal family of Travancore has, in fact, had eight girl adoptions since 1,300CE for the sole reason of keeping the lineage going on the woman's side. The Travancore queens were very famous for spearheading major social and intellectual freedoms for women. In 1682 Umayamma Rani adopted one male, Aditya Varma, and two females from the related Kolathunad Royal family. In 1868, Queen Gowri Lakshmi Bayi began vaccination campaigns, first vaccinating herself and the royal family to prove to orthodox opponents that the animal vaccine was neither sinful nor deadly. In 1925, Queen Regent Setu Lakshmi abolished animal sacrifice at Hindu rites and outlawed the local Devadasi temple dancer custom that had degenerated into little more than temple-sanctioned prostitution. These Queens deserved and earned all their accolades. They were true nobility.

Maharani Uthrittathi Thirunal Gowri Parvati Bayi was the Regent of the Indian state of Travancore who succeeded her sister Maharani Gowri Lakshmi Bayi from 1815 till her regency was relinquished in favour of her nephew, Maharajah Swathi Thirunal, in 1829.

Maharani Ayilyam Thirunal Gowri Lakshmi Bayi (1791–1815) was the Maharani of the Indian state of Travancore from 1811 till 1813 and Regent from 1813 till her death in 1815 for her son Swathi Thirunal Rama Varma. She was the only Queen of Travancore to have reigned in her own right for two years before becoming a regent.

Maharani Pooradam Thirunal Sethu Lakshmi Bayi, CI (1895 – 1985) was the ruler of Travancore as regent for her nephew, Chithira Tirunal from 1924 until late 1931. She is known for continuing the progressive tradition of the Travancore rulers preceding her with many social and economic reforms.

The **Arakkal family** was the only Muslim royal family of Kerala to control parts of the coast and Lakshadweep.The Arakkal family followed a matriarchal system of descent: the eldest member of the family, whether male or female, became its head and ruler. While male rulers were called Ali Rajah, female rulers were known as Arakkal Beevis.

Nair: The northernmost portion was dominated by the Matriarchal Naga dynasties. This period could be better known as Naga (Nair) or Samantha Era in Kerala ... of Kolathiri was thus the first to become Kshatriyas in the Vedic sense. Nâgas originated from Kashyapa, father of Surya from whom clan of Suryawanshi kshatriyas evolved. Thus Nagavansh is a sub-clan of Suryavanshi kshatriyas. In Rigvedic account of the Aryans there is mention of Naga (Serpent) race, Naga kings and Naga warriors. The matrilineal system in Malabar is based on the Tarwad-house, where all the matriclans lives. It is managed by karanavan, who is usually the eldest male; but in absence of a capable male, a woman could be a karanavan; his duties include economic management and ceremonial duties. In Malabar society there was a preponderance of female celebration. The Tarwad always bestowed greater attention to the females. Even now women in Kerala occupy very important positions in all walks of life; in fact women in Malabar enjoy equal rights and privileges with men. Descent is traced through the mother and property is divided equally among the children of a woman. Birth in a Taravad gives a member the right in share of the Taravad property consisting usually of land, trees, boats and buildings. This right passes through female members. "Among the Nayars, women are the mistresses of their homes. When a girl marries, she does not leave her home but the husband pays her visits in her own house. Descent and inheritance are counted through the mother and a father has no right over his child. The child is known by its mother's name and surname, which does not mean, however, that its paternity is unknown. Guardianship of children rests with the mother and the maternal uncle"[4]

Nagovisi: The Nagovisi are one of three tribes of South Bougainville, a large tropical island west of New Guinea and north of Australia. The Nagovisi are land-owning matriclans, which are themselves subdivided into localized, land-using matrilineages. The latter retain their localized character through uxorilocal residence (the practice, wherein a man, upon marriage, goes to live in the home community of his wife). In addition, the clans and lineages of the Nagovisi are the owners of other kinds of valuables, including shell money, and they were the focal points of most religious rituals and of much political influence. The shell money is kept as strands of shell disks or beads. Among Nagovisi the finest are heirloom jewelry, given from mother to daughter; the second best form is used in buying pigs, in marriage exchanges (if there were any), and in compensation for insult, injury, or death. Nagovisi women share leadership with men; a strong matrilineage system having political functions exists, with women playing significant roles in decision making and ceremonialism. Nevertheless, they have a dislike of chiefs and communal efforts.

Khasi: In the folktales of the Khasi, the earth Ka Blei is the mother of celestial bodies, fire and water. The sun is her daughter and the moon her son. Because of his bad behavior against his sister, the moon was punished and his face tainted by soot forever – a very similar story to the legend of

---

[4] Sharma U., Marriage in Indian society: from tradition to modernity, p.33,Mittal Publication,2005

the Japanese sun goddess Amaterasu and her unruly brother. The Earth Goddess has a prominent position in the religion of Meghalaya and Assam; she is often revered in the form of the Hindu goddess Durga. A Khasi clan mother is viewed as the worldly equivalent of the Primal Mother, Ka Blei. She is the most important person of the community, its chief and priestess, who administers the clan property. The high priestess of the village of Smit is the most powerful shaman in Northeast India, and she selects the dates of important ceremonies and appoints Khasi village chiefs. Every young Khasi girl takes part in a ceremonial dance where she absorbs the powers of the earth: girls dance in a large square protected by youths who wave yaks tails to keep evil spirits away.

Minangkabau: The Minangkabau are the largest and most stable matrilineal society in the world today. Numbering some 4 million people in West Sumatra, the traditional homeland of their culture, the Minangkabau are the fourth largest ethnic group in the archipelago. They are a proud people well known in Indonesia for their literary flair, democratic leanings, business acumen, and "matriarchal" ways. The matrifocality in Minangkabau society means that families live in matrilineal longhouses and all ancestral property goes to women. Women are the guardians of economy; they keep the key to the rice house. Matrilineage and household are conceived as the centre of power. The legends tell about a queen, Bundo Kanduang, who is a central figure in the folklore but her historicality is unclear.

Japan: Ryukyu Islands: In the Ryukyu kingdom, on Okinawa, women were religious leaders as shamans and priestesses, presiding all ritual life except mortuary rituals. Secular power was divided between the king and male officials, and corresponding female officials. The samurai envoys from the Japanese island of Kyushu got very annoyed when they had present their credentials to the women of the court in 1666. Women priestesses still function today in Ryukyu villages.

CONCLUSION

This matriarchal system can stop to a large extent the crimes and abuses on women and also can stop all the illegal activities happening which might in future affect the marriage system itself. The women of today are frustrated and depressed and a change in the society at this situation is a very important factor to the womankind. I am questioning the hidden crimes done against women in the name of patriarchal system in our society. There is only one way to stop this. We will have to take necessary steps to banish the prevailing patriarchal system in the society. A woman does not have to suffer at the hands of strangers but exert her full freedom in her own surroundings where her roots belong, and it is an example here I would like to mention that women are like trees, if the tree is uprooted from its place it will not survive, similar is the case with women. The matriarchal system helped women to free themselves of their inner confinements of their houses and come out into the world to contribute their intelligence for the society along with their male members.

BIBLIOGRAPHY

- Kumar H & Varghese J, Woman's empowerment, issues challenges, and strategies: a source book, p.36-37, 2005, Regency Publication.
- Sharma U., Marriage in Indian society: from tradition to modernity, p.33, Mittal Publication, 2005.
- Wikipedia, the free encyclopedia.

☆ ☆ ☆

4 Challenging Role of Indian Women from the Vedic to Modern Times

ABSTRACT

She has seen it all: sexual colonialism, violence against her, marginalization, ranked as second sex, from female circumcision in Africa to dowry deaths in India, battering, incest, assault, rape, economic helplessness, insufficient laws, an unending saga of oppression and hate. To have a better understanding of the present social structure and position of women there-in, it is imperative to know the operation of various historical, political, religious and cultural factors moulding the society.

To understand the present status of women, we must have a brief outlook at the past society because some of the norms and values affecting women today have their roots in the past. The attempt is only to provide a general overview and not to go into the details of periodisation and its controversies. It has been noted that there has been infinite variations on the status of women diverging according to the cultural milieu, family structure, class, caste, property rights and morals. As a result it is very difficult to construct a profile of Indian women.

In order to study the development of women's position, this paper has been divided into three broad periods, from 500 B.C. to 1800 A.D. described as the pre-colonial period is the longest one. The second covers from 1800 A.D. to 1947 i.e. the pre-independence period. And the third, the post independence period. Periodisation is arbitrary but the main purpose is to get an overview of the position, this scheme seems to be adequate.

Further, it is necessary to point out in this overview I have been able to give a generalized picture of basically Hindu upper caste women. The matrilineal society of Kerala, the matrilineal society prevailing among the Garos and the Khais in the northeastern part of country provide a qualitatively different social setting for the women in these areas. Muslim women or women of scheduled caste have different norms and problems. However, in this exploratory work it has not been possible to go into these diversities.

INTODUCTION

Plato wrote that "as far as the state is concerned there is no difference between the natures of men and women" human society has to march a long way before this dream of philosophers and this ideal of equality and freedom can be realized fully in actual life. The most remarkable thing about the story of women's progress is the strange uniformity of its pattern. From the Vedic to Modern, the obstacles that women have to encounter and surmount almost seem identical. It is this that makes a struggle not a national one but humane, this lends one kinship to our methods, ideals and achievements.

In the battles which I fight, I hold
The weapons, weapons that
Cannot rust, weapons
That cannot be sharpened, weapons
Of mud and plaster;
I roam in the circle of my defeats.

(Bhagya Jayasudarsana, 'For Akka')

Most of the norms that affect women today, have their roots in the past. Within the Indian sub-continent, there have been infinite variations on the status of women in diverging, according to cultural milieu, family structure, class and caste, property rights and moral. We don't have an authentic profile of Indian women. Sukumari Bhattacharya, a Sanskrit scholar, while unraveling the picture of women in the Mahabharata mentions that the Mahabharata presents two different pictures of women : one of which emerges from its perspective section and other from the core section and there is a clear dichotomy between the two. The women in the core epic behave with much greater freedom while those in other sections are presented as mere chattel.

NORMATIVE STRUCTURE OF TRADITIONAL INDIAN SOCIETY

The Vedic text and the Dharmashastras (the codes of sacred and social duties) are said to constitute the norms for Brahmanism and the religious practices for the upper caste. Brahmanism ,after the first millennium A.D., moved away from the centrality of sacrificial ritual, to worship through devotion to the deity and selfless action projected as the need to act in accordance with one's Dharma i.e. duty. This had to be performed according to one's 'Varna', 'Jati' and sect ,which differed according to each of these. Hindu philosophy further accepts pursuit of wealth and satisfaction of sexual desire as legitimate activities. The necessity of giving oblations to the departed by the male descendants sanctions marriage and rationalizes the necessity of a male child. Through legends, women have been highlighted as self sacrificing, pure image of women and through the ritual practices, which day in and day out emphasized the dominant role of the woman as faithful wife and devout mother.

The basic rules insisted that a woman must constantly worship husband as god, even though he is destitute of virtue or a womanizer. The ideal women are those who do not strive to break these bonds of control.

The first large group to be enslaved in early Indian history was women, as there is more frequent reference to dasis than dasas. The Rig Veda for examples, describes the Aryan women ruling over bipeds and quadrupeds; i.e. Slaves and cattles. The enslaved women's labor and sexuality were to be used. The possession of women slaves was clearly an element in the primitive accumulation of wealth.Also the myth of Rig Veda reflected an explicit relationship with demonic women or with apsaras. While the demonic women are a threat to their rituals and power, apsaras are free from male control.

Niyoga which was the privilege of the male kinship indicates that control over female sexuality was firmly established. Niyoga combines the utilization of the reproductive potential of women but under rules laid down by men to further cultured norms which privilege them. And it is noteworthy that there is no special value attached to chastity. Women's nature was always represented as sinful.

On the other hand, the birth of the daughter was not a source of anxiety, on the contrary it praises the birth of a scholarly daughter in these words: "A girl should be brought up and educated with great effort and care". (Mahanirvana Tantra); "All forms of knowledge are aspects of thee: and all women throughout the world are Thy forms". (Devi Mahatmya) Women who desired to undergo the sacred thread ceremony or Upanayana (a sacrament to pursue Vedic studies) which is only meant for males even to this day, were encouraged. The mention of female scholars and sages of Vedic age like Vac, Ambhrni, Romasa, Gargi, and Khona in the Vedic lore corroborates this view. These highly intelligent women were called 'brahmavadinis,' and women who opted out of education for married life were called sadyovadhus'. Co-education seems to have existed in this period and both the sexes got equal attention from the teacher. Moreover, ladies from the Kshatriya caste received martial arts courses and arms training.

Education of women, which was the accepted norm, slowly began to be neglected and later denied. The *Rig-Veda* shows abundant evidence pointing to the fact that women were totally equal to men as regards access to and capacity for the highest knowledge, even the knowledge of the Absolute or Brahma. The women seers were called *retinas* and *brahmavadinis*, the entire Rig-Veda is made up of Suktas and Hymns. The Rig-Veda speaks of the following rishikas (1) Romasa [I, 126, 7], (2) Lopamudra [I, 179, 1-6], (3) Aa [viii, 91, 7], (4) Kadru [ii, 6, 8], (5) Visvavara [v, 28, 3] and several others mentioned in the tenth mandala such as (6) Ghosha, (7) Juhu, (8)Vagambhrini, (9) Paulomi, (10) Jarita, (11) Sraddha Kamayani, (12) Urvasi, (13) Sarnga, (14) Yami, (15) Indrani, (16) Savitri, and Devayani.

The bramhmavadinis were products of educational discipline of bramacharya, for which women also were eligible. The Yajurveda (viii,1) similarly states that a daughter who has completed her bramhacharya should be married to one who is learned like her.

Female education was very must appreciated. The curriculum of female education comprised of Shastras, Puranas, Smritia, Sahityas, Kavya even the learning of music and dance was very much encouraged.

It is, therefore, no wonder that the wife enjoyed with her husband full religious rites and regularly participated in religious ceremonies with him, in fact the performances of such ceremonies would be invalid without wife joining her husband as his full partner. Thus the Rig-Veda accorded the highest social status to qualified women of those days.

There was no female infanticide. The profuse description of women as dancers, musicians, warriors, door keepers, and co-participants of men in observance of socio-religious festivities, as sellers in activity in market reveal the free moment of women in the society.

Legend loves to tell various stories about valiant princess. There is no denying the fact that during ancient times women enjoyed the position of sovereign monarchs. Not only they were great conquerors or generals, they were good administrators. Along with military training they were also trained well in the art of state craft.

A more interesting question is that of sati. In Mahabharata it is mentioned that one of the two wives of Pandu performing sati, but it is significant to note that in Ramayana, the custom was not followed by Dasaratha's wives.

A distinguished English man observed, writing in 1808, that remarked that though he had lived in India for many years and travelled extensively he had not come across a single case of sati. The idea that sati was generally practised among Hindu women during this period is altogether unhistorical.

Pre-puberty marriage was not prevalent at any time .In Kerala, Kashmiries kshatriya families it was never prevalent. It was, therefore, only a small section of people that followed this custom which came for some reason to be considered a special characteristic of Hindu life.

Motherhood is greeted with profound gratitude and the readiness for a poignantly high emotional investment in the child.

In short, though in the vedic period women had equal rights as man, gradually, in the Later period, she was considered to be in ferior to man and thus began the subordination of women.

CASTE SYSTEM AND RELIGION IN INDIA

Caste system in India has existed for a very long period and it has survived through major socio-historical changes. Features like caste endogamy as a mechanism of recruiting and retaining control over the labour and the sexuality of women, concepts of purity and pollution, segregation of groups and also regulating mobility of women are very crucial. Most serious punishment like excommunication and even death could be evoked for transgressing the norms. Another manifestation of caste inequality is the differential status of bride giver and bride taker, where the latter is always the superior. Mostly to climb high in the status ladder, the bride givers have to give compensations in terms of dowry.

Caste not only determines the division of labour but also sexual division of labour. Certain tasks have to be performed by women while certain other tasks are meant for men. The significant symbol of women in society is that the women of lower caste are accessible to the men of higher status while there is a very serious punishment for men of lower caste who dare to approach women of higher groups. The linking of women and Sudhras is more evidence of the low position of women. The prohibition of the sacred thread ceremony for both women and Sudhras, similar punishment for killing Sudhra or a woman, denial of religious privileges are some examples which indicate how caste and gender get entrenched.

In short, caste system not only provided a legitimization to the feudal relation of production but ideologically also provided justification for subordination of women.

The historical data is not enough to build up a detailed linkage. In this context I would like to point out that although the subordination of a women is a common feature of almost all stages of history, and is prevalent in large parts of the world, the extent and form of that subordination has been conditioned by the social and cultural environment in which women have been placed. The general subordination of women assumed a particular form through the powerful instrument of religious tradition which has shaped social practices. A marked feature of Hindu society is its legal sanction for an extreme expression of social stratification in which women and lower castes have been subjected to humiliating condition of existence.

The period from the invasion of India by Mohammed of Gazni to the establishment of British authority in Bengal in the second half of the 18th century, witnessed, in general, a deterioration of women in India. The continuous invasion led to vast migration of people, economic depression of social life, especially among women. The purdah system was introduced and rigorous seclusion of Muslim women became the rule.

Purdha is a bind of safety
The body finds a place to hide.
The cloth fans out against the skin
Much like the earth that falls
On coffin after they put the
Dead man in.
(Imtiaz Dharkar, 'Pardha I')

POSITION OF WOMEN DURING THE PRE-COLONIAL PERIOD

The decline of women's position dates back from the period of Manusmriti, i.e. 500 to 1800 A.D. Manav code provided a legal and ideological legitimization of a pattern of social structure which lasted for more than thousand years. The code laid down the basic framework for the hierarchical caste structure, the patriarchal joint family with the oldest male as the supreme head of the patrilineal kin group, and subordinate status for the Shudras and women. Even Bhagavat Gita, one of the most sacred book of the Hindus, places women Vaishyas and Shudhras in the same category and describe them all as being of sinful birth. According to Parasmriti, punishment for killing either a women and Shudra is identical (Manoranjan Mohanty; 2004)

The birth of a daughter became a source of disaster for father. Thus, it said that the birth of a son is bliss incarnate, while that of a daughter is the root of family misery. Education, which was an accepted norm began to be neglected, and later on totally denied. Vedic studies were prohibited in case of women and Shudras, thus closing the doors for any formal education to women .By Circa 8th century A.D. the marriageable age for girls was lowered to 9 or 10 years which not only gave a final blow to any effort at educating women but began the sinister practice of pre-puberty marriage. Finally, her life was confined to four walls and restricted to serve the kin members.

Since the main threat to the purity of the group came from female sexuality, it becomes vital to guard it. Most groups solved this problem by the custom of pre-puberty marriages. (Manoranjan Mohanty: 2004)

Nothing can be compared with the most tragic and subservient condition of a high caste widow. She was not only forbidden to remarry, but she was considered inauspicious and the harbinger of hard luck for the family. She had to forgo all good things in life so that she may not be attractive enough to lure any man.

Now, we come across two major religions, Buddhism and Jainism, described as shramanic religion, providing options to women from living such a servile life. Buddhism which flourished from the 5th century B.C. to 1st century A.D. kept open all alternatives. The first include the role of a wife or a mother, second as a devoted wife, third is of a courtesan. In Buddhist text, she does not seem to be suffering from condemnation, but still she is under the male control and dominance. As Bhikuni she had a greater freedom and more mobility, but inside the Sangha she experienced severe discrimination, which in a way perpetuated women's subordination.

Another liberal current which widened the horizon for women was Bhakti movement. They emphasized salvation through devotion and attacked ritualism; used vernacular as the language of communication, which in turn opened the gates of religion for women. To sum up, the overwhelming concern for the purity and maintenance of honor through woman resulted in undermining her role as a wife and mother. My effort is basically to highlight the formulation and influence of normative structure which are still persisting today. A woman during this span not only occupied an inferior position but was made to feel that her position is subordinate to men in the society.

POSITION OF WOMEN DURING THE PRE INDEPENDENCE PERIOD

During this period there were two important movements which affected the position of women: the social reform movement of the 19th century and the Nationalist movement of the 20th century. Both these raised the question of equal status of women. The social reform movement has been regarded as a key to the intellectual processes that went into making of modern India. The issues which attracted the reformists of the 19th century were Sati, ill-treatment of widows the ban on widow remarriage, polygamy, child marriage, denial of property rights and education to women. They felt that these social evils should be eradicated by raising consciousness and making people sensitive to the injustice perpetrated on women.

They thought that by giving women access to education, by enacting progressive legislation, social change could be initiated. Raja Ram Mohan Roy, Iswarchandra Vidyasagar, M.G. Ranade, Mahatama Phule, Lokahitawadi, Durgaram, and others from all parts of the country raised their voice against some of the unjust practices, while the revivalist like Dayanand Saraswati, Swami Vivekananda and Annie Besant, believed in reviving the old Vedic society for women.

Another powerful force which helped to change the position and attitude was the nationalist Movement. Women actively participated in the Non-Cooperation movement of 1921 and the civil disobedience Movement of 1930. Gandhiji had immense faith in the women's inner strength and vehemently criticized the custom of child marriage, temple prostitution, prohibition of widow remarriage, and custom of purdah. Under his leadership simple unsophisticated women also assumed leadership. Aparna Basu summarizes "Women indulged in various kinds of activities ranging from mass scale popular agitation, constructive work among Harijans and Adivasis, to formal electoral politics" (Manoranjan Mohanty: 2004).

Applying the rational and the humanitarian criteria to the problems they further laid stress on female education. All India Women's Conference in 1927 was a crucial event in women's march towards equality. Thus it marked a beginning to various aspects like, the Sarda Act (Child Marriage Restraint Act, 1929), women's right to property, legislation of limited hours of work, prohibition of night work, restricting work in mines, establishment of crèches etc.

An awareness of the need to remove the social disabilities of women was created. Doors of education were opened, emergence of women's organizations, political participation and finally, through various legal enactments, women's unequal position was tried to be rectified.

VIOLENCE AGAINST WOMEN IN INDIA

Remember those
Who have been forced to pay
In the high inflated currency of pain
For being born women.

(ketaki kushari Dyson ,
After reading Nawal El Saadawi's Book—
The Hidden Face Of Eve)

Though it is true that the violence towards women is not identical in all groups and communities, and that moral and social beliefs differ from group to group, I have concentrated on violence against women as perceived in general terms. There is no woman who has not suffered at one time or another the harassment, humiliation, exploitation and the violence that shadows her sex. A women's life lies between pleasure at one end and danger at other end .Even if all men are not potential kidnappers, rapists, batterers, molesters, and tortures of women, all women are potential victims.

Lama Abu Odeh in her report, the U.N special Rapporteur on violence against women records "Honor Crimes" against women where by the family kills a female relative deemed to defile the honor of the family. 'Washing away the shame or' 'bad conduct' constitute the motivation claimed by the perpetrators in most of the cases. Where the victim was single this variously meant the victim's loss of virginity, pregnancy due to illegitimate relationship, or marriage without knowledge, sometimes even on the matter of groundless suspicion. Here the criminal behaviour is not motivated by emotional factors alone, rather this emotional response is learned and acquired.

In sexual violence virginity is valued by man, yet it is man who violates it and commits rape. A very large number of such cases go unnoticed either because of victim does not dare to face the shame and humiliation poured on her family, or because of police harassment or threats of retaliation by the rapist. Many cases are thus hushed up and most of them are forced into prostitution.

The implementing of laws granting rights to women has been so slow, haphazard that socially, economically and politically they are kept behind men. They are discriminated, maltreated in hundred different ways. Constantly derived and mocked at, frequently bullied, sometimes assaulted and occasionally burnt to death, they remain victims in every role. In India, question is simply one- the survival of women. Children are also stigmatized. It is an important instrument used by men either to exploit women or to take revenge. In village it is a tool to terrorize their laborers. One survey on prostitution has revealed that 80% of prostitutes took up the profession after becoming victim of rape.

NGO's use court directives to create awareness among women. Female volunteers are harassed like Bhanwari Devi, a sathin from Rajasthan, who displeased many upper caste people by trying to prevent child marriage in her village. She was raped as a punishment and of course her rapist was acquitted by the court.

The number of abducted girls and women is less in number. Some rescued one is siphoned into the protection and correctional homes. A few are believed to become a part of network of trade in girls and women. The conditions in so called Rescue Homes were exposed and we are aware of the crude realities. Police station also offers very little protection to the rescued women. They are sometimes assaulted in police custody and surprisingly, in large number of cases the police manage to get away with it.

Of all crimes reported in India, the incident of torture is highest. Molestation, after torture is one of the major crimes against women. Eve teasing/ sexual harassment is also a crime that is increasing in the country. Importation of girls is not a significant crime in country. Sadly statistics on crime against women were not collected separately by the ministry of home affairs or the police research bureau till 1988. It was only in 1989 that data relating to crime against women began to be collected.

The performance of sati by 'Roop Kanwar of Deorala village of Rajasthan in September 1987 points how law proves ineffective in the face of crime. The Gulf countries have turned into a flourishing market place for Indian girls, sent under the veils like nurses, ayahs, and maids. Never has prostitution been reduced to such depths of animalist, as it has been in present India. As 'The Telegraph' Reported on 21st November 1992, on the Kuba Kabas village in Rajasthan, where every working woman is a prostitute. There is a lesser known inhuman system of 'Lausa' practised in Jaisalmer, Jodhpur and other adjoining areas, where women are forced to wear iron underwear which operates to lock and key system. The keys are obviously with the husbands, thus preventing her from indulging in any illicit sex in the absence of husbands. Thus, there is really no end to the sad saga of atrocities inflicted on Indian women.

CONCLUSION

Unless social economies, ethics change, unless women themselves show courage, social legislation is likely to fail to make a difference to the life of those who are in the danger of sexual harassment. Trade unions can play a vital role in encouraging women in reported cases of sexual harassment and then standing by them. Men should be sensitized and well educated. Most men recognize and appreciate the needs of laws and change.

The Indian women of culture, wedged between the old and new forces, the conflicts which threaten to crush her, nonetheless lives with spirit and courage which have won her a place in front rank of women's world. The cause of the problem is that the two sexes have never shared the world equally. Even today she is heavily handicapped though the situation is beginning to change. Almost nowhere in the legal status the women are never treated as same as men.

To eliminate this problem, we need a general plan of action for both the governmental and civil social institutions aimed at eliminating prevailing erroneous social and cultural assumption and practices that lead to inhuman treatment of women. We must aim at building a healthy society based on respect of mutual rights and obligations. Our agenda should be to illuminate the possibilities for future and criticizes the limitations of the present. It is a great fact that woman and man can never be separated from each other.

Together they recognize that sexism not only oppresses women but limits the potentialities of men. Together they provide a vision worthy of devotion. "Liberation is the best thing, as moon is best among the stars" so, let us march towards such a society where all the barriers fall to offer each member a world of opportunities regardless of the sex. Surely we will inhabit the place that we envision and promise ourselves and our children today.

I would like to end with the words of Barbara Starrett:

"Whatever we can imagine, is possible,
Whatever we will to be, will be
I know it is time to dream
Strong dreams
And to abandon them for
The dreams to come."

BIBLIOGRAPHY

A. Kumar *Indian Women A Historical Perspective.* New Delhi: Anmol Publications Pvt. Ltd. 2006.

Maitrayee Mukhopadhyay and Navsharan Singh. *Gender Justice Citizenship Development* Zubaan An Imprint of Kali for Women. 2007.

Zide Arlene R.K. *IN Their Own Voice.* Delhi: Penguin Publishers Pvt. Ltd., 1993.

Manoranjan Mohanty *Class, Caste, Gender.* Delhi: Sage Publication India Pvt. Ltd.

Ram Ahuja *Violence Against Women.* Jaipur and New Delhi. Rawat Publications, 2003.

Lynn Welchman & Sara Hossain. *'Honour' Crimes, Paradigms, And Violence Against.*

Women New Delhi. Zubaan an imprint Of Kali for Women. 2006.

☆ ☆ ☆

5 Challenging Role of Indian Women from the Vedic to Modern Times

INTRODUCTION

John Ruskin rightly states in the introduction to ***Lilies*** –

"Be thou glad, oh thirsting Desert; let the Desert be made cheerful, and

bloom as the lily; and the barren places of Jordan shall run wild with wood" [1]

Yes! education and opportunity will make the lilies of the world bloom. Over the generations prejudices, customs and superstitions have hindered their progress. Now they have achieved the pinnacle of their glory.

The cliché that we have taken for granted for generations has proved true.

"The hand that rocks the cradle
Rules the World"

In many spheres of life Eve has proved her superiority over Adam. They have truly brought ***'woe'*** to the male ego.

VEDIC PERIOD

There are stories of many women who excelled in all important spheres like civic affairs, politics, poetry, art, philosophy, architecture, education and justice Devi Leilama was the first established Guild in India and Dhanawantri who along with her husband was the foremost physician and surgeon in Sindh in 5000 B.C. and whose fame spread all over Bharat Varsha. Leelavati in 6000 B.C. spread mathematical love in India leading to decimal system. There are also stories of women who led Aryan contingents in foreign countries. [2]

In 5000 B.C. God was referred to as ***'She'***. The ancient prayer of that time was recited as something like the following:

---

[1] Isaiah xxxv, I. (Septuagint.)

[2] Return of the Aryans, Bhagwan S. Gidwani.

"Let us think of the splendour
Of her that is One Supreme
She that is one without second
That she may inspire our minds
Our words, thoughts and deeds"[3]

In the Vedas, the attainments of women in the intellectual field are to be inferred from the fact that some of the hymns are attributed to the female Rishis. They learnt the Vedas and were entitled to recite them too. They were teachers as well as learners. They were the poetesses, preachers and scholars of the day.

There were no child marriages held around that time. The bride's right to select her own consort was exercised through a ceremony called ***'swayamvar'***. Monogamy prevailed and widows were also allowed to remarry. This shows the amount of freedom that the females living during that time enjoyed.

POST VEDIC PERIOD

During the post Vedic period, women started losing her status in society. She became a subject of protection. Manu, the progenitor of the Hindu race stated that a woman should be kept day and night in subordination by the males of the family – the father (in childhood), the husband (after marriage) and the sons (in old age). He felt that women had no right to the study of the Vedas or for the use of mantras in performing sacraments except the ritual of marriage. He regarded women as being more of the emotional type rather than the rational. Further, he went on to conclude that women love ornaments and wealth and possess impure desire, are dishonest and are an example of bad conduct. So he contemplated equality between man and woman in different walks of life. Also, Manu felt that women do not need to get educated. He was also against inter-caste marriage. Both polygamy and monogamy were prevalent during this period. Brahmins were allowed to possess 3 wives, the Kshatriyas 2 and the Vaishyas only 1 respectively. Besides, a Shudra wife was meant to be for all. Evidence regarding the presence of widow remarriage during this period is conflicting. There are cases of permission and prohibition. A widow was usually not allowed to remarry.

Women living in this society were not seen capable enough to possess property. If she dared to assert her rights she was signed off as being a witch or sorceress possessing evil thoughts and intentions.

Manu insisted that a husband should be constantly worshipped (even if he was not an ideal husband) in the form of God by his faithful wife. The birth of a son in the family was very much important from a religious and spiritual point of view. This was because it helped pay off the debts which one owes to his ancestors. ***'Putra'*** or ***'a son'*** symbolized one who saves a person from being doomed to land in hell.

Mughal Rule: During the Mughal Rule, the socio - economic status of the Hindu women wss very much lowered. She had to depend on the Hindu male in each and every

[3] Ibid., pp. 70.

activity. Social evils such as the *'purdah'* and *'child marriage'* came into force. Lack of education, early marriage, non – existence of employment opportunities, absence of absolute property rights were the main causes of inequality of the sexes in the socio – economic field. Economic dependence made the Hindu woman socially backward. Incidents of *'sati'* and *'female infanticide'* were prevalent.

Women were being regarded of being the same status as that of the Shudras. Sons were looked upon as the builders of the family's prestige and prosperity.

British Rule: Rani Lakshmibai (1828 – 1858) is referred to as India's Joan of Arc. She studied self defense, horsemanship, archery and formed her own army with her female friends at court called *'Nari Sena'*. She lost her 4 month old son followed after two years by her husband. However, it was her able administrative skills that kept Jhansi calm inspite of all the unrest in the empire. She was one of the leading figures of the *Indian Rebellion of 1857* and a symbol of resistance to *British rule* in India.

Inspired by Gandhiji, women from different parts of India played a predominant role in the Swadeshi Movement. On the anniversary of the Amritsar massacre, a frontline of seven people including 2 women Kamaladevi Chattopadhyay and Avantikabai Gokhale stepped on to the beach to light fires and boil sea water to break salt laws. Kamaladevi remembered that day.

"This was their (women's) first appearance in any modern militant political campaign and I could hardly suppress my excitement at the enormity of the occasion and my own good fortune to be amongst the first..........it seemed such a stupendous moment in my life, in the life of the women of my country."[4]

Women sold salt on the streets and went from house to house asking housewives to buy swadeshi products. They made merchants sign a pledge not to sell foreign cloth.

In Bengal, the Mahila Rashtriya Sangha begun in 1928, was the first formed organization to mobilize women for political work.

In 1931, Santi Das wrote letters to women members of district Congress asking each to elect 10 delegates. These women organized meetings, elected their delegates and held discussions about social reform issues.

Sarladevi Chaudhurani explained why women needed a separate Congress for them. Women's point of view had never been identical to men but men had not shown interest in understanding women. Now was the time to speak publicly about their status and join the worldwide Women's Movement.[5] Summing up women's experience with politics, she said Congress ***"assigned to women the position of law breakers only and not law makers."***[6] She concluded what was certainly the most forceful feminist speech of the 1930s with a call for legal, economic, social and educational equality.

---

[4] Kamaladevi Chattopadhyay, *Inner Recesses/Outer Spaces:Memoirs* (New Delhi, Navrang, 1986), pp. 152-3.

[5] "Srimati Saraladevi Chaudhrani's Speech at the Bengal Women's Congress," *Stri Dharma,* 14, (August 1931), pp. 506-10; "Women's Congress" *ABP* (May 3, 1931), p. 7.

[6] "Bengal Women's Conference," *The Hindu* (May 3, 1931), p. 9.

In Madras, Krishnabai Rao organized the Desh Sevika Sangha under the aegis of the swadeshi lead. Dressed in orange sarees and blouses, D.S.S. women picketed foreign cloth shops with men volunteers standing at the entrance of the shops. They stopped customers and pleaded with them ***"India is already downtrodden. Please do not help in its further degradation by buying foreign made goods."***[7]

The women, who joined the revolutionary movement worked closely with men, wore disguises, travelled alone in the company of strangers and learnt how to shoot, drive cars and make bombs. Gandhiji called them ***"unsexed".***

Significant numbers of women were in the workforce by the 1920s but work did not become a women's issue until the 1930s. In 1929, *Women in Modern India,* edited by Evelyn C. Gedge and Mithan Choksi was published with a foreword by the doyen of women's organization and nationalist movement Sarogini Naidu. She called the book the ***"authentic voice of modern Indian womanhood"***[8]

The first women doctors faced a number of challenges as they embarked on their careers. First, it was difficult to combine family life with professional demands yet society had little tolerance for single women. Second, they had to contend with sexual harassment. In Ahmedabad, in the early 1930s, the case of Dr. Miss Ahalyabai Samant, the Director of the Municipal Dispensary of Nadiad was reported.

Dr. B. Harishankar Bhatt, the Municipal Councilor abducted and assaulted Dr. Samant. The District and Session judge sentenced Bhatt to one year in prison hoping that this would make it clear that women doctors were to be treated with respect. The Chief Justice of the High Court overturned the decision and simply fined Bhatt. According to the Chief Justice ***"If women engaged in professional work come out into the open world, they must adopt the standards of the ordinary men and women of the world. They cannot expect to retain the hyper – sensitive notions of modesty which their ancestors in purdah may have possessed."***[9] Thus the Chief Justice's opinion revealed the prejudice that men have against professional women.

Indira Gandhi (1917 – 1984) – No essay on challenging roles played by Indian Women would be complete without mention of the ***'Iron Lady of India'.*** Having a premonition of her violent death, she had said – ***"If I die a violent death, as some fear and a few are plotting, I know the violence will be in the thought and the action of the assassin not in my dying."***

Indira Priyadarshini Gandhi, Prime Minister (1966 – 1977; 1980 – 1984) will be remembered for her commendable efforts in the development and progress of science, space exploration, irrigation as well as policies like the nationalization of banks and the 20 point programme.

Neera Desai (1925 – 2009) was the pioneer of Women Studies in India. She joined the SNDT University in the late 1950s and served as Professor and Head of the PG department and

---

7 *Smrutika: The Story of My Mother as Told By Herself,* the story of Shrimati Kamala Bai L. Rau, trans. from Tamil by Indirabai Rau (Pune, Dr. Krishnabai Nimbkar, 1988), p. 47.

8 Evelyn C. Gedge and Mithan Choksi, eds., *Women in Modern India* (Bombay, D. B. Taraporewala Sons and Co., 1929), foreword.

9 "Professional Women and Professional Standards, " *ISR,* 41 (August 1, 1931), p. 761.

Joint Director of PG Studies and Research Centre for Women Studies. She was also the Officiating Vice Chancellor. She not only built institutions but also feminist and women's studies scholars.

Kamala Surayya (Kamala Das) (1934 – 2009) was an Indian writer who wrote both in English and Malayalam. She openly and honestly discussed and wrote about the sexual desires of Indian women which made her an iconoclast of her generation. She expressed an independence of mind and body at a time when Indian women poets were still expected to write about fantasies of eternal, bloodless, unrequited love. Her works are available in French, Spanish, Russian, German and Japanese. She has also held positions as Vice Chairperson in Kerala Sahitya Academy, Chairperson in Kerala Forestry Board, President of the Kerala Children's Film Society, Editor of the poetry section of *Illustrated Weekly of India.*

Successful women in science have had to work hard often fighting difficult personal battles to reach senior positions. Kalpana Chawla went on a space shuttle ***'Columbia'*** for a 16 day out of the world experience. The NASA Chief called her ***"a terrific astronaut"***. Dr. Aditi Pant was the first Indian woman to participate in the cruise to the icy continent Antarctica.

The super woman of India today is a tough young woman who is not conditioned into gender – biased upbringing, of a girl being ***'allowed'*** to venture into a man's job. The same goes for the girls who aspire to qualify in jobs that were unthinkable for girls to take up a century before. They are virtually into everything.

Rani Jadhav, a retired bureaucrat is the full-time Head of the Port Tariff Regulatory Body ***"This is the first time a woman has been chosen to head TAMP. 12 years after the regulator was created in 1997, when India opened its door to private investment in the ports sector."***[10]

Lakshmi Venkatachalam, an Indian Administrative Officer from the Karnataka cadre is India's Director General of Shipping.

Ambika Soni is the Union Information and Broadcasting Minister. About her experience Soni says that the journey was ***"as tough as it could get.........Women in general are vulnerable and there are people who want to hit where it hurts the maximum..........and I fought."***[11]

Nirupama Rao, Indian Foreign Secretary knew when she was 12 that she would do it. Today, she says that she has realized that being a bureaucrat in a position of power is actually ***"being in a position of great responsibility. You have to put things in perspective, build consensus and utilize peaceful means to accomplish your goals. It is public service in the real sense of the word."***[12]

A topper in the 1973 batch, Nirupama has worked in Indian missions in Washington, Moscow, Sri Lanka and China. She was the first woman to be appointed Official Spokesperson of the Ministry of External Affairs when relations between India and Pakistan were tense. When

---

[10] *Women in key maritime roles*, P Manoj, *Mint*, pp. 5, (Friday; Oct 16, 2009), Mumbai edition.

[11] *Women of Power*, Tavishi Paitandy Rastogi, cover story, *HT Brunch*, pp. 10, (Sept 27, 2009), Mumbai edition.

[12] Ibid., pp. 7, Poonam Saxena.

[13] Ibid.

asked if it irritates her to be upheld as an example of her gender success, she says ***"Well, women do have a long way to go to fulfill their potential...........women in positions of high responsibility is a relatively recent phenomenon so the attention is inevitable. But it could be a catalyzing process for other women to take up other professions. There is a larger national goal here that we mustn't lose sight of."***[13]

Agatha Sangma, Minister of State Rural Development makes decisions that affect lakhs of people. She did her Masters in ILS Law College, Pune and went to the University of Nottingham for a Masters in Environmental Management. Returning to India, she joined the law firm Fox and Mandal in Noida. She was first elected to the 14th Lok Sabha in 2008 and was re – elected in 2009 to the 15th Lok Sabha. According to her, ***"My prime agenda is to completely utilize the youth of the country. They are an important productive resource."***[14]

Chanda Kochhar (48) MD and CEO of ICICI Bank feels that ***"women are the best people to work in banking. After all, banking requires a lot of thinking from the customer's point of view and women are good at putting themselves in other people's shoes."***[15] She proves that with careers gender does not matter. As the head of India's largest private bank, which is also India's second largest bank overall, Kochhar, who featured in the ***'Forbes'*** list of the ***'World's Most Powerful Women'*** proves her individual ability. In her 25 years, ICICI grew and diversified into many new businesses. So she has done many different jobs, many ventures like an entrepreneur. The bank makes finance available for projects affecting all of us.

Missile scientist Tessy Thomas states that ***"Science has no gender."*** The Associate Project Director for AGNI 3 may look like an epitome of the traditional Indian woman but her job is the least traditional. Attached to the DRDO (Defence Research & Development) in Hyderabad, her work has contributed significantly to India's security. The 3500km range AGNI 3 ballistic missile can strike at targets in the heart of China.

"It is a very challenging job." she says. ***"There is nothing routine about it. Sometimes the hours are very long. You have to keep updating your knowledge. In science, something new comes up everyday, it is never ending."***

Taslima Nasreen, the Bangladeshi writer had to go underground as the fatwa dangling above her head has militated against all social, religious and political onslaughts on the courage she was born with. This has made ***'Lajja'*** possible.

She expounds at length, the atrocities committed by the Islamic majority of Bangladesh on Hindu structures, shops, establishments, temples, homes and markets. The threat to her life is an attack on freedom of thought and expression. According to Taslima – ***"Religion is one of the many tools evolved by the patriarchal society to be used, misused and abused while being directed at women."***[16]

Meira Kumar (64) was elected unopposed as the first woman speaker of the Lok Sabha on 3rd June, 2009. She is a lawyer and a diplomat. She had been elected to the 8th, 11th, 12th and 14th Lok Sabha wherein, she remained as the Cabinet Minister in the Ministry of Social Justice

---

14 Women of Power, *Leading Ladies:* Parul Khanna, pp. 7, *HT Brunch,* (Sept 27, 2009) Mumbai edition.

15 Ibid., pp. 8, Kushalrani Gulab.

16 *Indian Women: From Darkness to Light,* Shoma A. Chatterji, Section 5, 6th part – 'Taslima X – Rayed: Herione or Vamp?', pp. 218.

and Empowerment 2004 – 2009. She is a keen sportswoman and holds medals for rifle shooting. She is also a poetess.

Pratibha Patil was sworn in as the President of the republic of India on July 25, 2007 and is the first woman to hold this office. She began her political career in 1962 at the age of 27. She was the Deputy Minister for Education in 1967 and the Deputy Chairperson from November 1986 – 1988. After Rajiv Gandhi's demise, she won the election for the 10th Lok Sabha. She has also served as the Director of National Federation of Urban Cooperative Banks and Credit Society. In November 2004, she became the first woman Governor of Rajasthan.

CONCLUSION

Equality is shedding its elitist mystique to reach down to the grassroots - women who are born with toughness in their genes. Many young girls of today in the city, town or village will not grow up into women or mothers striving to strike the delicate balance between work and home, because, their priorities are clear. They have to prove themselves only to themselves and this is achieved through work not home. Women have moved from being objects of legislation to initiators. For many women, the family no longer exercises total control over their destinies. A general awakening has begun and it cannot be permanently suppressed.

BIBLIOGRAPHY

Books:

- The New Cambridge History of India; Women In Modern India; Geraldine Forbes; Second Reprint 2000; Cambridge University Press.
- Indian Women: From Darkness to Light; Shoma A. Chatterji; First Published in 2000; Parumita Publications; Calcutta.
- Empowering Rural Women; Minakshi Sudarshan Mehta; First Published in 2006; Anmol Publications Pvt. Ltd; New Delhi.
- Women & Politics: An International Perspective; Vicky Randall; Second Edition; Macmillan Education Ltd.
- Feminism and Citizenship; Rian Voet; First Published in 1998; Sage Publications.
- Feminist Review; Edited by Vicki Bertram; Published in 1999; Printed by Bell & Bain Ltd., Glasgow.

Journals:

- Hindustan Times; Brunch; Sunday Magazine; September 27th, 2009; Mumbai Edition.
- Mint; Friday; October 16th, 2009; Mumbai Edition.

Internet:

- *www.doc.stoc.com*
- *www.tribuneindia.com*
- *www.jhulelal.com*
- *www.wikipedia.org*
- *www.indiragandhi.com*
- *www.ruskin.classicauthors.net*

☆ ☆ ☆

PART - B

SLEF HELP GROUP WOMEN EMPOWERMENT

1 Micro Finance - The Role of Women Empowerment

ABSTRACT

Microfinance is the extension of small loans to the people who are too poor to qualify for bank loans as they cannot offer any security. A Self-Help Group is a socially and economically homogenous group of 10 to 15 people who voluntarily come together to achieve common goals. Upto 2006 in India 22 million SHGs were financed by the banks. A total of 165 million poor people have gained credt to 11 lakh SHGs, most of them are women SHGs. Micro finance has emerged as an important tool for improving and vitalizing the economy by reducing poverty. SHGs help the poor households to realize their dreams by engaging them in some economic activities which can give some return on investments. This paper gives a brief idea of SHGs, their role in empowering women and elimination of poverty, despite the outdated technology used by the SHGs.

MICRO FINANCE – ROLE OF SHG IN WOMEN EMPOWERMENT

Can a mere Rs. 500 change a life? This sounds unbelievable. But numerous villages in India, especially Tamil Nadu and Andhra Pradesh, thousands of poor women are using small loans to rewrite their and future with the help of microfinance. As Sheila Diskshit, Chief Minister of Delhi, says Micro finance will be the future mantra for alleviation of poverty. I had met women who say that Rs. 500 - Rs. 800 makes all the difference as it dramatically changes their standard of life "Micro finance and micro credit have become famous only one decade ago. The Declaration of the Micro Credit Summit held in Washington D.C. in 1997, defined Micro- credit programmes as those "extending small loans to poor people for deployment of projects that generate income, allowing them to care for themselves and their families".

The Micro finance institutions in India are working on the same pattern as that in Latin America, Africa and Asia. A self –Help Group is a socially and economically homogenous group of 10-15 people who voluntarily come together to achieve common goals.This article tries to throw light on micro credit as a device to remove poverty as well as role played by SHG in micro financing and women empowerment.

Objectives of the study: The main objectives of the study are:

(1) To find out the outreach of microfinance in India and study the changes that took place in the economic status of the SHG members after credit linkage with the bank.

(2) To study the functions of SHGs.

(3) Also to find out the limitations of SHGs in financing.

(4) To make suggestions for removing the limitations.

Research methodology: The present study covers the micro credit programs offered by NABARD. The study is purely based on the secondary data collected from journals, newspapers like Indian Express , Economic Times and Business lines as well as websites.

Limitations of the study: (1) SHG linkage with NGO, village Panchayat etc are not dealt in detail.

(2) This study made only in relation with secondary data available from institutions like NABARD and SIDBI, due to time constraint.

Literature Review: A study made by Dr. K. C. Sharma highlighted the challenges and status of micro finance in India. He has specifically explained the different dimensions of micro finance such as out reach, sustainability, impact and reglations in the Indian context. Mr. Aloysius Fernandez, the Padmashree awardees who pioneered SHG movement in Bangalore in 1980s is of the opinion that micro finance can play a crucial role in development of rural India. He being the promoter of an SHG called Myrada, got about Rs. One Million from NABARD to train the members of SHG and match their savings.He says micro finance can play a crucial role only when the poor get access to resources, market, political power, confidence, management skills, and social class.

Another study made by Dr. Kishore C. Padhy, Director, Institute of Management Studies Bhubaneswar, in Orrisa concluded that 96% of members of the SHG are women and they could avoid money lenders easily.

An article which is published by Ms. Ramalakshmi, in Economic & Political Weekly opined that in Andhra Pradesh above 5.6 million women were covered under micro credit with a saving of a rupee per day and the financial institutions extending loans upto 4 times the amount of group savings. Recently commercial banks even reduced the interest rates to SHGs and increased the amount of loans offered to the extent of Rs. 1000 Cr.

In the year 2006 financial services reached about 35 million households which rose to 59.5 million households in the year 2008. This is a remarkable achievement in this model of SHG Bank linkage. Usually micro financing is done at a subsized rate of interest than the market rate. According to an estimate, about 75 million poor households in the country which have received the micro finance out of which 60% belong to rural India. This is a great achievement for the government when they aim at inclusive financial growth. According to a research conducted by NCAER, 2008, 60% of SHG-Bank linkage customers belond to BPL category.

Features of SHGs:-

- Small savings will be collected which ensures the habit of thrift among the customers. This is true especially in the case of women customers.

- 98% of the members make savings regularly as per the norms given by SHGSs.
- Majority of consumers in India, about 90% of members of SHG, are women and they are very prompt in repayment, compared to their other counter part.
- It is formed with simple rules.
- The end use is not so rigid which makes the facility quite interesting.
- Micro financing is a very effective strategy to neutralize poverty and SHGs are the medium through which savings can be mobilized.
- SHGs improve the self confidence and self esteem of members.

STRUCTURE OF MICRO FINANCING IN INDIA

Some Statistics: In the year 1990 micro financing started with a few million dollars which rose to 20 billion by the year 2007.The data available from NABARD website, the Microfinance Information Exchange report and the reports of Sa-Dham show that about a thousand micro finance institutions (MFIs) have reached 14.1 million people,with an outstanding loan portfolio of Rs. 59.5 billion. Whereas 3.48 million self help groups (SHGs) with a membership of 58 million , have been linked to banks with an estimated loan portfolio of Rs. 80 billion with three banks.

In India SHG Bank linkage is the largest single micro finance program which has got an outreach of 59.5% in the year 2008. These SHGSs are essentially informal associations of 10-20 people formed with a common objective, raising and managing their collective savings for the benefit of all members. According to NABARD the number of participating banks in the SHG linkage was 585 that included 44362 branches of commercial banks, 158 RRBs and 340 co-operative banks. The banks will monitor the functioning of SHGs and evaluate them. On this basis banks give credit about four times of the savings of SHGs. The savings bank account as well as the loan account will be maintained by the bank in the name of the group.

The SHG Bank linkage can function in three different models which can be represented diagrammatically as follows:-

(Source: Reasearcher's own Contribution)

NGO based Model : In this model the NGO will be taking initiative in forming the groups and connecting them with the banks. Banks will be giving loans and advances to the members of the group to NGO.

Bank Staff Based Model: According to this model, groups promoted by NGO and Micro finance insititutions (MFI) NGO-MFI group will raise bulk amount of loan from the bank and the banks charge some fee from the group will disbursing loans.

All these methods are working very well, NGO based system is working with great success.If the NGO is strong how far Microfinance will be suitable in the long run depends on the quality of SHGs, rate of interest charged and subsidy offered by the government as per Bharat Microfinance report of Sa-Dhan in March 2008, the 223 member MFIs of Sa-Dhan had an outreach of 14.1 million clients with an outstanding Microfinance portfolio of Rs. 5954 Cr.

NABARD launched the Micro Enterprise Development Programme (MEDP) for skill development in March 2006. The basic objective was to enhance the capacities of matured SHGs to take up Mirco Enterprise to skill upgradation during 2007-2008. 394 MEDPs were conducted covering 9182 SHG members on activities like Bee keeping, mushroom cultivation, horticulture, floriculture, vermicompost etc.

Impact of Micro-finance and SHGs: Micro finance has a very positive influence among the poor and the underprivileged.

Apart from NABARD, SIDBI even RBI has taken several initiatives to give further boost to the micro finance movement in India. The impact of credit can be analyzed as follows:-

- Two different models SBLP model and MFI model are widely practised and SBLP model has maximum coverage in the world.
- The credit needs of the poor by combining flexibility and sensitivity.
- Micro finance has developed mutual trust and confidence between bankers and the rural poor.
- SHGs have improved the habits of thrift among rural and urban poor.
- They have helped to accept door step banking and even encouraged the lady members in the families for prompt payment of the monthly installments.
- The main benefit received by the bankers was reduction in costs in relation with appraisal and supervision.
- Money lenders have been successfully eliminated by all SHGs.

One of the SHGs of women is formed to enable women below the poverty line to have an access to micro finance so that they can live with dignity. Bridge Trust an NGO, has started and motivated more than 4000 poor women in Thane district to form 370 SHGs. These SHGs take up projects such as starting micro enterprises, and income generating activities such as goat rearing, poultry, carpentry, masala and papad, candle making, vermin composting etc. Thus SHGs help women in economic empowerment.

ECONOMIC EMPOWERMENT OF SHGS

Most of the women belonging to the SHG take up economic activities related to agriculture and allied activities. The main activities are vegetable and flower cultivation, milk and milk products, handcraft and handloom production.

Public private partnership is adopted in promoting opportunities for SHG members by accepting them as dealers for the sale of products manufactured by MNCs. The companies in return help the SHGs in giving training in finance management, packaging and pricing of the products. These methods can be adopted by all SHGs which can empower them economically, which in turn can empower their members.

The areas of concern: There is a negative side to the story of micro finance. The demand for micro finance is Rs. 500 billion. Only Rs. 18 billion of this has been generated so far. World bank study says 56% of people below poverty line borrow from money lenders even now.

There are ceratin major areas of concern in the field of SHG financing in India; such as :

(1) The demand for self financing and the supply of it shows a major gap.It is revealed that the demand is estimated to be Rs. Two Lakh Crore whereas supply is for a sum of Rs. 7000 crores.

(2) SHGs charge a high rate of interest which ranges between 12 to 36%.

(3) Measuring the impact of micro finance is very complicated and therefore studies were made by comparing borrowers and non borrowers.

(4) Because micro lenders naturally choose to work in areas where the prospects of success are maximum, millions of low income group are still outside the system of micro finance.

(5) The SHGs are understaffed and lack sufficient capital. Due to this the growth of SHGs is also restricted.

Suggestions & Recommedations:

- The interest rate charged by SHG is quite high when it is compared with the income level of the poor. This should be reduced to less than 10% so that it can become an incentive.
- A proper legal and regulatory environment is urgently needed in order to control the SHGs.
- Suitable products with proper staffing pattern for the SHGs should be provided.
- Concentration of SHGs at one particaulr place or state should be avoided. It should be widespread all over India.
- There is a long gap between the demand for finance and its supply. The rural banks and co-operative banks can help in this endeavor by encouraging SHGs towards this end.
- The loans provided by SHGs are in too small amounts, in most of the cases upto Rs.5000 which is a meager sum to make any dent in poverty alleviation.
- Quality of SHGs can be improved only when they exercise good corporate governance.
- Many SHGs suffer from absence of financial discipline and internal controls. This can be avoided only through structured practices and a good system.
- Many SHGs do not cater to the accounting norms. It should be made compulsory to publish their audited annual accounts through national news papers so that they can prove their integrity.
- Accounting is done manually since low income customers have small accounts. With the help of centralized computers accounting can be done systematically as well as regularly. This can help them to publish their accounts even half yearly.
- Capacity building training is organized by NABARD as well as SBI, which do not have good frequency. Training can be done by the banks of NABARD continuously with the help of sponsorship from the help of Central Government.
- Economic empowerment of SHGs can be made by educating them, creating awareness about the social evils, public private partnership, development programmes, utilizing IT.
- SHG are to be encouraged to get PCs, which can be used to display their products either as pop ups or as advertisements or in the portals of e-commerce companies.

CONCLUSION

The micro credit programme as a major policy instrument of the RBI has been under implementation for more than a decade. A study conducted by NABARD which covered 560 members households from 2-3 self help groups spread over 11 states have shown positive results which indicate that SHGs play an important role in micro financing. Micro credit is a useful weapon in allleviation of poverty through empowering women and SHG if apply corporate governance can serve the nation in a better manner. To conclude, Dr. C. Rangarajan, Chairman,Economic Advisor Council of Government of India, points out that Micro Finance aid employment and sustain household giving them those opportunities they never had before.

"The time has come to recognize microcredit as a powerful tool in the struggle to end poverty and economic dependence".—Micro Credit Summit Declaration, Feb 1997.

BIBLIOGRAPHY

- Article published by Ms. Ramalekshmi, Commissioner, Women Empowerment And Self Employment, CEO, Employment Generation Mission in Economic and Political Weekly in Volume XXXVIII Nos 12 & 13, March 22-28 & March 29-April 4, 2003.
- Economic & Political Weekly Vol.XLIV No.30, Various articles.
- N. Srinivasan (2009), Microfinance India, State of the sector Report, 2008, Sales publication, New Delhi.
- Professional Banker, Dr. Kishore C. Padhy, February 2008, Microfinance-A window of opportunity, pp-53-56.
- Research paper by Dean Karlan and Jonathan Zinman, July 2009, Expanding Micro Enterprise Credit Access : Using Randomized supply decision to estimate the impact in Manila.
- The Economist Newspaper Limited 2009.

☆ ☆ ☆

2 Self Help Groups (SHG) - Role in Women Empowerment

Women empowerment is an important tool for social development and this can be achieved when the society recognizes women as one among the social partners, provide them all with equal rights to education, health and all the facilities which will empower them to participate, along with men, in all walks of life. According to Sushila Jain empowerment is as much a function of structural change as of attitudinal change. Along with the legislations, constitutional amendments and changed planning strategies need to be designed to change the culture of gender hierarchy which has still a strong control over the common man.

Women in India today suffer from discrimination in various forms at every stage of life in comparison to men. After independence many laws and acts were passed by the parliament. Inspite of all these laws and acts a lot more needs to be done to ensure that the women are not deprived of equal rights as men. The upliftment of status of the women rests on their empowerment which comes through education, employment and awareness. Since progress of the nation depends largely upon the improvement of status of women it is imperative to take positive a step towards this goal.

Sidney Schuler and Sayed Hashemi in Bangladesh describe that an inductive approach is well suited to look at empowerment. It includes participation in groups, sense of self and vision of future mobility and visibility, economic security, status and decision-making power in the household, an ability to interact effectively in public spheres and participation in non family groups.

Self-help groups (SHGs) are emerging as a powerful tool that aimed at empowering women and eradicating poverty in a sustainable manner. It is a major mechanism of development and empowerment of women in the third world. In India since the Ninth five year plan, most of the development programmes are channelled through SHGs. In all the parts of the country, SHGs are organised by governmental and non-governmental organisations. The government departments, banks, and NGOs facilitate them by providing revolving fund, organisational base and training, credit etc. It is worthwhile to call SHGs a mass movement on a national scale for development and empowerment of the poor and downtrodden in the country.

Based on the concept of "self-help," small groups of women have formed into groups of ten to twenty and operate a savings-first business model whereby the member's savings are used to fund loans. The results from these self-help groups (SHGs) are promising and have become a focus of intense examination as it is proving to be an effective method of poverty reduction.

The present paper studies the role of SHGs in empowering women in Vasai taluka of Thane district. The focus is on development parameters that include and allow for the gender factor, at all levels of social and economic initiative, in order to bring women into the mainstream of development. The paper highlights the SHG model, overview of SHGs in India, Emergence of the SHG Movement in Vasai, a case study of "Jivhalla Assumption Social Centre" to assess the impact of SHGs on empowerment of women from the perspectives of socio-economic status.

REVIEW OF LITERATURE

H. D. Dwarakanath (2006) says that SHGs are mostly informal groups where members pool savings as a thrift deposit and re-lend in the group on rotational basis. The SHGs have been able to provide primitive banking services to its members that are cost effective, flexible and without defaults based on local requirements. The SHGs have undertaken entrepreneurial activities at smaller level with minimum capital requirements. It has successfully demonstrated how to mobilize and manage thrift, apprise credit needs and enforce financial self discipline. The SHGs have the potential to ignite socio-economic revolution in rural India.

Lalrinliana, Joseph and Easwaran Kanagaraj (2006) say that Self-help groups (SHGs) are emerging as major mechanisms of development and empowerment of women in the third world. In India since the Ninth five year plan, most of the development programmes are channelled through SHGs. In all the parts of the country SHGs are organised by governmental and non-governmental organisations. The government departments, banks, and NGOs facilitate them by providing revolving fund, organisational base and training, credit etc. it is worthwhile to call SHGs a mass movement on a national scale for development and empowerment of the poor and downtrodden in the country.

METHODOLOGY

The study is descriptive and is based on the primary data collected by personal interview. The unit of study is the members of women SHGs. The study is confined to seven panchayat units randomly selected from Vasai taluka of Thane district in Maharashtra. All thirty five SHGs are under Jivhalla Assumption Social Centre of Vasai taluka are selected for study.

THE SHG MODEL

Structure of SHG: A SHG is a group of about 10 to 20 people, usually women, from a similar class and region, who come together to form savings and credit organization. They pooled financial resources to make small interest bearing loans to their members. This process creates an ethic that focuses on savings first. The setting of terms and conditions and accounting of the loan are done in the group by designated members.

SHG Federation: SHGs have also federated into larger organizations. In SHG Federation, about 15 to 50 SHGs make up a Cluster /Village Organisation (VO) with either one or two representatives from each SHG. Depending on geography, several clusters or VOs come together to form an apex body or an SHG Federation. At the cluster and federation level, there are inter-group borrowings, exchange of ideas, sharing of costs and discussion of common interests. There are typically various sub-committees that deal with a variety of issues including loan collections, accounting and social issues.

OVERVIEW OF SHGS IN INDIA

India is a vast country with multi-layered regional, cultural, religious, lingual and level of economic development variation. A Self-Help Group (SHG) is a registered or unregistered group of micro entrepreneurs having homogenous social and economic backgrounds, voluntarily coming together to save regular small sums of money, mutually agreeing to contribute to a common fund and to meet their emergency needs on the basis of mutual help. The group members use collective wisdom and peer pressure to ensure proper end-use of credit and timely repayment. This system eliminates the need for collateral and is closely related to that of solidarity lending, widely used by microfinance institutions. The Suwaran Jayanti Gram Savyam Rozar Yojana (SGSRY) is a Central Government Scheme implemented through the District Rural Development Agency under the Rural Development Department with the aim of alleviating poverty. The scheme was initiated in 1999.

In all the parts of the country SHGs are organised by governmental and non-governmental organisations. The government departments, banks, and NGOs facilitate them by providing revolving fund, organisational base and training, credit etc. it is worthwhile to call SHGs a mass movement on a national scale for development and empowerment of the poor and downtrodden in the country.

The rise of SHGs and more formal SHG Federations coupled now with SHG Bank Linkage have made this a dominant form of microfinance in addition to microfinance institutions (MFI). The policy environment in India has been extremely supportive for the growth of the microfinance sector in India. Particularly during the International Year of Microcredit 2005, significant policy announcements from the Government of India (GoI) and the Reserve Bank of India (RBI) have served as a shot in the arm for rapid growth. SHGs have spread rapidly due to their ease of replication. SHG Bank Linkage has provided the capacity for SHGs to increase their capital base to fund more members and bigger projects. Today, it is estimated that there are at least over 2 million SHGs in India. In many Indian states, SHGs are networking themselves into federations to achieve institutional and financial sustainability. Cumulatively, 1.6 million SHGs have been bank-linked with cumulative loans of Rs. 69 billion. In 2004-05 alone, almost 800,000 SHGs were bank-linked. However, the state of SHGs identifies key areas of weakness which undermine the sustainability of SHG movement, namely, areas such as financial management, governance and human resources range from weak to average quality for a majority of SHGs. While the spread of the movement is impressive, these are key areas that need to be addressed if any external intervention is to be effective.

The formation of common-interest groups consisting primarily of women has had a substantial impact on their lives. The impact of SHGs on women's empowerment and social security has been invariably an improvement from the status quo but there is a need for support in several areas which are analyzed in this report. The status of women has generally improved as they have developed stronger confidence which has changed gender dynamics and their role in the household. In south India, significant improvements in fertility rates, female literacy, participation in development programmes and economic independence are evident. Women are able to fight for their rights and entitlements and have emerged as a force to be reckoned with. Further, SHGs are becoming more than just financial intermediaries, instead they have emerged into a more political and social unit of society.

More importantly, the penetration of microfinance to the poorest of the poor is still weak and needs a wider reach. The areas of support to further the SHG impact are varied and the report describes areas for NGO technical and government policy support. The need for a coordinated and comprehensive support strategy is imperative as the financial management issues of SHGs need to be addressed, otherwise the benefits of the civil society impacts will be lost as SHGs will become overburdened and un-sustainable.

Emergence of the SHG Movement in VASAI

While no definitive date has been determined for the actual conception and propagation of SHGs, the practice of small groups of rural and urban people banding together to form a savings and credit organization is well established in Vasai. In the early stages, NGOs played a pivotal role in innovating the SHG model and in implementing the model to develop the process fully. It was in 1999, SHGs were started by panchayat samitis and Gram Panchayats under SGSRY. Till date there are 685 BPL SHGs working under panchayat samitis and Gram Panchayat and about 1200 SHGs are run by various NGOs. The policy makers took notice and worked with development organizations and bankers to discuss the possibility of promoting these savings and credit groups. Their efforts and the simplicity of SHGs helped to spread the movement across the taluka. State governments established revolving loan funds which were used to fund SHGs were viewed by state governments and NGOs to be more than just a financial intermediation but as a common interest group, working on other concerns as well. The agenda of SHGs included social and political issues as well. The spread of SHGs led also to the formation of SHG Federations which are a more sophisticated form of organization that involve several SHGs forming into Village Organizations (VO) / Cluster. The NGOs are engaged in organizing women's group, encouraging thrift habits among them, promoting and supporting them to improve their living conditions. One such case is Jivhalla Assumption Social Centre, which is working in Vasai.

Jivhalla Assumption Social Centre

Mission: Towards New Horizons of Self-Reliance and for a Sustainable Development.

The members, of Jivhalla Assumption Social Centre are dedicated to serve the poorest of the poor, marginalized and oppressed people with a purpose to give them dignity, equality, justice and love through people's full participation. It aims at the integral development of people by enabling them to commit themselves towards becoming self-reliant by education which will lead them to personal and collective action. In all the efforts to educate and develop the poorest of the poor, they aim to collaborate and network with like minded individuals, government and non-governmental organizations (NGOs).

Jivhalla Assumption Social Centre is a registered NGO whose purpose is the promotion of life through various educational, social, political, psychological, economical i.e. all-round development of the poor. They have been working for 40 hamlets in and around Rajodi, in 7 Gram Panchayats. At present 35 SHGs are formed and run by them. They have started Cluster/ Village Organisation by combining 10 SHGs together.

This Centre is situated in Rajodi, in Vasai Taluka of Maharashtra State. It is not only in the interior but also in the coastal area, 80 km away from Mumbai. Vasai has different communities belonging to different religion and cultures as Hindus, Muslims Adivasis and Dalit. The Adivasis (the tribal aboriginal population of India) especially warlis are a small group who are hidden from the main-stream of development. In this area, they are migrant labourers who have neither land nor house. They are exploited by the land owners. They have no access to get out of the bonded labour system and are caught in the vicious circle of poverty and illiteracy. Around 80% of them are illiterate. They can't read, write or even sign. These forces conspire them in their present state of under-development for they contribute cheap, docile, dependable labour. 80% of them don't have their names in the electoral roll. Many of them do not have below poverty line card (BPL) or ration card. Many of the Adivasi villages do not have the basic necessities of life such as drinking water, electricity, Healthcare Centres, road access etc. The unhygienic conditions of living make them prone to different kinds of illnesses. The life span of these people is forty to fifty years. Due to frustrations and helplessness many of them commit suicide.

The youth are addicted to alcohol and gambling. In the early childhood, children are taught to drink alcohol. They continue this practice all throughout their life. Women are the most docile and vulnerable, due to the low status which makes them live with domestic violence, illiteracy, ignorance, superstitious beliefs, no decision making power, no saving, no freedom to move out of their houses. The early marriages, and thereby the early responsibilities affect their health badly. The girls are treated like goods that are only useful for doing the household work and later to be married. Thus their education is neglected. Poverty, hunger, malnutrition and disease seemed to be their painful fate. There seemed to be the condition of sheer hopelessness.

ACTIVITIES

Jivhalla Assumption Social Centre believes in Education, which is the way to progress and empowering the people with life promoting values. To reach this goal they have undertaken following activities:

(1) **Development of SHGs:** Women form group to open Saving Accounts in the banks. To start one group, it needs a lot of time and numerous meetings, but the results are obvious: they learn financial interaction, they increase their self view-point, get the freedom from money lenders and gradually start income generation programmes. Once the saving Account is opened, the work continues with various meetings and training programmes every month.

(2) **Educational & developmental programmes for women:** Group building sessions on different topics are held to strengthen the groups to take up issues together. They organise seminars to make them aware of girl child, child care and understand the importance of the education, legal awareness, importance of health care, nutritious food and so on. The sessions are also organised so that they may understand themselves to be better persons. Gradually the change is visible. They learn to talk with others, to get out of home for the meetings to go to bank etc. Their decision making power has really increased.

(3) **Supplementary Classes for Children:** Supplementary classes are necessary to support the education of the poor, for the motivation of the children, and their parents. These classes are run in their own villages, in the rooms provided by the villagers themselves. The teachers are chosen from the village itself who have studied minimum, thus there is need for intensive training. They arrange monthly training sessions for the teachers.

(4) **Awareness Programmes on the Rights and Environmental Issues:** They organise awareness programmes on environmental issues such as the use of solar energy, tree plantation including medicinal plants, ill-effects of the excessive use of plastic and the like.

(5) **Educational Activities:** One of the most important problems of these women and children is their character. They are timid, frightful with a low self-image, as a result of the marginalization lived for so many years. With these programmes, they stress on healthy relations. They learn to face challenges of life with courage.

(6) **Issue based Activities:** They work hard to help the people to get the ration card, BPL card, to insert their names in the electoral roll, to make aware of schemes for widows etc.

(7) **Other Activities:** Home visits, survey of villages, starting of federation of SHGs, study tours, camps, meeting and discussion with leaders of the villages, bank managers, and government officials are arranged in order to empower the marginalised.

CONSTRAINTS

- Lack of support from male members (of the families) as well as banks
- Large magnitude of the target group of poor people
- Attitudinal rigidities
- Difficulty in creating awareness among people
- Limited resources with the NGO
- Large requirements of training and sensitization of issues

ACHIEVEMENTS

- Maintenance of proper accounts by the SHGs
- Regular meetings of the SHGs members to tackle problems among themselves
- Healthy relation and coordination between SHGs, NGOs and banks
- Generation of small savings in the rural sector among women
- Use of local knowledge and resources in productive activities
- Nearly 100% recovery of loans

CONCLUSION

Self-help groups are playing a vital role in women empowerment that leads to total community development in Vasai taluka. The capacity building by SHGs has led to many positive socio-economic changes not only among its members, but also among other members in the rural community. Training programmes for members of women SHGs, community based organisations mobilisation and management of micro finance, law as a tool of women's empowerment, climate change, etc., are conducted by the NGO. Besides making their own savings and credit portfolio, the SHG members have also started establishing small micro finance institutions encompassing members from cluster of villages. The members are now slowly involved in initiating income-generating economic activities.

The number of women involved in politics is low. But, the trend is definitely moving up. Their presence today is affecting the perception of women and their role in the political arena. They are being recognized as an important group with serious concerns.

The role of SHGs is both as inspiration and as a financer. Impoverished women develop greater language and financial skills through the SHG which provides the building blocks for higher levels of confidence to engage the world.

SHGs not only empower its members but also wield a powerful political role as a group as well. At local village meetings, the leaders of SHGs are often invited to attend and speak.

The impact of SHGs on social harmony has also been mixed. While it has been observed that in groups with mixed membership they had group leaders that came from a variety of the social groups. In the vast majority of instances, group leaders were almost exclusively from the dominant social groups' category. This demonstrates a lack of equality and unity across caste divisions.

SHGs resolve disputes between members and the community at large. These instances include initiating legal action, arbitration, divorce and others. There are significant contributions from SHGs to education, family planning, eradication of child labour and hygiene. The SHG demonstrated a clear leadership role and rallied the support of the entire village. This demonstrates that given the opportunity, SHGs, assuming they have the capacity, can act as director of community development. The perception of a women's based organization taking a leading role for the betterment of society has monumental impact on the local community. Gender dynamics begin to balance in instances such as these.

SUGGESTIONS

There is an urgent need for coordinating NGOs and government policy support to increase sustainability of benefits of SHGs to the society. Livelihood measures should be an area that is vitally important to SHGs along with social empowerment. Hence, it is necessary to emphasise more on income generating activities among the women of the group, to improve their livelihood so that they can receive greater and steadier cash flows. In rural areas, livelihood ranging from agriculture farming, animal husbandry, dairy and various other goods and services activities should be promoted. Along with development of entrepreneurial skill, training regarding the market activities should also be improved. Moreover, communication and leadership skills should be given more importance, to improve personality development and group discussion skill for real empowerment.

BIBLIOGRAPHY

- Dr. Daniel Lazar, Prof. P. Palanichamy, Micro Finance and Poverty Eradication, New Century Publication, New Delhi 2008.
- H. D. Dwarakanath, Rural Credit And Empowerment of Women under Self Help Groups – A Study of Ranga Reddy District. 2006.
- H. Parameshwar Hedge, Modern Women and The Society, Mohit Publication, New Delhi 2005.
- Kropp, Dr. Erhard W. & Suran, Dr. B.S., Linking Banks and (Financial) Self Help Groups in India – An Assessment, November 2002.
- Lalrinliana, Joseph and Easwaran Kanagaraj (2006) "SHGs and Tribal Development in Mizoram". Kurukshetra, (January): 37-48
- M. R. Biju, Women's Empowerment, A Mittal Publication, New Delhi. 2006.
- Rathindra Nath, Pramanik Ashim, Kumar Adhikari, Gender Inequality and Women's Empowerment, Abhijeet Publication, New Delhi. 2006.
- Sukanya Nihal Singh, Prospectus for Women Empowerment Dynamics of Enablement, Commonwealth Publishers, New Delhi 2001.
- Tara Singhal, Working Women and Family, RBSA Publishers Jaipur. 2003.

☆ ☆ ☆

3 SHG - As a Catalyst in Empowerment of Rural Women

ABSTRACT

The women's empowerment refers to the process by which women acquire due recognition, at par with men, to participate in the development process of the society. This decision making can be in many forms. In the form of political participation, in the form of social and domestic activity and in the form of entrepreneur in small and tiny enterprise.

The lifestyle of rural, urban and pseudo urban is strikingly different so also the power of decision making. The women still work either under the shadow of men or has to be anti-men. But the concept of decision making is not family disharmony in particular and social disharmony in general.

Panchyat raj (73rd Amendment Act, 1992) played a vital role in empowering rural women and paved the way to women decision making and exposure of rural women to each other's point of view and experience in all phases of life.

This exposure and group activity led to formation of meaningful groups (SHGs) which worked as a catalyst in setting economic activities where savvy business decisions are to be taken for economic gain. SHG can be precisely viewed as a vehicle for women's economic development which works as a catalytic factor in sharpening women's decision making power and leads to the development of savings habit among the women. More importantly, the SHGs consists of members who are below poverty line.

With economic empowerment, the role of women as a decision maker went beyond the four walls of the kitchen and made her an important party in household decision in the social sector too.

In this paper an empirical study was carried out using primary as well as secondary data obtained through personal interviews and government gazettes. The focus of study was on rural women who were basically poor (BPL). The constraint of social and economic factor was considered and a comparative analysis was made. Finally some recommendations were made for positive improvement of the women.

Indian culture as well as tradition respects women as 'Shakti', the source of power. She serves be in the form of Mother, Sister, Wife and Daughter. Days have passed. Now she is free of every burden and has proved herself quite capable. After the successful political role of women in the Panchayati Raj system, for which Late Biju Patnaik deserves all the credit, now they have proved their excellence in economic sector being a part of family's income source through Mission Shakti. Groups constituted under Mission Shakti are basically non - formal organizations. In order to get rid of financial crunch, this idea was conceived in the mind of the poor people. They assembled themselves and initiate such effort. 36,000 WSHGs were there in the State of Orissa prior to the launching of 'Mission Shakti'. Banking organizations, Co-operative Banks, Private Banking sector, N.G.Os and both the Union and State Governments extended a helping hand. Where Banking organizations were reluctant to sanction individual loans apprehending the uncertainty in repayment there they cheerfully grant group loans and also double the loan amount. Group loans generally grow with small business, agriculture and consumer loan including repayment of the previous loan from the private money lenders (Sahukar) and for medical treatment etc. Most of the people, who were below poverty line, now by this way, have been excluded from the B.P.L list. The definition of the word 'poor' impacts in a certain directive to their mentality and they try to come out of the said depressive word with self-confidence. According to CARE India and SIDBI, there are over 16 lakh Self Help Groups throughout the country. An amount of over Rs. 6500 crore has been sanctioned towards these S.H.Gs. The aforesaid statements were expressed by the said Organisations in the year 2005.

The basic aim of the SHGs can be summarised as a logical extension of Government's advocacy for sustainable development of women.

(1) Increased participation by women in local governments and decision making processes.

(2) Greater spread of community based organizations, including women's group.

(3) An increasing focus of poverty alleviation programmes for women; a mandate to eliminate discrimination against girl children and adolescents in matters of food, health, education and child labour.

(4) Recognition of the need to sensitize all levels of bureaucracy, legislator and law enforcement agencies to gender issues.

(5) The promotion of income activities and thrift and credit through self help groups for women.

SHG AND WOMEN EMPOWERMENT - AN OVERVIEW

Operationally, women empowerment is also defined as a mental state where the process has been identified as resultant of two basic components. The first is social mobilization and collective agency, as poor women often lack the basic capabilities and self confidence to counter and challenge existing disparities and barriers against them. Often change agents are needed to catalyze social mobilization which needs to be accompanied and complemented by economic freedom and security. Both the factors jointly strengthen the confidence level which in turn expands the number of choices for the women.

The orign of SHG during early 1980s, and experimental attempt was made in the neighboring country of Bangaladesh by Dr Md. Yunus to encourage landless and marginalized women known as beggars, to undertake petly trade with little loan given from his own pocket at the initial stage. This effort was turned into a grand success with its innovative approach to the motive. The rural poor and unprevieleged women inculcated banking habits through small savings and credit activities, which at present has attained a global campaigns "Bangaladesh Grameen Bank".

In Indian context, women Self Help Groups are actively performing the role of reorganizing the village as well as the country. Saving of an amount nearing Rs. 200 crore has been possible through Women S.H.Gs whereas more than Rs. 55462.18 lakhs have already been sanctioned as loan assistance towards 2,22,142 A/c holders by the end of March-2006. The Units run by S.H.Gs are in Cattle rearing, Goat farm, Poultry, Bee keeping, Horticulture, Tissue culture, Floriculture, Pisci-culture, Vegetable and Mushroom cultivation, Sewing, Handicrafts, Making of soft toys, Cottage industries' products handicrafts, Pickle and Spice production etc. S.H.Gs. are also carrying out labor-intensive Programmes. Selling of control kerosene and L.P.G has also been handed over to these S.H.Gs. In many cases the Government (e.g Government of Orissa) has directed to the Health and Urban Development Department for purchasing phenyl and pesticides prepared by the S.H.Gs.1080 S.H.G candidates have been imparted with Computer Training. During a natural calamity, S.H.Gs are being engaged in relief and restoration works. Panchayati Raj and Horticulture Departments are also one step ahead in providing special loan assistance to some selected S.H.Gs.

OBJECTIVE OF THE STUDY

The objective of women empowerment (typically rural poor women) through SHG approach is to make the rural women empowered in all respects in general but specifically the objective may be pointed out to be;

- To develop awareness about different affairs relating to their social, economic, health, cultural and political matters.
- Linkage and orientation of supporting agencies (like RRBS, Govt agencies. Panchayat and NGOs)
- Inculcation of saving and credit habit among the members
- Exposure to office administration
- Scientific approach to various activities (like marketing and financial management)

SIGNIFICANCE AND SCOPE OF STUDY

This study tries to find out how women once engaged only in household work are now generating income for their family. By the help of the S.H.Gs, women in village are discussing themselves regarding the day-to-day development in social, political, economical, cultural and spiritual fields. They also discuss their personal and family problems and find a way for solution to their impediments through S.H.Gs. Participating in the process of development and welfare of their village they successfully perform their role.

In Adivasi populated areas, the S.H.Gs are fighting against illiteracy, poverty, superstitions and sale and distillation of spurious country liquor. They also create public awareness regarding the eventuality bursts out of drinking wine or using other excised goods. People can escape their problems by helping each other. It does mean not only to the fiscal but also to every aspect of life. The moral power of women representatives in Panchayati Raj system becomes strong and decisive owing to these S.H.Gs as they certainly create congenial atmosphere for the co-operative movement as well as social reforms. The 'zoolum' of the 'Sahukar' lessens by this way. Programmes and preparations undertaken by the Government for proper health-service towards women and children are successfully being implemented; infant mortality rate has been reduced and "care of the pregnant one helps in bringing out a healthy child" is well taught in the areas where, S.H.Gs are active.

BRIEF PROFILE OF THE STUDY AREA

Nayagarh district is located in the central part of Orissa. The district of Nayagarh was formed on the basis of 1981 census, taking the old Nayagarh Subdivision of Puri district for recognition of Puri into 4 different districts. The district of Nayagarh comprises of one subdivision, eight tahasils and eight C.D. Blocks, four towns, two NACs, one hundred and seventy nine Gram Panchayats and seveteen hundred two inhabited villages. This is one of the backward districts of Orissa. There are sizable tribal and SC numbers who constitute 20 to 25 per cent of the total population. They are scattered over all the territories of the district. It is needless to say that tribals as well as SCs are underdeveloped and malnourished.

Table 1:

Total population, Rural and Urban Population by sex in different blocks and Urban areas of Nayagarh district.

S.No	Block / Urban	Male	Female	Total	Sex ratio
(1)	Bhapur	47973	45948	93921	958
(2)	Dasapalla	47452	45045	92497	949
(3)	Gania	18031	16619	34650	922
(4)	Khandapara	51843	47775	99618	922
(5)	Nayagarh	69115	63529	132644	919
(6)	Nuagaon	43872	40377	84249	920
(7)	Odagaon	79579	74031	153610	930
(8)	Ranapur	76044	74149	150193	975
Total rural		433909	407473	841382	939
	Urban				
(1)	**Khandapara**	**4530**	**4227**	**8757**	**933**
(2)	**Nayagarh**	**7720**	**6594**	**14314**	**854**
Total Urban		**12250**	**10821**	**23071**	**883**
Grand Total		**446159**	**418294**	**864453**	**938**

The population of the Nayagarh district in the year 2001 was 864,453 (Table 1). The rural population was 841332 and urban population was 23071. It occupies 2.75 per cent of the total land area of Orissa. In 2001 census there were 1,21,000 (approx) inhabitants belonging to Scheduled Castes and 51,000 (approx) belonging to Scheduled Tribes. The sex ratio was found to be 938 females per 1000 males as shown in Table 1. The density of population of Nayagarh district was 223. The literacy rate of Nayagarh district was 39 per cent in 2001 census. Out of which 52 per cent males and 26 per cent are females. The literacy rate of Scheduled Castes and Scheduled Tribes were 21% and 15 per cent, respectively (*District Statistical Handbook*, 2001). The workforce of the district as obtained from 2001 census were 2,88,503, out of which 2,05,676 were main workers, 82,377 were marginal workers, (All inclusive of cultivators agricultural labourers too). About 17 per cent employment is generated under SGRY, out of which 4.87 per cent were SCs, 8.85 per cent were STs and 2.78 per cent were OBCs. There are 2469 groups working throughout the district of Nayagarh and the number of women participants was 33,206. Out of them 823 groups are working under NGOs, 1534 groups are working under the ICDS (Integrated Child Development Schemes), 25 in Block level and 87 groups are working independently.

LITERATURE REVIEW

Few studies are available on SHG and micro-finance and women empowerment. The researcher has tried to review the following:

Osman (2000) in his article remarked that micro-finance schemes alone cannot alleviate poverty. The battle for total eradication of poverty requires combining micro-finance schemes with parallel, complementary programmes addressing the social and cultural dimensions of want, privation, impoverishment and dispossession. **Kapur (2001)** in her study tried to discuss, analyse and answer the challenging questions as to why despite all the efforts and progress made, still there continues to be so much of gender discrimination and what strategies, actions and measures to be undertaken to achieve the expected goal of empowerment. She opined that women's empowerment is much more likely to be achieved if women have total control over their own organisations, which they can sustain both financially and managerially without direct dependence on others. **Pattanaik (2003)** in her study reveals that SHGs are continuously striving for a better future for tribal women as participants, decision-makers and beneficiaries in the domestic, economic, social and cultural spheres of life. But due to certain constraints like gender inequality, exploitation, women torture for which various Self Help Groups are not organised properly and effectively. **Malhotra (2004)** in her book has examined how women entrepreneurs affect the global economy, why women start business, how women's business associations promote entrepreneurs, and to what extent women contribute to international trade. It explores potential of micro-finance programmes for empowering and employing women and also discusses the opportunities and challenges of using micro-finance to tackle the feminisation of poverty. According to her, the micro-finance programmes are aimed to increase women's income levels and control over income leading to greater levels of economic independence. They enable women's access to networks and markets, access to information and possibilities for development of other social and political role. They also enhance perceptions of women's contribution to household income and family welfare, increasing women's participation in household decisions about expenditure and other issues leading to greater expenditure on women's welfare. **Narasaiah (2004)** in his study mentioned that the change in women's contribution to society is one of the striking phenomena of the late twentieth century. According to him micro-credit plays an important role in empowering women. Giving women the opportunity to realise their potential in all spheres of society is increasingly important. **Cheston & Kuhn (2004)** in their study concluded that micro-finance programmes have been very successful in reaching women. This gives micro-finance institutions an extraordinary opportunity to act intentionally to empower poor women and to minimise the potentially negative impacts some women experience. **Manimekalai (2004)** in his article commented that to run the income generating activities successfully, the SHGs must get the help of NGOs. The bank officials should counsel and guide the women in selecting and implementing profitable income generating activities. He remarked that the formation of SHGs has boosted the self-image and confidence of rural women. **Sahu and Tripathy (2005)** in their edited book view that 70 per cent of the world's poor are women. Access of the poor to banking services is important not only for poverty alleviation but also for optimising their contribution to the growth of regional as well as the national economy. Self Help Groups (SHGs) have emerged as the most vital instrument in the process of participatory development and women empowerment. The rural women are the marginalized groups in the society because of socio-economic constraints. They remain backward and lower position of the social hierarchical ladder. They can lift themselves from the morass of poverty and stagnation through micro finance and formation of Self-Help Groups. **Das Gupta (2005)** in his article commented that a paradigm shift is required from "financial sector reform" to "micro-finance reform". While the priority sector needs to be made lean, mandatory micro credit must be monitored rigorously. Simultaneously, space and scope have to be properly designed for providing competitive environment to micro-finance services. Extensive database needs to be created by the RBI for understanding micro-finance. **Sinha (2005)** in his study has observed that micro-finance is making a significant contribution to both the savings and borrowing of the poor in the country. According to him the main use of micro-credit is for direct investment. There is of course some fungibility, depending on household credit requirements at the time of loan disbursement. Some studies reveal that micro-finance programmes have had positive as well as negative impacts on women. Some researchers have questioned how far micro-finance benefits women (**Goetz and Sen Gupta, 1996**). Some argue that micro-finance programmes divert the attention of women from other more effective strategies for empowerment (**Ebdon, 1995**), and the attention and the resources of donors from alternative, and possibly more effective means of alleviating poverty (**Rogaly, 1996**). In some cases, women's increased autonomy has been temporary. It only benefits women who are already better off. But in most cases the poorest women are least able to benefit because of their low initial resources base, lack of skill and market contact.

As per report prepared by **TOWARD** there are 234 SHG under DWACRA and 230 under SGSY in the district of Nayagarh.As per **Orissa Review 2004** Mission Shakti was lunched in 2001 to bring and create 1 lakh WSHGs in rural Orissa in four years. By the end of 2003 threre were 99661 groups with more than 13,00,000 members with a total capital asset of Rs. 68 crores. It surpassed the target by the end of 2004. At present around 24 lakh families are involved in this movement with more than 2,40,000 WSHGS and Rs.343 crore loan assistance (**Orissa Review 2006**).

FOCUS AREA OF STUDY

The broad objective of the study is to examine the role and performance of WSHGs (Mission Shakti in Orissa) in promoting women's empowerment in the study area i.e District of Nayagarh. However, the study has some typical objectives. They are:

(1) To analyse the economic gains derived by the members after joining the WSHGs.
(2) To examine the change in social status of the members.
(3) To analyse the modus operandi of SHGs for the mobilization of saving, delivery of credit to the needy, management of group funds, repayment of loans, in building up leadership, and establishing linkage with banks.
(4) To suggest any changes through policy intervention for the effective performance of SHGs.

PROCESS OF STUDY (METHODOLOGY)

Selection of Study Area and Sample Units: The study was carried out in selective clusters spread over five blocks of Nayagarh district in Orissa.

It is noteworthy to mention here that the Women Self-Help Groups (Mission Shakti) in nayagarh district are encouraged by government and promoted by NGOs as well as Government agencies. Due to time constraint the researcher has selected the SHGs promoted Under umbrella of Mission Shakti by a particular NGO. At present this NGO is working in all 8 community development blocks. There are 356 Self-Help Groups promoted by This NGO in the eight blocks. The researcher has chosen 6 SHGs each from each block promoted by the NGO. In total the study covers 48 SHGs with 691 members.

Table 2.

Sampling Frame of the Study

Block	SHGs	SHG Members
Bhapur	6	90
Dasapalla	6	75
Gania	6	100
Khandapara	6	86
Nayagarh	6	80
Nuagaon	6	90
Odagaon	6	85
Ranapur	6	85
Total	**48**	**691**

Data Collection and Analysis

In order to collect and gather primary data, field observation and structured questionnaire survey methods were employed. In addition, information was also collected through discussions and interviews with local NGOs and government's grass roots level workers. Secondary data gathered from the records of SHGs and NGOs and government offices were supplemented by the primary data collected from the group. A wide range of information such as composition of membership, savings mobilised, loans disbursed, interest rates, recovery procedures, assets created, external assistance received etc. were ascertained from the SHGs and their members. Besides, different books, newspapers, articles, journals, magazines and web sites were also referred for the purpose. The data collected from each block regarding the structure and profile of SHG members, savings and loans of SHGs, economic and social benefits derived by SHG members, etc. has been processed separately and averages of each block are being taken. The analyses obtained from different blocks are compiled and compared to draw the inferences about the performance of the SHGs in the study area.

DATA ANALYSIS

Structure of SHGs

The structure and characteristics of Self-Help Groups in the study area is presented in Table 3. It is noted that the average membership per SHG was 16.75. The study reveals that in the Nayagarh and Ranapur blocks the average membership of the Self-Help Group is the highest (18) and Gania block had the lowest membership (15). Most of the members agreed that their motives in joining SHGs were to save. Some said they joined the SHG to get credit to meet the unexpected cash demand for consumption and other purposes. Few opined that it led to social empowerment. The average savings per SHG was Rs. 13,532. It varied from Rs. 8003 in Ranpur to Rs. 18225 in Daspalla block. The per member savings was around Rs. 939.

The frequency of group meeting by SHG indicated that fortnightly meetings were the most common followed by monthly and weekly. Meetings are arranged regularly by NGOs, government agencies and Groups. They are held in the middle of the street. The absentee member has to pay a fine of Rs. 5.

Table 3.

Structure of SHGs in the Study Area

Item	Bhapur	Daspalla	Gania	Khandapara	Nayagarh	Nuagaon	Odogaon	Ranapur	Overall
Membership average (No.)	15	18	15	16	18	17	17	18	16.75
Savings per SHG (in Rs.)	13217	18225	14637	17564	16367	10456	9876	8003	13532
Loan (Avg.) (in Rs.)	19752	19177	16040	17758	18000	11370	10190	9134	13756
Frequency of group meeting (percentage):									
Weekly	6	15	7	12	17	8	11	10	10.75
Fortnightly	60	68	70	35	28	56	69	28	51.75
Monthly	10	17	15	12	17	24	24	12	16.375

Source: Obtained from primary data collected.

Profile of SHG Members

The average age of WSHG members in the study area is presented in Table 4; it is observed that the average age of SHG members was 34 years, lowest being 32 years in Daspalla block and highest being 37 years in Nayagarh block. Regarding the caste profile of SHG members, the table shows that majority of members belong to non-SC or Non-ST category. However sizable tribal and SC members are there (9.5% and 18.5%, respectively). Highest number of tribals are in Khandapara block and highest number of SCs in Gania block. Educational background of the WSHG members shows that most of them are illiterate. Only 10 per cent of them have studied up to primary level. So far as the occupation of the members is concerned, almost equal number of them are engaged in agricultural as well as non-agricultural activities. As regards to average income per SHG, it was around Rs. 7904. It was highest in Nayagarh block (Rs. 8948) follo)wed by Daspalla block (Rs. 8823) and lowest in Ranapur block (Rs. 7182).

Table 4.

Profile of SHG Members

Item		Bhapur	Daspalla	Gania	Khandapara	Nayagarh	Nuagaon	Odogaon	Ranapur	Overall
Age (years)		34	32	33	35	37	35	33	34	34.12
Percentage of STs		5	12	15	17	7	8	7	5	9.5
Percentage of SCs		15	22	32	25	15	12	14	15	18.75
Percentage of Other Castes		70	56	52	58	78	80	79	80	69
Literacy (%)		6	12	8	16	15	8	10	12	10.87
Occupation	Agri (%)	72	36	40	45	37	47	63	52	49
	Others (%)	28	64	60	55	63	53	37	48	51
Income (Average)		7867	8823	7657	7824	8948	7345	7589	7182	7904

Obtained from Primary data collected

Utilisation of Fund through Credit

Generally, after six months operation of savings account, the saving is pooled and used for internal lending among the members. The amount of loan and number of loans are decided by the members themselves depending on their need and urgency.

Table 5.

Credit Demanded by WSHG Members and utilisation (In%)

Item	Bhapur	Daspalla	Gania	Khandapara	Nayagarh	Nuagaon	Odogaon	Ranapur	Overall
Domestic consumption	28	29	15	61	52	27	31	35	34.75
Health	12	21	10	8	12	17	13	8	12.625
Festivals	16	10	9	6	12	14	11	19	12.125
Repayment of old debts	16	11	11	6	11	16	16	13	12.5
Investment	15	12	12	7	8	12	15	17	12.25
Others	13	17	43	12	5	14	14	8	15.75
Total	**100**	**100**	**100**	**100**	**100**	**100**	**100**	**100**	**100**

Source: Obtained from primary data collected

The utilisation of credit demanded by the WSHG members from the WSHGs is given in Table 5. It is observed that most of the members have demanded credit for domestic consumption purposes. It is highest in Khandapara block (61%) followed by Nayagarh (52%). The credit requirement for health and festival appears to be almost the same so also for repayment of old debts and investment. Around 16% credit is for other purposes.

Economic Activities Covered by SHG Members

Table 6 revels that most of the WSHG members are engaged in the agro-base activities. These include broom making, cashew processing, food processing, turmeric processing, tamarind,), coir, seasonal pickle, etc. Some of the members are engaged in forest based activities like tendu leaf collection, Mahul collection, palm gur processing and preparing leaf plates. They are also engaged in poultry, dairy and goatery business. Some are engaged in other activities like making haldi. powder, wax, making bags, vegetable business, tailoring, pan shop, etc. As there is a good demand for milk products, they are preparing sweets with milk, ghee, etc. and are getting a good price. They earn about Rs. 800 to Rs. 1200 per month through these activities.

Table 6.

Economic Activities Covered by the SHG Members

Item	Bhapur	Daspalla	Gania	Khandapara	Nayagarh	Nuagaon	Odogaon	Ranapur	Overall
Forest based	18	28	22	18	16	15	18	23	19.75
Agro based	43	39	52	54	49	51	43	46	47.125
Goatery	18	12	11	11	14	15	10	12	12.875
Dairy	12	10	9	9	12	8	14	8	10.25
Others	9	11	6	8	9	11	15	11	10
Total	**100**	**100**	**100**	**100**	**100**	**100**	**100**	**100**	**100**

Source: Information obtained from primary data

Loan Support to SHGs by Banks

There is a bank linkage programme established to WSHGs. The WSHG members opened their accounts in various nationalised banks such as State Bank of India, Indian Bank, Bank of Baroda, Union Bank of India, Andhra Bank, etc. and also some local banks like Puri Grmya bank (Nayagarh was initially a part of Puri District) and Cooperative Banks. And under Mission shakti NABARD extends loan directly to Rural Co-operative Banks to help in Micro finance advances to WSHGs.

Under Mission Shakti WSHG members are getting both internal loans and external loans under the security and guidelines NABARD through NGOs. They are paying .2% interest. They are also maintaining cashbook, membership register, loan register, individual passbook register, etc. They are entitled to avail loan for both production and consumption purposes. Banks have advanced loans of upto tune of Rs. 2,66,324/- to Dasapalla block the least being Rs. 1,12,324 at Ganiablock.

So far as loan repayment is concerned, the WSHG members of Bhapur Block have repaid 82 per cent of their loans followed by Nayagarh block with 81 per cent. The repayment percent is in sitys in case of Nuagaon and Odogaon block (**Table 7**). It shoul be noted that under scheme of NABARD loans are to be disbursed to WSHGS under Mission Shakti without any collateral.

Table 7.

Loan Support to SHGs from Various Banks (for WSHGs under Study)

Name of the Block	Total SHGs	Loan availed	Loan Repayment
Bhapur	6	Rs. 1,26,212	82%
Dasapalla	6	Rs. 2,66,324	75%
Gania	6	Rs. 1,12,324	62%
Khandapara	6	Rs. 2,13,567	58%
Nayagarh	6	Rs. 2,04,634	81%
Nuagaon	6	Rs. 1,19,315	65%
Odagaon	6	Rs. 1,12,567	66%
Ranapur	6	Rs. 1,90,372	78%
Total	**48**	**Rs. 13,45.315**	**70%**

Source: Annual Audited Report of WSHGs

Benefits Extended by Panchayat

As 30% of the seats in panchayat are reserved for women, it worked as a positive impetus in order to get benefits like ease of formation of SHG, enhancing the leadership quality, active participation in panchayat sponsored (supervised) activities like PDS and decision making capacity.

Benefits Derived by SHG Members

Variety of benefits are derived by the members of SHGs as presented in Table 8

Table 8

Item	Bhapur	Daspalla	Gania	Khandapara	Nayagarh	Nuagaon	Odogaon	Ranapur	Overall
Habit of Savings	72	81	66	76	77	72	68	66	72.25
Economic independence	70	64	69	62	72	64	62	68	66.375
Self-confidence	81	87	84	68	86	68	70	59	75.375
Social cohesion	70	76	74	67	77	79	82	77	75.25
Asset ownership	53	64	26	56	60	51	60	45	51.875
Freedom from debt	49	56	77	70	65	58	53	63	61.375
Additional employment	32	35	39	44	63	66	62	23	45.5

Source: Compiled from primary data (in %)

The members opine that the best benefit they received is a to boost self confidence and social cohesion. Sizable number of members have developed a habit of savings. Generation of additional employment is not that encouraging.

Findings of the Study

Based on the primary interaction with the group members, field workers of the local NGO and group questionnaire survey results, the following findings emerged.

The social profile of SHG members indicates that majority of members are non-tribal; however, sizable tribal involvement is there in WSHG under Mission Shakti though the literacy rate is very low.

It is found that the operational efficiency and group dynamics of the SHG is not the same in all blocks. This could be attributed to several factors like background of SHG formation, internal problem, support provided by the promoters, government mechanism effective leadership, etc.

It is observed that the average membership in WSHG under Mission Shakti was around 16.75. Membership is the highest in Nayagarh and Ranapur block and the lowest in Bhapur and Gania block. However, the disparity is not significant between rural and urban divide.

The members had joined the group in order to earn more income, promote savings habits and to develop collective economic and social activities.

So far as the frequency of group meetings are concerned, it is observed that fortnightly meetings were the most common.

The Groups maintain cashbooks, passbooks and attendance registers. The members in-charge of accounts are being given training in book-keeping by the NGOs as per guidelines of

NABARD. But the member who looks after all these secretarial work is not paid any financial incentive.

From the study, it is found that individual members contribute Rs. 15 to Rs. 65 per month. 70 per cent of SHG circulated thrift and their period of circulation was monthly. Accumulated savings by members to group funds per SHG were to the tune of Rs. 13,532, against this loan disbursed amounted to Rs. 13,756.

The SHG disbursed loans both for consumption and production purposes. Purpose-wise disbursement of credit by SHG indicates that, domestic consumption received maximum share of 34.75 per cent, followed by others (15.75%). It is found that credit demanded for investment purpose is low.

As far as external loan is concerned, the Banks under scheme of NABARD have advanced loans to the tune of Rs. 13 lakhs as a whole(of which 70% has been repaid). The members have invested the loan in different economic activities like broom making, *khalli* stitching (leaf-plates), preparing eatables like *bodi*, *papad*, etc. They are also engaged in poultry, dairy and goatery business. In Gania block, the members are preparing milk products like sweets, ghee, *khoa*, etc. and getting good price. They earn about Rs. 600 to Rs. 1000 per month through these activities. The study reveals that the members are not skilled enough to run various units.

Members perceived several benefits through their membership in SHGs such as economic independence and self-confidence, promotion of savings habits, social cohesion and freedom from debt.

The study also reveals that WSHGs had set a new agenda for financial intermediation by banks in the form of micro-credit. It has infused dynamism among its members to climb up socio-economic ladder in the development process. Thus, WSHGs have served the cause of women empowerment, social solidarity and socio-economic betterment of the poor for their consolidation.

CONCLUSION AND SUGGESTIONS

Considering the findings of the study, the following suggestions were prescribed.

- Literacy and accounting training is needed for the poor women to benefit from the micro-credit schemes. Training in legal aspect, rights and gender awareness are important complements to micro-credit for the empowerment of women. The members should be given necessary training and guidance for the successful operation of the group.
- The members of the WSHG should be more active, enthusiastic and dynamic to mobilise their savings by group actions. In this process NGOs should act as a friend, philosopher and guide.
- The office bearers managing the group should be given nominal financial benefits, which will motivate them to be more involved in the activities of the Group.
- The bank should advance adequate credit to the WSHG according to their needs and repaying capacity. Uniformity should be maintained in formation and extension of financial assistance to them by banks in all blocks.
- The procedure of the banks in sanctioning credit to WSHG should be simple and quick.
- Marketing facilities for the sale of products of WSHG may be created.Periodical

exhibitions at block-level may be organised where the products of SHG can be displayed.

- Meetings and Seminars may be organised where the members will get a chance to exchange their views and be able to develop their group strength by interactions.
- Active intervention (not interference) by district administration, professional bodies and voluntary organisations is precondition for the successful conception of micro enterprises in terms of skill training, designing products, providing new technology and access to market.
- Panchayats should also come forward to prepare cluster of training centres so that better and practical training can be imparted to SHG members based on local requirement.

POLICY IMPLICATIONS

In this twenty-first century, we must take along an active people-centred and growth-oriented poverty (the word itself an insult to human dignity) alleviation strategy – a strategy which seems to incorporate women's aspirations (thereby a family's inspiration), dynamism and involvement. It is envisaged that self-help groups in the umbrella of Mission Shakti will play a vital role in such strategy. But there is a need for structural orientation of the groups to suit the requirements of new business.

Micro credit movement has to be viewed from a long-term perspective under WSHG framework, which underlines the need for a deliberate policy implications in favour of assurance in terms of technology back-up, product market and human resource development. Hence, there is a need for the development of an innovative and diversified micro-finance sector, which will make a real contribution to women empowerment.

BIBLIOGRAPHY

- Annual Report of CCD, 2003-2004.
- Bosch, Ellie (2002), *Micro-finance: New Wine in a New Bottle, A Supplementing Role for Cordaid and IICO*, March.
- Censuses of India, C series, RGI, New Delhi, 2001.
- Cheston, Susy and Lisa Kuhn (2002), "Empowering Women Through Microfinance", Unpublished Background Paper for the Micro-credit Summit 15, New York, 10-13 November (www.microcreditsummit.org).
- Dasgupta, Rajaram (2005). "Microfinance in India: Empirical Evidence, Alternative Models and Policy Imperatives", *Economic and Political Weekly*, 19 March.
- *www.govtof orissa.nic.in*
- Kabeer, N. (2001), "Resources Agency Achievements: Reflections on the Measurement of Women's Empowerment – Theory and Practice", SIDA Studies, No. 3.
- Kapoor, Pramilla (2001), *Empowering the Indian Women*, Publications Division, Ministry of Information and Broadcasting, Government of India.
- Malhotra, Meenakshi (2004), *Empowerment of Women*, Isha Books, Delhi.
- Manimekalai, K. (2004), "Economic Empowerment of Women Through Self-Help Groups", *Third Concept*, February.

- Narasiah, M.L. (2004), *Women and Microcredit*, Sonali Publications, New Delhi.
- Orissa Review 2004 (I & PR Department, Government of Orissa)
- Osman, Khalil, "Microfinance Institutions: Effective Weapon in the War against Rural Poverty", www.muslimedia.com.
- Pattanaik, Bijoy Kumar, "Smaranika, 2003", *e.*
- Pattanaik, Sunanda, "Smaranika, 2003", *Empowerment through SHG: A Case Study of Gajapati District.*
- Sahu and Tripathy (2005), *Self-Help Groups and Women Empowerment*, Anmol Publications Pvt. Ltd., New Delhi.
- Sinha, Frances (2005), "Access, Use and Contribution of Micro-Finance in India: Findings from a National Study", *Economic and Political Weekly*, April 23.
- Yunis,Muhammad(2002)"Grameen Bank II : Designed to Open New Possibilities", Available at *http://www.grameeeninfo.org/bank/bank2.html.*

☆ ☆ ☆

4 SHGs & Role in Women Empowerment

INTRODUCTION

Recognition of the importance of Micro Finance as a crucial development tool for poverty reduction has increased during the last two decades. The UN in its General Assembly Resolution 52/94 passed on 18th December, 1997 noted in particular, that in many countries of the world Micro Finance Credit programmes have succeeded in creating self employment by providing access to small capital for people living in poverty, as well as increase in participation in the main stream economic and political process of society.

Most Micro Finance programmes are aimed to promote and protect income and empower specific sectors of the population. Poverty is multi dimensional and its reduction depends on many factors. Micro Finance is taken as one tool, among many development tools for alleviating poverty. Thus Micro Finance is an efficient tool to combat poverty through self-help.

FAILURE OF RURAL BANKING:THRUST ON MICRO-FINANCE

Since the 1950's the Government of India has been experimenting with a large number of grant and subsidy based poverty alleviation programmes. Various studies show that these mandatory and subsidized programmes, implemented through Banking Institutions have not been successful in meeting social and economic objectives as the main features of these programmes were:

(i) Target orientation
(ii) Based on grant /subsidy
(iii) Credit linkage through Commercial Banks

However, these programmes were not,

(1) Sustainable
(2) Perpetuated dependent status of the beneficiaries
(3) Depended ultimately on Government employees for delivery
(4) Led to misuse both of credit and subsidy
(5) Were treated as poverty alleviation intervention

Banks too never looked upon them as a profitable and commercial activity.

In India, the Financial Institutions have been unable to reach the poor households and particularly, women in the unorganized sector. There is no orientation of these Institutions towards recognizing the needs of the poor for credit. The problem is aggravated by the low level of the influence of the poor, either about their credit worthiness or their demand for saving services. Low levels of recovery have been further eroded due to loan waiver programmes leading to institutional disenchantment with lending to small borrowers.

India has world's most extensive **banking infrastructure**. Today there are about **60,000 outlays** of formal banking sector comprising **12,000 branches** of district level co-operative banks over **44,000 branches** of RRB's and over **30,000** rural and semi-urban branches of commercial banks in addition to **1,12,000** co-operative credit societies at the village level.

There is at least one retail credit outlet on an average for about 5000 rural people or every 1000 household. This is a remarkable network, capable of meeting the financial needs of the entire population. However, poor credit deposit ratio, unsustainable lending and high level of NPA's give often cripple much of this infrastructure.

All these gave rise to the concept of 'Micro- Credit' for the poorest segment along with a new set of credit delivery techniques. With the support of NGO's, an informal sector comprising small SHG's started mobilizing credit of their members and lending these resources among the members on a micro scale. The potential of these SHG's to develop as local financial intermediaries to reach the poor has gained recognition due to their community based participatory and sustainable recovery rates have been significantly higher than those achieved by the Commercial Banks in spite of loans going to poor, unorganized individuals without collateral security.

After nationalization in 1969, the Government of India launched an ambitious programme to improve access of the rural poor to formal credit and saving opportunities. As on **June 2005, 49%** (32,538) of all scheduled Commercial Bank Branches were in rural areas accounting to **31%** of the total deposits in rural India. The number of people per Branch also reduced from 64000 in June 1969 to 15000 in June 1997.

According to 1995 World Bank estimates, in most developed countries the financial system reaches only the top 25% of the economically active population- the bottom 75% have no access to financial services except money lenders.

All these gave rise to the Micro Credit to the poorest segment of the population with a new set of credit delivery techniques supported by the NGO's through Self Help Group's.

MICRO CREDIT –GLOBAL SCENARIO

Micro credit is a part of microfinance. Apart from loans, it includes savings, micro insurance and other financial innovations.

- In **1959, Dr. Akhter Hameed Khan** as the founder of Pakistan (now Bangladesh) Academy for Rural Development introduced the revolutionary idea of Micro credit.
- In the 1970s, experimental programmes in Bangladesh, Brazil and a few other countries extended tiny loans to groups of poor women to investment in micro business.
- In **1971, Al Whittaker** established Opportunity International's first US office in Washington DC for extending micro loans.

- Al Whittaker and David Bussau of Indonesia formed the global organization, Opportunity International that provides opportunities for people in chronic poverty to transform their lives by creating jobs, stimulating small businesses and strengthening communities.
- In **1973, Accion International**, a Peace Corps like group, started to switch their focus towards providing economic opportunity to poor people and began to offer micro loans to poor people eager to start small businesses.
- Around **1974** in Bangladesh, **Muhammad Yunus**, a U.S.- educated professor of economics started a similar experiment. He extended small loans from his personal money and discovered that very small loans could make a significant difference in a poor persons ability to survive.
- In **1976**, Yunus founded the **Grameen Bank** to make loans to poor Bangladeshis. Since then the Grameen Bank has issued more than $5 billion in loans to several million borrowers-at the close of 2005 the number of outstanding loans is more than 4 million.

MICRO FINANCE- CONCEPT AND MEANING

Money begets money. More than two hundred years back **Adam Smith** in his famous book "The Wealth of Nations" said, 'money', says the proverb 'makes money'. When you have got a little its often easy to get more, but the great difficulty is to get that little. It very difficult for the poor to get small working capital from the formal banking system, so Micro Credit enables the poor to take a great leap forward.

According to **Asian Development Bank, Micro Finance is the provision of a broad range of services, money transfers and insurance to poor and low-income households and their micro enterprise.**

Micro Finance is defined as, the provision of appropriate financial services to significant number of low-income people with an end object of poverty reduction. The credit provided is expected to be invested in income generation activity as working capital or as productive assets.

PRINCIPLES OF MICRO FINANCE

Commonly, micro finance practitioners follow six general principles in the establishment of micro finance programmes, these principles are:

(1) Serve the poorest clients to promote social and economic justice among the poor communities and providing them opportunities

(2) Link loans to savings, is a means to connect the size of the client's loan to the amount of the client's savings to ensure that they build capital as they borrow

(3) Use solidarity guarantees wherein a group guaranteed loans replace collateral security

(4) Practice participatory management wherein the self elected group undertakes the task of management and administration of the financial services that they receive

(5) Invest in scale and self-sufficiency, to ensure building capacity of key players in the process right from the genesis. Achieving scales this way is reinforced which is critical to advances the mission of micro finance of serving the poor

FEATURES OF MICRO FINANCE

The main features of Micro Finance services are:

(1) It a tool for empowerment of the poorest

(2) Delivery is normally through self help groups

(3) It is essential for promoting self employment, it increases the productivity of self employed in the informal sector of the economy

(4) It is not just a financial system but a tool for social change, specially for women- it is potentially welfare enhancing

(5) Because micro credit is aimed at the poorest, micro finance lending technique needs to mimic the informal lenders rather than the formal sector lending. It has to: (a) provide for seasonality (b) allow repayment flexibility (c) eschew bureaucratic and legal formalities (d) fix a ceiling on loan sizes

Micro Finance approach is based on certain truths, which are not always recognized. These are:

- That the poor are bankable: successful initiatives in micro finance demonstrate that there need not be a trade off between reaching the poor and profitability. Micro Finance constitutes a statement that the borrowers are not 'weaker sections' in need of charity: but can be treated as responsible people on business terms for mutual profit.
- That almost all poor households need to save small amounts, regularly and are willing to save provided they are motivated and facilitated to do so.
- That easy access to credit is more important than cheap subsidized credit which involves lengthy bureaucratic procedures.
- 'Peer pressures' in groups helps in improving recoveries.

SELF HELP GROUP's (SHGs)- BANK LINKAGE

In India the commercial Banks have adapted to the new product segment of micro finance or SHG-Bank linkage. More than **90%** of **SHG-Bank linkage** in regard to volume and **87%** in regard to numbers of SHG is delivered by public **commercial banks** and Regional Rural Banks. They operate within existing structures, which are relatively inexpensive and require low level of capital investment.

The NGOs are contributing to the wide coverage to the SHG-Bank linkage product. They are performing the role of facilitators in about **70%** of all linkages, while banks are providing the financial services. The micro finance scene is dominated by SHG-Bank linkage programmes for more than a decade to extend their outreach to the poorest among the poor. Though the SHG existed even before the linkage programmed the banks could not recognize their potential as business clients and both operated independently without knowing the strength of the other. **NABARD** intervened in forging this linkage in the emergence as the very strong micro finance in the country.

The SHG-Bank linkage programme was conceived with the objective of:

(1) Developing supplementary credit delivery services for the un-reached poor.

(2) Building mutual trust and confidence between the bankers and the poor.

(3) Encouraging banking related activity both on thrift as well as sustaining a simple and formal mechanism of banking with the poor.

The banks have externalized what would otherwise have been high transaction costs for mobilizing savings of the poor, appraisal and sanction of loans and improved loan recovery through the financial intermediaries role played by SHGs.

According to the latest estimates there are yet **260 million** people below the poverty line. Government of India launched the **Swarn Jayanti Gramin Swarojgar Yojna in 1999** where the major emphasis is on forming SHGs, social mobilization and economic activation through micro finance. Simultaneously the Government supports the NABARD to take up activities related to SHGs micro finance activation.

Besides this, the **Rashtriya Mahila Kosh** (National credit fund for women) have their own programmes to provide micro credit for economic development of the poor. The year 2001-02 marked a decade of SHG-Bank linkage programme in India. With the growing of micro credit through SHG-Bank linkage in India, the Reserve Bank of India included financing to the SHGs as main stream activity of the banks under their priority sector lending.

It has been estimated that India has the world's largest micro finance programme in terms of outreach with **7-8 million** households accessing credit through **17085** branches of the formal banking system under the micro credit finance programme. Between **2003-2004 361,731** new SHGs were formed and received **US$ 412 million** in bank loans in the context of the programme as on **March 31st 2006** over **22.35 lakh** SHGs were linked with banks. **90%** of them were women groups and **Rs. 113.98 billion** has been disbursed to **32.98 million** poor households. The average loan per group in this programme is **Rs. 50,917** and per household **Rs. 3,456.**

STRUCTURE & WORKING OF SHGs

With traditional loss making rural banks shifting their portfolio away from the rural poor in the post reform period, SHG based micro finance nurtured and aided by NGOs, has become an important alternative to traditional lending without incurring operating and monitoring cost.

An SHG is an informal organization of up to 20 people from poorer sections of the society, organized, owned, operated and controlled by the members based on solidarity, reciprocity, common interests and resource pooling.

SHG is the newfound concept in the micro finance and there are already over a million groups in the country with a membership of over 10 million (mainly poor women). These are informal credit groups consisting of 10-15 members formed voluntarily and managed democratically where members save a few rupees regularly and then lend amongst themselves with repayment rates exceeding 90%.

CHARACTERISTICS OF SHGs

- Each SHG is a registered unit.
- Micro finance services are accessed by forming into a group of minimum 5 members.

- A President, secretary and treasurer is elected from the group.
- The group usually creates a common fund by contributing their small savings on a regular basis (Rs50-500).
- Most of the groups themselves or with the help of NGOs evolve a flexible system of working and managing their pooled resources with participation of every member in the decision-making.
- The group meets every morning on 10th or 15th (periodic meetings) and requests for loans are considered by consensus.
- Loans are given mainly on trust with a bare minimum of documentation and without any security.
- The amount paid as loan are small if borrowed singly (Rs. 1000) but if in group (Rs. 25, 000 to 50,000).
- The loans cover a variety of purposes, some of which are non- traditional.
- Rate of interest is (approx 13-14%) differs from group to group.
- Interest charged is generally higher than that charged by banks and lower than that charged by moneylenders.
- Some SHGs are linked with banks.
- Deposits the money with banks and not have to withdraw at least for 6 months.
- A periodic meeting of members also serves as a forum for collecting dues from members.
- Defaults are erased mainly due to group pressure and intimate knowledge of end use of credit.

Thus SHG is a social design in which people participate by making themselves socially and economically accountable to each other.

Process of Micro Financing The Poor: SHG-Bank Linkage and NABARD

The poor need financial services but the majority of them lack access to savings and credit delivery. India has taken a middle-path approach in micro finance whereas the commercial banks have adapted to the new product segment of micro finance or SHG.

It has linked close to **1.6 million SHGs** with a total credit outstanding of **Rs40 billion**, serving approximately 24 million individuals. The output level is a modest **1.3%,** which is laudable.

The number of SHGs linked banks rose from barely **500** in **1990** to **8,00,000** in **2004** (Basu and Srivastava 2005). During **2006-07** as many s **3,46,000** new SHGs were linked to banks and the total bank credit to SHGs was **Rs3,082 crore 48 Commercial banks, 196 RRBs and 316 Cooperative banks** are now actively involved in the programme.

With a view to developing a supplementary credit delivery mechanism to reach the poor in a cost effective sustainable manner, the guiding principle behind NABARD micro finance has the following contours:

- Offer cost effective approaches to formal institutions for expanding outreach to the poor.
- Develop collateral substitute.

- Focus on rural poor.
- Facilitates empowerment of the poor.
- Effectively pursues the macro economic objective of growth.

NABARD introduced a pilot project for linking 500 SHGs, with banks in 1992. As on 1994, 637 groups have established credit linkage with 16 Commercial banks and 12 RRBs. The total loans sanctioned by banks amounting to Rs7.9 million. The list of State wise numbers of SHGs linked with banks and loan sanctioned is given in the Table-1.

Table-1.

Pilot Project on SHG –summary progress report

State	No. of SHGs	No. of women SHGs	Bank loan Sanctioned (Rs)	NABARD Refinance (Rs)
Gujarat	19	-	398	310
Karnataka	172	97	1232	1232
Madhya Pradesh	14	14	168	148
Orissa	180	180	1906	1906
Assam	2	-	75	-
Andhra Pradesh	139	131	2660	2553
Rajasthan	16	5	224	222
Tamil Nadu	74	63	881	864
Bihar	2	2	20	-
Maharashtra	17	15	376	376
Kerala	2	2	32	32
TOTAL	**637**	**509**	**7971**	**7643**

Cumulatively as at the end of the **June 2004, Rs 26.98 Cr (Rs 269.80 million)** has been sanctioned as Revolving Fund Assistance to **31 NGOs**, micro finance institutions and Rs **0.58 Cr (Rs 5.8 million)** as grants have been sanctioned to various NGOs. The amount excludes **3.4 million** sanctioned under SHG post office linkage programme in Tamil Nadu. The NABARD continues to provide **100%** refinance assistance to Banks to finance SHGs. During **2004-2005 Rs 29942.25 million (696 million US dollar)** was disbursed as loan to SHGs.

Cumulatively, till **31st March 2005** the Bank loan disbursed to SHGs aggregated **Rs 68984 million (1604 Million US dollar)**. Cumulatively as on **31st March, 2005** NABARD sanctioned a grant assistance of **193.87 million** covering **1048 NGOs**, for promotion, nurturing and facilitating credit linkage of **1,39,513 SHGs**.

NABARD micro finance initiative emerged as the **largest micro finance** programme in the world. The **Corporate Mission** for micro finance set by NABARD envisages reaching banking services to **1/3rd** of the very poor section of the country i.e. a population of 100 million rural poor through **1 million SHGs** by the year 2007-08.

The overall strategy adopted by the NABARD relies on two planks:

(1) Expanding the range of formal and informal agencies that can work as SHG promoting institutions

(2) Building up capacities of the increasing number of stake holders.

Banks find it easier to lend money to the groups as the members have developed a credit 'cold' (outside) money get added to the own 'warm money' in the hands of the groups which have become structures which are able to enforce credit discipline among members.

MICRO FINANCE & POVERTY ALLEVIATION

Since independence, India has pursued a planned approach as a level of social and economic change thereby actualizing all round economic development. The **Planning Commission of India** in the **10th Plan** announced that **26.10%** of India's population is **below the poverty line. 836 million (77%)** of India's population lives on income below Rs 20 per day. Successive governments have grappled with poverty reduction through a plethora of schemes, spending 100s and 1000s of crores of Rupees.

As a part of poverty alleviation method Government of India launched various self-employment programmes like **IRDP, TRYSEM, DWCRA, SITRA, GRY & MWS etc**. In 1991, Government of India launched the Swarn Jayanti Gram Swarojgar Yojana by merging the above programmes. The basic objective of SGSY is to bring poor families above poverty line by providing them income-generating assets through a mix of Bank credit and government subsidy. The programme aims at establishing a large number of micro enterprises. The programme has been conceived as a holistic self-employment programme through SHGs.

Up to **March 2003, 13.38 lakh** groups were constituted in **33 states** and union territories of which **33436 SHGs** only could take up economic activities for their sustenance.

TACKLING POVERTY

Microfinance (used interchangeably with microcredit) has emerged as a powerful tool to tackle poverty. This movement started with Grameen bank in Bangledesh by Prof. Mohammad Yunus. Research tells us that in Bangledesh when 15 million families were benefited from small loans of other financial products as a microsavings and micro insurance 40% of the overall poverty has been reduced due to microfinance.

FIELD WORK –METHODOLOGY

The present study assesses the benefits of microfinance through SHGs. A specially designed Questionnaire (comprising of 21 questions) was prepared and personal interviews were conducted. The available data was analysed and inferences were drawn on circumstantial evidence. A survey was conducted in the interiors of Mumbai in Ambarnath and Badlapur 60 kms away from Mumbai.

The field study tried to assess the benefits in terms of higher income and to analyse whether the people have been benefited by such income generating activities.

The study has been divided into Two Groups:

GROUP A- Consisting of Central Government Sponsored programme under SGSY (40 Members)

GROUP B- Where the SHGS are operating without any support of the Government (30 members)

Both the groups have taken up economic activities of this choice of income generation. The second group comprising of 30 members build up their own corpus and taken up internal lending to the members of the corpus.

FINDINGS OF THE STUDY- (Analysis of the Table 1.1 to 1.4)-GROUP A

(1) Out of 40 members 13 members are in the age group of 35 Years, 17 members are around 45 years and 10 members are above 45 years.

(2) All these members have joined SHG lately (2003,04,06).

(3) 75% of the beneficiaries are qualified upto primary level & 25% of the beneficiaries have secondary level education.

(4) 95% of the beneficiaries husband's are employed and among them 7 members draw Rs 1000 salary. 20 members i.e 50% draw salary in the range of Rs 2000-3000. 27.5% draw a salary about Rs 5000. The head of two members are unemployed.

(5) Out of 40 members 21 members (52.5%) contribute Rs 100 per month and 19 members (47.5%) contribute Rs 500 per month.

(6) All the members have raised the loan under SGSY Scheme. 25% have raised Rs 1 lakh, (10 members) 47.5% (19 members) have raised Rs. 1.5 lakh and 27.5% (11 members) have raised Rs. 2.5 lakh loan for undertaking income generating activity.

(7) 22.5% of beneficiaries have taken loan for running a canteen. 27% purchased vehicles for giving on rent. 25% have taken the loan for selling garments and 25% for selling snacks.

(8) Before joining SHG only 1 member was earning just Rs 150 per month and one more member was earning Rs 200 per month.

(9) After joining SHG and undertaking income generating activity 50% of the members have started to earn Rs 500 p.m 27.5% Rs. 600 p.m. % 22.5 % of Rs 1000/-

(10) The lending rarely varied. 27.5 % are paying 13% and 72.5 % of members are paying interest between 14 – 15%.

(11) 75% of the repayment is regular and 25% is irregular.

(12) There are no defaults.

GROUP-B (30 MEMBERS)

FINDINGS OF THE STUDY (Analysis of the Table 1.5 to 1.6)

(1) Out of 30 members, 10 members are in the age group of 25 years 15 members in the age group of 35 years and 5 members above 45 years.

(2) 10 members joined SHG in 2002 and 20 members in 2000.

(3) 66.6 of percent of beneficiaries have primary level education 33.3 have secondary level, none of the member has reached higher education.

(4) 33.3% (10 members) have 2 children, 50% (15 members) have 3 children and 16.6% 5 members) have more than 3 children.

(5) 33% of children are at primary level education 50% have secondary level education and 16.6% have College level.

(6) 72.5% of the head of family are employed and 12.5% are retired.

(7) The monthly contribution of all the 30 members is Rs. 100/-

(8) These 30 members have built up their own corpus and put the contribution in Banks. So out of 30 members, 10 members have raised Rs.1,000 and 20 members have raised Rs.2,000.

(9) 49.9% have raised loans for selling snacks, 16.6% for selling vegetables, 33.3% for tailoring activity.

(10) 20 members earn income between 1,000 – 3,000 (66.6%) and 10 members (33.3%) earn approximately Rs. 350 per month.

(11) The rate of interest charged is 4 – 5%.

(12) 20 members repay loan on a regular basis and 10 members irregularly.

FINDINGS OF THE STUDY

Microfinance has been beneficial to women by –

(i) **Supplementing the family's Income** which has helped them to perform a better role, in terms of health, education and nutrition. (Millennium Development Goals).

(ii) Creating curiosity to know more about the various schemes and **becoming aware** about the benefits because of **Group SHGs**.

(iii) **Increasing women's employment** in micro enterprise has raised the productivity of women's income generating activities.

(iv) **Enhancing** their **self confidence and status** within the family as independent producers and providers of cash resources to the household.

SUGGESTIONS

(A) Increase outreach and coverage both total number of poor as well the depth of poverty estimates is needed.

(B) To increase the competition between various forms of financial institution like SEWA, BASIX, SHARE and banks like ICICI, HDFC, IDBI, SIDBI, CITY GROUP etc which can increase the access to the clients.

(C) The rate of interest has to be reduced by MFI's.

(D) Market studies information and data have to be gathered about clients so that microfinance can reach the rural poor and uplift them above APL.

(E) An independent assessment of MF is needed to know its real impact of to reduce poverty.

BENEFITS

(1) The main benefit of micro credit appears to be: reduce vulnerability of the poor to adverse circumstances; increase consumption in the same group and empowerment of women.

(2) The major spin off of the micro credit movement at the grass root level has been the fact that women have used the system to come out and join in main stream activities in villages. In many areas particularly where there has been support from NGOs of strong SHGs, women gained a voice and have been able to use this space to come out of their traditional role into a more 'pro active' male space.

(3) Women have been able to mobilize capital and in the process have acquired skills that have enhanced their economic, social and political power.

CHALLENGES

(1) To bring in mobilization of savings under a **regulatory framework** in order to prevent unscrupulous element to enter the sector and exploit the hard earned savings of the poor.

(2) The MFIs charge interest rates, which perceived as exploitative by many and so the MFIs should reduce the rate of the interest.

(3) There is an urgent need for structured long term financing to the sector to fully address the important issues and smoothly transition into a well-functioning mature industry.

(4) Technological innovation, such as, **smart cards**, **biometry ID'S** and **rural Kiosks**, that can help control costs are crucial for a safe and rapid scale-up.

(5) The management of micro-credit institutions require **skilled human resources**, and **management** of other issues such as **flexible product design**, **reducing transaction cost**, ensuring adequate management information system, standard credit information, accessing alternative financing, expanding into under served area, and dealing with regulatory hurdles and political risk.

CONCLUSION

The microfinance **institution demand** for credit is estimated to be around Rs. **2,00,000 crore** against which a meagre **Rs 7,000 crore** is flowing through the channels of banks. The microfinance in India is still too small to create a massive impact in poverty alleviation, but if pursued with **proper institutional arrangement** and **policy preparation** we can change the Socio Economic face of the poor.

Bibliography

- NABARD 1997 Annual Report, National Bank for Agriculture and Rural Development, Mumbai India.
- Nanda Y.C-Micro finance: an important tool for empowerment of poor women, NABARD, Mumbai India.
- Sinha S.J. Samuel and B.Quinones. Jr 2000, micro finance in India; adjusting to economic liberalization.
- World Bank 2000 World Development Report 2000\2001 Attacking poverty World Bank, Washington D.C.
- Rose Kalima 1992 were women leaders: The SEWA Movement in India, Zed Books, London.

☆ ☆ ☆

ANNEXURE-I

QUESTIONNAIRE

(1) Name of SHG_

(2) Year of Establishment-

(3) Whether Sponsored-Yes\No

(4) If Yes by whom- Central Govt\State Govt.

(5) Formation of SHG-Individual\Group.

(6) Whether subsidy Received-Yes\No.

(7) Personal details (beneficiary)

(a) Name

(b) Age-

(c) Status-Married\Unmarried.

(d) Qualification- (a) primary level (b) Secondary level (c) Higher level

(e) No> of children- (i) One (ii) Two (iii) More than Two

(f) Children working- Yes\No

(g) Status of Husband- employed\Unemployed

(h) If employed salary drawn- (i) 1,000 (ii) 5,000 (iii) Above 5,000

(8) Year of Joining SHGC (Beneficiary)

(9) Purposes of Joining SHG-

(10) Total members-5\10\20 members.

(11) Amount of Contribution- (i) Rs.50 (ii) Rs.100 (iii) Rs.200-500\-

(12) Mode of contribution- Monthly\Quarterly\Yearly

(13) Have you taken loan-Yes\No

(14) If Yes- Purpose- Consumption\Production

(15) How many times loan taken- Once\Twice

(16) Amount of loan-

(17) Rate of Interest-

(18) Income earned monthly-

(19) Payment of loan-Regular\Irregular

(20) Still a member- Yes\No

(21) Is there any default-Yes\No.

ANNEXURE-II

GROUP A TABLE – 1.1

Group size (1)	Age (2)		Education of Beneficiary (3)		No. of children (4)		Education of children (5)	
	Members	Years	Level	%	Members	Children	Level	%
40	13	35	Primary	75	5	2	Primary	75
	17	45	Secondary	25	34	3	Secondary	12.5
	10	>45	College	Nil	1	>3	College	12.5

TABLE – 1.2

Period of operation (6)		Head of family (7)		Monthly contribution (in Rs.) (8)		Amount of loan (in Rs.) (9)		Nature of Economic Activity (10)	
Members	Year	Nature	%	Members	Amount	Members	Loan amount	Activity	%
9	2003	Employed	95	21	100	10 (25%)	1 lakh	Operating canteen	22.5
21	2004	Unemployed	5	19	500	19 (47.5)	1.5-1.25 lakh	Vehicle on rent	27.5
10	2006					11 (27.5)	>1.25 lakh	Selling garments	25.0
								Snacks	25.0

TABLE – 1.3

Earlier Income (11)	Present Income (Rs.) (12)		Lending rate (13)		Repayment (14)		Default (15)
	Income (Rs.)	%	Percentage	Rate of interest	Repayment	%	
1 member only Rs.150 per month	500	50	27.5	13	Regular	75	Nil
1 member only Rs.200 per month	600	27.5	72.5	14-15	Irregular	25	
	1000	22.5					

ANNEXURE-III

TABLE 1.4

Group size (1)	Age (2)		Education of Beneficiary (3)		No. of children (4)		Education of children (5)	
	Members	Years	Level	%	Members	Children	Level	%
30	10	25	Primary	66.6	10	2	Primary	33
	15	35	Secondary	33.3	15	3	Secondary	50
	5	>45	College	Nil	5	>3	Higher	16.6

GROUP B
TABLE 1.5

Period of operation (6)		Head of family (7)		Monthly contribution (in Rs.) (8)		Amount of loan (in Rs.) (9)		Nature of Economic Activity (10)	
Members	Year	Nature	%	All	Rs. 100	Members	Loan amount	Activity	%
20	2000	Employed	72.5			20	2000	Snacks	49.9
10	2002	Unemployed	Nil			10	Nil	Vegetables	16.6
		Retired	12.5					Tailoring	33.3

TABLE 1.6

Earlier Income (11)	Present Income (Rs.) (12)		Lending rate (13)		Repayment (14)		Default (15)
	Members (Rs.)	Income	Members	%	Members	Regular	
Nil	20	1000-2000 (66.67%)	20	4-5	20	Yes	Nil
	10	350 (33.33%)	10	Not taken loan	10	Not taken loan	

☆ ☆ ☆

PART - C

WOMEN AND CORPORATE ERA

1 Work Participation of Women - Challenges and Initiatives

INTRODUCTION

Empirical studies on women in India are recent in origin. However, many of the contemporary studies on women are rooted in the past. Hence it is necessary to make a historical survey of the changing status of women.

Literary and historical researchers claim that women had a position equal to men in almost all spheres of life in the early Vedic period (2500-1500 B.C.). Degradation began in the Brahmanic period (1500-500 B.C.), and it was during the period of Sutras and Epics (500B.C. - 500A.D.), that the position of women deteriorated to a great extent due to various socio-political factors, foreign invasion and misinterpretations of the old religious texts. This situation continued in the period of later Smritis (500 A.D- 1800 A.D.) After 1800 A.D. various socio-cultural and politico-economic circumstances, protest movements, social reform movements, freedom movement and the call of Gandhiji during freedom movement in 1920s brought about some improvements in the position of women through education, socio-economic and legislative measures. After independence, the makers of the constitution very seriously took up the task of improving the status of women.[1]

Contemporary scholars working on the status of women opine that many changes have occurred in the traditional conception of role and status of women through new opportunities for education and employment, emergence of new socio-economic pattern and privileges of equal legal and political rights. Women are competing with men on an equal footing and have entered into occupations which were considered as the domain of men (Desai, 1957; Dube, 1963; Kapoor, 1972; Mahajan, 1982; Kaur S, and Punia, 1988; Seth, 1990)

Clem Tisdell, on his theoretical survey of relationship between economic development and status of women, organizes his discussion around pessimistic and optimistic views about the nature of relationship. In the former case, he states that primitive societies are generally egalitarian and sometimes even matriarchal. European colonialism and the socio-economic institutions introduced by them have shown to have a negative effect on the status of women in the colonies. There are also other examples to show that economic development has impaired the status of women. Like economic development may create new opportunities but development

[1] Savita Thakur Joshi, "Women and Development" Mittal Publications, New Delhi, 1999, pg 2,3

patterns have been such that women have lost their traditional role and still are unable to seek more than a marginal role in the labour market. According to the optimistic view, subsistence economies are generally patriarchal and in the absence of growth women cannot gain independence, while the proliferation of the market system which is inherently non-discriminating, open up new opportunities for activities outside the household and hence for improvement in the socio-economic status of women. This reinforces the fact that economic growth results in better education and employment opportunities, healthcare and so on for women.

In all, Tisdell concludes that there may be a U shaped relationship between economic growth and status of women. When the growth is low the relationship may be negative but as there is increase in economic development the relationship turns positive.

This paper concentrates on understanding the participation of women in organised work force, challenges faced by women, industry practices that are pro-women and intitatives to enhance work participation of women.

WORK PARTICIPATION OF WOMEN ACROSS THE WORLD

- Globally, female labour force participation rates continued to rise significantly, currently at 56.6 per cent.
- However, in Asia Pacific the picture is mixed. In South Asia the female labour force rate is just 43.5 per cent (only in the Middle East and North Africa is lower). In East Asia and the Pacific the rate is 61.2 per cent.

Some countries have particularly disturbing gender gaps. In India only 26 per cent of women are participating in the labour force compared to 84.1 per cent of men – a gap of more than 58 points. In Brunei Darussalam, Indonesia and Malaysia the equivalent differential is more than 30 points. A cause for concern is that projections for 2015 and 2020 show these differentials closing only slightly; in both Brunei Darussalam and Indonesia, the gender gap is still predicted to be greater than 30 in 2020.

A study by a non-profit organization Catalyst in the US, recently reported that big companies with the greatest number of female board members on average have significantly better financial performance than those with fewer women. The study looked at financial results such as return on equity, return on sales and return on invested capital, at companies in the Fortune 500 over the 2001 to 2004 period and found that those with at least three women directors had notably stronger financial performance.

Female unemployment rate

Worldwide, when women do enter the workforce they are often more likely to be unemployed than men or to work in the informal economy (meaning they lack the benefits and regular income of formal work). Globally the female unemployment rate in 2004 was 9.3 per cent and the male 8.2 per cent. In South Asia it was 8.1 per cent for women (4.1 per cent for men) and in East Asia and the Pacific the rate for both sexes was 5 per cent.

Pay Differences

There are also important differences when it comes to pay. In South Asia the percentage of employed women working without pay is the highest in the world, at 60 per cent (and another 20 per cent are self employed). In East Asia and the Pacific more than 11 per cent work unpaid and a further 12 per cent are self-employed. Those who are paid often suffer differentials. Female manufacturing workers in the Republic of Korea and Japan are paid less than 60 per cent of the wages of their male counterparts. In Singapore, Taiwan (China) and Hong Kong (China) they are paid 30-40 per cent less.

A key measure of the improvement in the situation of working women is the quality of the work they take up, notably the number in legislative, senior official or managerial (LSOM) positions. Overall the Asia Pacific region still lags behind the global average of 28.3 per cent of LSOM jobs held by women. In East Asia and the Pacific 24.8 per cent of these positions are held by women, up from 20.9 per cent in 1995. South Asia has the lowest percentage of any region, at 8.6 per cent, although this is an increase from 4.6 per cent in 1995. The report notes that a country's stage of economic development does not seem to play a key role in determining how many women are in LSOM roles.

Women at work in India

An Assocham survey (2007-08) says 66.3% urban Indian women prefer to work rather than keep house, though only 16% of them work for a living. Yet, paradoxically, according to available data (2004), Indian women had cornered 14% of senior business posts. However, they still have a long way to go. Says Janet Gasper Chowdhury, principal consultant, Pricewaterhouse Coopers: "While Indian companies are moving in that direction, they still have a long way to go. We do see more women joining companies, but as we move up the hierarchy the numbers start dwindling. The lapse is not by companies alone. Our socio-economic background does have a major role to play."

Although Assocham data mentions that 17.7% of women in India tend to give up their work in middle-management positions, many companies have taken care to ensure that the female talent is retained. Says Chitra Ramakrishna, managing director, National Stock Exchange (NSE): "About 50% NSE staff is women and that has been a way of life with us. At junior levels, we employ 40% to 50% women professionals; they progress up the ladder and at middle and senior management levels, we have 30% women. Also, the fact that if women take maternity leave, it has not gone against their promotion has helped."

Liberalisation, globalisation and the consequent business expansion have raised the aspirations of women. In tandem, several industries have taken steps towards positive discrimination of women.

Work participation of women in India

Table - 1.
Economic Participation and Opportunity for women in India-Global rating

Score	0.3977
Rank	122

Source: Report of World Economic Forum-2007

The economic participation and opportunity ranking of India is 122 out of 130 countries surveyed, which shows a very dismal picture.

Table - 2

Women work participation and women employed in managerial positions in India

Women work participation	Women employed in managerial positions
26%	14%

Source: Assocham survey-2004

The figures in both the tables don't really portray a favourable picture of Indian women despite the economic development the country is boasting about. Yet given the socio-economic profile of our society these figures are very encouraging.

However, in India most of the top business women have made inroads into the financial sector which generally is considered a man's domain. Today, we have women heading banks, commercial and investment-insurance companies, asset management mega corps, housing finance behemoths and even at SEBI and RBI. They are cutting deals, raising resources and monitoring markets and currencies without much ado. This is absolutely creditworthy for the Indian Women.

Women in leadership positions in corporates

Indian women may not have proportionate representation in companies, but they are better off than women elsewhere. **Eleven per cent of 240 large companies — Indian-owned as well as multinational, private as well as state-owned — have women CEOs,** according to a study carried out by executive search firm EMA Partners. In comparison, only 3 per cent of the Fortune 500 companies have women CEOs. In Germany, over 25 per cent executives are women, in the UK more than 30 per cent and in France over 35 per cent. Thirty-five per cent of the women CEOs, according to EMA Partners, are also promoters of their companies. The other 65 per cent are professional CEOs.[2]

Table - 3

Industry	Percentage of women in top leadership position in India	Percentage of women in leadership position in fortune 500 companies
Financial Services	54	7
Media	11	NA
Pharmaceuticals	11	NA
Consultancy	8	NA
FMCG	8	48
Manufacturing	4	13
IT & IT enabled services	4	13

Source- Statistics compiled from report of Executive Search Firm, EMA Partners as published in Business Standard on 30th Nov, 2009.

[2] Business Standard, 30th Nov, 2009

Following are names of some Indian women who steer the destiny of many corporates

Chanda Kochhar is the Managing Director and CEO of ICICI Bank, ex-ICICI Prudential chief Shikha Sharma heads Axis Bank and Kalpana Morparia is the country head of JPMorgan. Renuka Ramnath, the former CEO of ICICI Ventures, will run a yet unnamed fund. In addition, Naina Lal Kidwai occupies the corner office at HSBC and Meera Sanyal at ABN Amro. Manisha Girotra heads UBS, Ashu Suyash Fidelity Fund Management. Kiran Mazumdar-Shaw is the Chairman & Managing Director of Biocon and Villoo Morawala Patel is the founder, Chairman & Managing Director of Avesthagen. The big names in FMCG are Vinita Bali of Britannia, Sangeeta Talwar of Tata Tea, Leena Nair of Hindustan Unilever and Nadia Chauhan of Parle Agro. The largest personal computer company in the country, Hewlett-Packard, is headed by Neelam Dhawan.

Women entrepreneurs in India

It is estimated that women entrepreneurs presently comprise about 10% of the total number of entrepreneurs in India, with the percentage growing every year. If the prevailing trends continue, it is likely that in another five years, women will comprise 20% of the entrepreneurial force. With corporates eager to associate and work with women-owned businesses, and a host of banks and non-governmental organisations keen to help them get going, there has rarely been a better time for women with zeal and creativity to start their own business.[3]

Thus it can be said that as compared to the women in developed nations, Indian women have still a long way to go to carve a significant place in India Inc. But the already available statistics on this is quite heartening and shows very progressive symptoms.

Challenges faced by women at work place

Even though there is enough evidence of progressive transformation in the society and the status of women in workplace, still the trends in this direction are not satisfactory. A working woman of today still struggles with the harsh realities of discrimination, exploitation and violence in organizations, societal and family pressures, and suffer from bitter effects of the balancing act which she is expected to perform for handling official and household chores. Following are the challenges generally faced by working women across the globe irrespective of the economic development of the country that she belongs to. The problem may only vary in degree from country to country.

- **Glass Ceiling**

  Women have made inroads into areas which were male dominant like pilots, astronauts and so on. However the problem of glass ceiling still poses an enormous threat to a woman who wishes to achieve newer milestones in her professional career. Glass Ceiling could be regarded as a situation in which the professional advancement of a person within the hierarchy of an organization is restricted on the grounds of gender or race. Women are also subjected to **Glass Walls**- a situation where women who manage to reach the senior managerial positions are usually deprived of accessing responsibilities into strategic areas. Moreover, the contemporary woman also grapples with the problem

---

[3] The Hindu, December 14 2005

of **Glass- Elevator** in which the male counterparts are rapidly promoted, especially senior managerial positions against female employees.

According to the survey findings of Accenture 2006, Glass Ceiling doesn't carry negative consequences for the women only, but it equally affects the organizations, as they fail to maintain their reputation, retain quality workforce and optimize the growth potential.

- **Societal perceptions**

  Society finds it difficult to accept the role of a woman as a caretaker as well as provider. There has been a rigid and age old perception, that the woman must take care of the home and children and she is looked down upon by the society if she attempts to strike a balance between her family and profession.

- **Childcare and work-Life Balance Issues**

  The poor childcare facilities both in India and abroad pose a severe restraint for women in continuing their jobs after the birth of a baby. In India normally the working women depend on the extended family network for childcare purpose. Further many professional women juggle with domestic and professional responsibilities during their mid-age period which co-incidentally happens to be one of the most productive periods of their careers. And it is during this period that women either take a temporary break or permanently give up their jobs.

  Working women confront the challenges such as relocation, restriction in travels, limitations imposed by the nature of work itself as they aggravate the constraints of work-life balance problems.

- **Self-imposed restrictions**

  Many women lack confidence and maintain a tendency of underestimating their competencies in a professional market, which makes them a victim of pay inequalities in leading organizations.

- **Cultural Challenges**

  According to a recent survey report, "The Leaking Pipeline: Where are our female leaders?" published by the Gender Advisory Council, a specialized wing of Pricewater house Cooper, lack of female role models, lack of proper mentoring facilities, lack of proper awareness or communication opportunities, lack of clear career path, lack of skills or experience and gender stereotyping are some of the reasons which keep women away from leadership positions.

- **The Double-Bind Dilemma**

  The Catalyst-2007 highlighted that women in leadership positions believe that they are expected to achieve higher standards in their professional field and for this reason they should work hard in comparison to their male counterparts.

- **Glass –Cliff**

  Women also face the problem of high levels of burnout which occurs because of the excessive stress on reaching higher positions where they have to struggle to balance work-life and personal life.

- **Mini-me Syndrome**

  Martha Frase Brunt discovers the social phenomena of Mini-me syndrome which was published in HR Magazine, 2003. In this case the executives choose successors who are similar to themselves in terms of age, style and most importantly gender. The women community faces this challenge through the succession planning process in their organization due to which they are deprived of climbing up the ladders of success in the organizational hierarchy.

Initiatives to improve status of women at work place

It certainly cannot be denied that a nation's economic progress can be improved by providing a conducive climate for women at workplace to not only work effectively but also to progress and realize her complete potentials. Following are some initiatives suggested:

- **Forum for women**

  It is important that working women unite to represent their issues through various fora so that their feeling of isolation reduces and their voices heard well.

- **Providing supportive culture**

  Providing a supportive culture which offers women an opportunity to share their experience and practice skills through individual or group mentoring, coaching or networking.

- **Developing leadership skills**

  Women and business organisations can develop leadership skills which would offer women a broader perspective in handling the professional matters and addressing stereotypes successfully.

- **Developing a fair and transparent succession planning**

  Developing a fair and transparent succession planning will ensure optimum career opportuinities for women professionals.

- **Initiating women employee friendly HR policies**

  Some pro-women employee HR policies could be flexible working hours, compressed work weeks, paid leave, part-time, staggered hours, adjusted hours/time-off during summer seasons, sabbaticals or career leave, floating holidays, vacation buying/borrowing/sharing etc. Other flexi-work options could include telecommuting at home, working at off site locations, shift swapping, job sharing etc.

- **Providing childcare privileges**

  This may include on site/near site childcare, sick child or odd-hour care, holiday/summer childcare, homework assistance programs etc.

Best Practices in Organisations for Women Professionals

Following are best practices in some business firms which offer women a leading edge in the war of equality at work place and enable them to cope with all the challenges that they face.

PepsiCo, US

A strategic support and resource group, **PepsiCo's** *Women of Color Multicultural Alliance* focuses on attracting, retaining, and developing women of color in the middle and senior management ranks at PepsiCo. This initiative highlights women of color as a strategic priority and works on building deeper, more authentic relationships across all levels. The success of the program is clear: key findings include that, from 2002-2006, the number of women of color at the senior management/director/VP level has increased; representation for women of color on the board of directors has doubled.

Tata Group, India

Tata introduced a Second Career Internship Program (SCIP) for women professionals who preferred opting for a career break and wish to get back to their profession. The entire endeavour involves an experiential pedagogy as the company provides a live project to a woman based on her domain expertise and interest for tenure of 5-6 months of a total duration of approximately 500 hours. During this period the woman professional may perform on a flexi-time basis and the guide and trainee explore their mutual interests and along with that the trainee may also earn a lucrative stipend to the tune of Rs. 4 lakh.

William-Sonoma Inc, US

William Sonoma Inc offers its employees a privilege of reduced work schedule once the female professional returns from the maternity leave under their phased return program provisions. This program aims at maximizing employee retention by taking care of the pressures of the new working mothers, which they confront due to the early and difficult feeding schedules. These programs also explore the possibility of part time arrangements and normally reduce the working schedules by 50% in the initial two months based on mutual agreement.

Deloitte and Touche and LLC, Swiss

These organizations are the main champions of Alumni networking and Consulting programs and Mass Career Customisation programs for the employees. Through Alumni Networking, these companies maintain close contact with the employees who prefer to leave their career for personal pursuits for a certain period of time. These companies maintain links with such employees by keeping their mailing accounts active, inviting them to attend corporate parties and providing them an access to free trainings for kepping their skills fresh and providing part-time or consulting opportunities. This initiative helps the organization to retain valuable and talented pool of women employees. Through the Mass Career Customisation Module, the organization works in conjuction with the employees by understanding their custom career goals on the basis of career advancement, place, role and schedule and help them out for working in tune with their career path.

Best Buy, US

Best Buy championed the Results Oriented Work Environments (ROWE) program, in which the employees get ample autonomy for handling their work requirements as they are allowed freely to decide how, when and where they can get their job done. This inititative tackled the problem of employee discontentment due to work-life imbalance issues and excess of repression from the management through excessive control and helped the women employees to a great extent.

CSC India

This organization offers utmost freedom and flexibility to its women professionals at work due to which there has been an impressive rise in the number of female workforce by around 21% in 2006 in comparison to 13% in 2004. The firm has introduced an exclusive website for women professionals known as Planet W. The site serves as a forum for exchanging ideas and sharing problems. Moreover, the organization also provides different courses on dieting and personal grooming for improving the lifestyle of the female workforce.

Scotia Bank, UK

Through research which demonstrated that women had the skills, proven performance levels, and aspirations to contribute at more senior levels, **Scotiabank** found a strong business case to support the creation of its *Advancement of Women Initiative (AoW)*. The organization's most senior women started this business-focused imperative that improved women's representation by leveraging existing processes, programs, and platforms, thereby reinforcing the business value of the work. Through this initiative, Scotiabank has significantly improved senior women's representation at the bank: the number of women at all senior levels – from vice president and above – nearly doubled from 2003 to 2006.

CONCLUSION

Economic Development of a nation certainly affects the work participation of women. It has been observed that countries with higher levels of economic development project more favorable figures of women at workforce. However, irrespective of these statistics, working women across the globe face similar impediments which can be overcome only if business organizations play a proactive role in framing policies that are women friendly. A working woman of today still struggles with the harsh realities of discrimination, exploitation and violence in organizations, societal and family pressures, and suffer from bitter effects of the balancing act which she is expected to perform for handling official and household chores. The organizations which successfully address these challenges and tackle the issues of diversity will be able to attract and retain talented women professionals and ultimately gain a competitive edge. This will further fasten the pace of economic development of the nation.

BIBLIOGRAPHY

- Verma S.B., Status of Women in Modern India, Deep & Deep Publication, New Delhi, 2005.
- Thakur Savita, Women and Development- The changing Scenario, Mittal Publications, New Delhi, 1999.
- HRM Review, September 2008, Women at Workplace, The ICFAI University Press.
- ILO Report, May 2007.
- *http://editorial.careers.msn.com/articles/womansplace,* accessed on 4th Sep, 2008.
- *www.ilo.org,* accessed on 4th Sep,2008.
- Business Standard, 30th Novemeber, 2009.
- *www.economictimes.indiatimes.com,* accessed on 5th Sep, 2008.

☆ ☆ ☆

2 Challenges faced by Women in Corporate World

INTRODUCTION

A woman is the mother of the race and liaison between generation, it is truly said," the hand that rocks the cradle rules the world". In the emerging complex social scenario, a woman has a pivotal role to play ......They can no longer be considered mere harbingers of peace but are emerging as the source of power and symbol of progress.

The role of women worldwide is undergoing a dramatic change. Women today share a podium with men in almost all fields, be it in kitchen or defence. Women in India are also poised to take off. They are standing on the threshold of a new era. Working women are no longer a rarity and are now accepted as an integral part of the working force. Indian organisation has experienced a steady increase in number of women employees and this pattern is bound to continue in the future as well.

Gone are the days when we hardly could see any women in the core management of organisation. Women are increasingly taking up superior position in the corporate world, thereby turning down all the male bastions. In the corporate world women have shown the perseverance and determination to break the glass ceiling. There are women who have taken the lead role in the corporate world like- Indra Nooyi - CEO- Pepsico, Naina Lal Kidwai- M.D – HSBC India, Lalita Gupte – COO-ICICI, Chanda Kochar-CEO-ICICI Bank, Pragya Raman – Group Executive President of Aditya Birla Group- to name a few. It is also estimated that women heading the corporate sector presently comprise of 10% of the total number senior management positions in India with the percentage growing every year according to the study conducted by the forum for women in leadership (WILL Forum).

Some of India's top companies are now giving specific mandates to fill the middle and senior management roles with women candidates. Bharti Enterprises and American Express have mandated their recruitment agencies to have certain percentage of women candidates at interview stage. While American Express asks for at least one third representation among those appearing for job interviews, it is 25-30% of Bharti Enterprises. These efforts of promoting diversity are being appreciated in the corporate world.

Despite all this feel good news, Indian companies seriously lack women in senior management roles. There are stunning statistics which include the corporate world. According to a recent study conducted by KPMG a top audit and consulting firm only 26.1 percent of the listed companies (392 of 1,500) have women on their boards. Out of the 278 directors on the BSE sensex companies, there are only 10 woman directors. Apart from this, women executives in India earn 40 percent less than what men earn over their entire career. Even when compared to global counterparts, corporate India stands below average. Over 77 percent of the 200 largest companies in the world as ranked by Fortune, had at least one woman director on their board as of 2006. Only 36 percent of Indian companies have women holding Senior Management positions as compared to 91 percent of Companies in China. These figures force us to ponder on how successful women have been in breaking the barriers which obstruct them from reaching the top.

In March 1986,"the wall street Journal "discussed work related phenomenon experienced by women and termed it as the "glass ceiling". The term struck and ever since, the limited presence of women, compared to the over powering presence of men in top level management positions has come to be described as the "Glass ceiling".

Term "Glass ceiling" refers to a situation where the advancement of a person within the hierarchy of an organisation is stopped at a lower level because of some form of discrimination, most commonly sexism. It is believed to be an unofficial, invisible barrier that prevents women and minorities from advancing in business.

The term "glass ceiling" has been thought to have been used to refer to invisible barriers that impede the career advancement of women in the American workforce in an article by Carol-Hymowitz and Timothy Schellhardt in the March 24, 1986 edition of the Wall Street Journal. The situation is referred to as a "ceiling" as there is a limitation blocking upward advancement and "glass" (transparent) because the limitation is not immediately apparent and is normally an unwritten and unofficial policy. This invisible barrier is distinguished form of formal barrier to advancement, such as education or experience requirement. Mainly this invisible barrier seems to exist in more of the developing countries.

However, this glass ceiling tends to cripple working women the most, this barrier prevents large number of women, from obtaining and securing the most powerful, prestigious and highest grossing Jobs in the work force. This barrier makes women feel as they are not worthy enough to have these high-ranking positions but also they feel as if their bosses do not take them seriously or actually see them as potential candidates.

Fig. 1

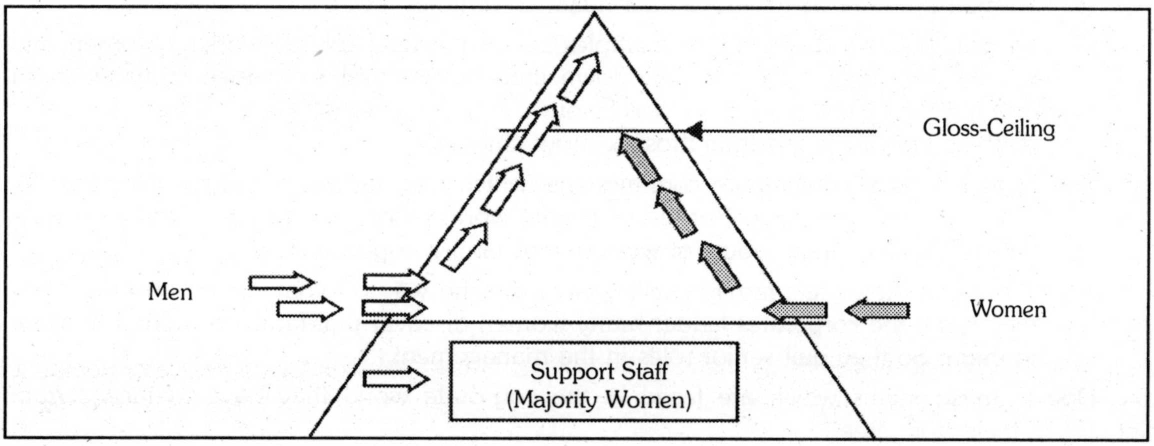

TYPES OF GLASS CEILING BARRIERS

- Different pay for comparable work.
- Sexual, ethnic, racial, religious discrimination or harassment in the work place.
- Lack of family, friendly work place policies.
- Exclusion from informal networks, stereotyping and preconceptions of women's role and ability, failure of senior leadership to assume accountability for women's advancement, lack of role models and lack of mentoring.

"Glass walls" is also another barrier which is faced by women managers who have managed to reach high level managerial positions. Here, they are mostly restricted to areas less central or less strategic areas such as product development or finance.

"Glass Elevator" or **"Glass Escalator"** is also another barrier. This term means there is a rapid promotion of men over women especially in female dominated field such as nursing where men are less common, they receive differential treatment that favours them to exert their authority and control in the work place and are therefore promoted with ease in these fields.

"Glass Cliff" is a situation where in some one has been promoted into a risky, difficult job.

Although an increasing number of women are proving that when it comes to taking up of corporate challenges they have much more than just a pretty face to show. But still Indian companies seriously lack women in senior management roles as they have certain myths relating to women.

CERTAIN MYTHS APPLIED TO WOMEN IN THE CORPORATE WORLD

(1) Society is biased against women in executive positions.

(2) Women fall apart in a crisis.

(3) Women are too concerned with the social aspects of their jobs and cannot be trusted with important matters.

(4) Women are more concerned than men about working conditions.

(5) Women are not ready to travel or relocate more extensively for the organisation.

(6) Women put their heart above their head, so at times they become emotional.

(7) Women have to deal with the complexities of the dual role as working women and mother and many a times slow down their careers and so women managers with children are often looked on as less favourable as they are viewed to be less committed by the corporate world than those without children.

(8) Higher roles ask for higher commitments which may include working more than 40 hours of work per week. But the corporate world is sceptical whether women will be able to dedicate more hours of work due to family responsibilities.

(9) Many corporates feel family challenges get in the way of women's advancement. As they climb the corporates ladder many women discover that family is more important to them. So they quit senior roles in the management.

Due to these myths which are faced in the corporate world they have to face certain setbacks in their work area.

CERTAIN SETBACKS IN THEIR WORK AREA ARE

(1) Glass ceiling is a situation which women managers have to face in a corporate world and so are unable to advance their careers.

(2) Women often have to secure positions that have designations with little power or supervisory authority.

(3) Mentoring is often limited to women which in turn results in a lack of access and training that aids in the advancement within the organisation.

(4) Many a times, there is a difference in compensation of women as women executives are paid far less than their male counterparts.

(5) Many a times when women are assertive and take charge, people often react negatively, but if she fulfils the prescribed stereotype of being a kind and gentle woman, she may be regarded as a poor leader.

These factors often act as obstacles thereby barring women from climbing the corporate ladder.

FACILITATING WOMEN'S PROGRESSION TO MANAGEMENT AND EXECUTIVE POSITIONS REQUIRE –

(1) High level commitment to change the existing culture within the firm or organisation through sensitization programmes. All levels of the hierarchy should be geared to refute the myths surrounding the women's capabilities and dedication to work, improving manager understanding to gender and family issues, and endorsing the value contribution women can make to an organisation's image and to its productivity.

(2) Women should have access to management training and line experience, mentors and role models at the highest levels as well as admittance to formal and informal networks and channel of communication at work.

(3) Integrated and sustained efforts are also needed to be made to ensure that components of equal employment opportunity policies (including recruitment, job assignment, career planning, grading wages, transfer and promotions) are closely monitored and that the procedures are transparent objective and fair.

(4) One of the main characteristic of professional and managerial work is the extended working hours that are entailed to obtain promotion. Family – friendly policies (including flexible working hours, parental leave for men and women, child care facilities etc) should be important elements in any integrated package of measures supporting women at work.

(5) Strategies to encourage female students to widen their study choices by eliminating sex stereo typed images of women and men in all areas of society.

(6) Women's equal participation in all areas of society (through teaching methods and teaching materials) should be instilled into children's consciousness from an early age.

(7) Sensitization programmes for teachers, focussing on removing discriminatory practices and attitudes from teaching and vocational guidance and awareness rising campaigns among students, families and friends and among the community at large.

(8) Employers need programmes to help them recognise the benefits women can bring to their business.

(9) Programmes are needed to improve the presence of female mentors and role models in the academic hierarchy.

However, success today requires organisation to best utilize the talent available to them irrespective of the gender and so to do this we have to redefine and restructure the organisation systems to respond to the dilemmas faced by women managers.

Some organisations have, but many organisations have yet to recognize that female executives offer a wealth of talent and certain skills with which many times women have become "Super women" to respond being equal.

One of the strongest skill is their ability at multitasking. Women managers also bring with them a different style and different skills and research has confined that they can handle more contradictions, can tolerate more and deliver more than men.

Some of the stereotyped beliefs that women managers are uncertain of themselves, look for constant reassurance and tend to be aggressive are baseless. The reality is that women in general and women managers in particular have different value system, which they bring to the organisation.

A study conducted in November 2007 by KPMG a top audit and consulting firm and by a forum for women in leadership (WILL forum) an independent organisation brought together women executives from across the corporate India and multinational companies globally, for collective thinking and an open dialogue.

The survey roped in 104 men and women who are under the ambit of top management in public and private sectors companies across different disciplines-IT, hospitality, financial services, advertising, pharmaceuticals, and manufacturing among others. The proportion of women respondents was higher (66.3%) than that of men.

Sangeeta Singh, executive director, human resource, KPMG in India said, "our research evidence reveals that women leaders are self critical on their own strengths and weakness and tend to rebound gracefully from set backs. They tend to be intuitive crisis managers, enabling fair and sound judgement. They drive a democratic, inclusive approach by nurturing talent."

Anu Aga-director of Thermax said "women are doing extremely well in the family owned business and elsewhere and few have made headlines in the corporate sector, but by and large, there is still a bais against women" while stressing that women are capable of doing any job in the corporate sector, she said that every girl should be given equal opportunities right from childhood to focus on her career. She should be encouraged as much as a boy is boosted in a family. There should be no favour and no hurdles for women in climbing up the corporate ladders on merit.

Argued Poonam Barva, convenor of the Forum for women in Leadership that the survey suggests that corporate India seems to be working on the traditional definition of a hierarchal conservative leadership, while women professionals are definitely on the rise. They are paving the way to redefine leadership for future generations.

Singh and Barua explained that while research has been conducted on Gender stereotypes. The survey explored the personality and motivational factors that are at the core of underlying gender differences. Over the last decade leadership styles in corporate India have been revolutionised with emphasis on inclusive growth.

The survey shows that 87 percent of respondents agree that striking a judicious balance between corporate and family life is a challenge that women management contenders are confronted with another 82 percent stated that Gender stereotypes are barriers that women executives have to break to reveal their true leadership potential.

Women have an openness and willingness to listen and learn. A woman takes the concept of nurturing from home to the organisation. They are focussed and goal oriented and take the group along as they are good listeners. Despite being soft they can quietly take tough decisions.

They have broken stereotypes. By providing themselves, they have earned respect of others and proved to be good leaders said Suneeta Reddy, Executive director-finance Apollo Hospital.

Women in the Corporate Era are aware of the constraints they work under and obviously try to make the best of bargain. They typically bear a disproportionate amount of responsibility for family and home and thus have more demand on their time outside the office. And when they do reach the managerial level, they bring with them both silver lining and dark clouds.

But they flower if they are allowed to flower despite all the obstacles which are mainly societal and perceptual. So let us all strive to give women the place they so richly and rightfully deserve in the society.

BIBLIOGRAPHY

- Amarnath, Nischinta; Ghosh, Debashish; (2005), *The Voyage to Excellence: The Ascent of 21 Women Leaders of India Inc., Pustak Mahal.*
- Robbins, P. Stephens; (1999), *Organizational Behavior – Concepts, Controversies, Applications*, Prentice Hall of India Private Limited, 8th Edition.
- Sekharan, Uma; (2004), *Organisational Behavior – Text and Cases*, Tata McGraw-Hill Publishing Company Limited, New Delhi, 2nd Edition.
- K. Shanti (1998) "Empowerment of women" Published by Anmol Publications New Delhi.
- Lathica Menon 1998 "Women Empowerment and Challenge of Change "Published by Kaniska Publishers, New Delhi.
- Indu Prakash Singh 1991 'Indian Women:The power trapped 'Published by Galaxy Publications, Kalkaji, New Delhi.
- R. P. Sharma 1995 "Women in Hindu Literature" Published by Gyan Publishing House, New Delhi.

☆ ☆ ☆

3 Women and Corporate Era

Empowerment is truly the idea of power sharing, enabling an environment of trust, sharing power alongside men. In developing countries especially in Asian region it was the culture which did not allow the women to work. In India specially marriage and male chauvinism had stopped women from building their career. Empowering of women presupposes a drastic, dynamic and democratic change in the perception of and expectation from women in our society.

To help women to attain economic independence is the first priority for such a change. When she attains economic independence she becomes author of her own decisions. Empowerment of women is essential for sustainable development of a community, which implies equilibrium in factors related to human life. This may be social, political, economic, or environmental. The concept was introduced by women from south at the International Women's Conference in Nairobi in 1985 as a counter- project to the integration concept for advancing women. The empowerment concept makes clear the political and economic gap between social classes and between men and women.

Women empowerment in the organisations is now gaining momentum as more women managers have become successful in leading companies worldwide. Ignoring women as a valuable asset is ignoring over a quarter of the value of one's organization is realized by corporates.

So corporates are now not hesitating in treating them at par with men. But organisations and work culture must be sensitive enough to understand the needs of the women employees, so that it becomes a better place to work. Skill and competencies of the person must be given priority than the gender.

To empower the women, the corporates must create the structure that works for the women. It may include flexible schedule, time or job sharing; structures that are friendly, which will create opportunities for women. It is also necessary to provide them with needed training and resources. As we cannot expect any employee to move ahead into greater opportunities without providing the necessities it takes to get there. This is true for women too. Finally, create a culture of respect. So all employees will have little issues with gender conflicts.

Now the situation is slowly changing, for women power sharing along with men has become common in all the fields. Women are proving to be effective in taking decisions and leading organisations, though sociologically, they face the burden more in the family balancing demands of working place and family life.

Since 1980 onwards the I.T. software and service industry has emerged as the biggest contributor towards India's exports. If the same global business scenario continues, this industry can contribute up to 35% of country's total exports and 8% of G.D.P. Impressive growth rate of software sector as a whole, as well as its increasing share in the various national parameters has been possible mainly due to software exports. Software sector has become country's engine of growth in terms of employment, foreign exchange, development of infrastructure, foreign investment etc.

Attainment of this growth was possible only with the help of Human Resource. In the year 2002 around 1.7 lakh people were involved in software industry. By 2004 this figure reached 2.6 lakh. In case of I.T. enabled services this growth is much faster around the year 2000. There were hardly 25,000 people employed but by the year 2002 figure reached one lakh and by 2004 it reached 2.45 lacs. It is expected that growth in future is expected to continue at the same rate.

I.T. is one sector which recognises the importance of women in the development of the industry and tries to empower them by taking all possible care, physical as well as psychological. Survey shows how this important asset is being nurtured and taken care of by I.T. industry. It has played important and active role in empowering today's women treating them on par with men. Equal opportunities are being provided to them by this sector.

STATUS OF WOMEN EMPLOYEES AND THEIR FUTURE IN THE INDUSTRY

India being a developing economy has seen major changes in social and economic status of women employees over the past few decades. Today's woman likes to assert her independence and explore her potential. They have now practically dominated every field of economic activity.

I.T. industry is one challenging field where the women have made entry. They have equipped themselves with the necessary qualifications and technical skills. The man to woman ratio in the software industry was 76:24 in 2006 which increased to 65:35 by the year 2007.

Thus women in I.T. are here to stay and more are expected to join. It is, therefore, imperative to see their present status in the industry and look into their future in it.

It is interesting to note how preciously this resource is being used by the I.T. industry and how in innovative ways companies are taking all possible care of their professional and family problems and making all out efforts to retain this asset.

Following measures are being taken by the companies especially for women employees.

Fig. 1

CORPORATE SUPPORT

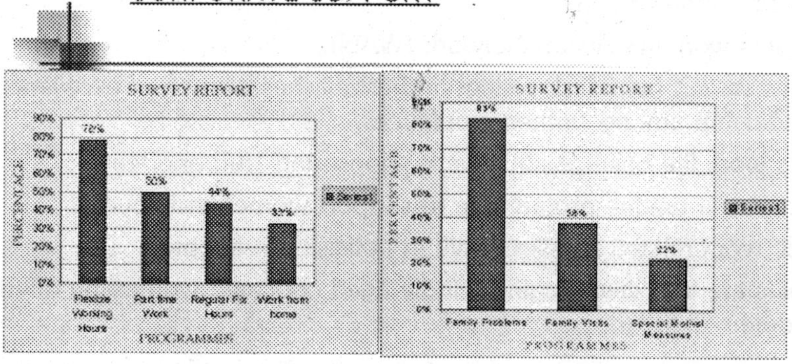

- Flexible working hours.

  78% of the companies offer such facility to suit individual requirement.
- Facility of part time work.

  Only 50% of the company's offer this facility.
- Fixed working hours.

  44% of companies offer this facility to women employees. Though it is difficult in this industry to provide this facility as projects have dead lines.
- Work from home.

  33% of the companies are allowing women employees to work from home. Still this concept has not gained popularity in India.
- Attend to family emergencies.

  83% of the companies allow women employees to attend to such emergencies. This shows humanitarian and sympathetic approach towards women employees.
- Arrangement of family visits.

  38% of the companies make such arrangements though percentage is less it is a good beginning. Family as a whole feels proud about it.
- Special motivational measures.

  22% of the companies undertake special motivational measures.
- Cell to deal with abuse.

  44% of the companies have separate cell to deal with the cases of mental and physical abuse.
- Cell for general grievances.

  39% of the companies have such cell to deal with other general grievances of women employees.

All these measures indicate how companies are sensitive towards women employees.

EXAMPLES OF SENSITIVE APPROACH

Measures undertaken by specific companies also indicate the same approach. A few examples are:

- Infosys has set up an Infosys women's net work, a forum that looks into various issues being faced by the women.
- At Cisco it is women's Action Network (WAN).
- Zenser has started help desk system and establishes women of excellence(WE) forum to foster leadership among women employees.
- IBM at its work life balance initiative is sponsoring "fun and learn".
- Accenture has a unique programme to support women employees.
- To handle work related stresses, Walk in policies are adopted.
- Companies are also encouraging middle aged educated women by offering a four hour job schedule.

- There is also a trend graded re-entry of women employees into work force post maternity, lasting over a period of six to nine months.
- Companies also ensure safety of women employees travelling by cabs. Character of the cab driver is checked. They have also devised a system where a first person picked up and last person dropped is not a woman. Some have GPS tracking devices in their vehicles. In late night shifts a senior male member is instructed to drop all women employees first.

Thus I.T. sector has played a great role in empowering women not only by providing training to compete the jobs but has provided maximum opportunities in software sector and other I.T. enabled services like B.P.O, Call Centers, medical transcription, Animation, Web Designing etc.

BIBLIOGRAPHY

- Field Work is part of Research work done for Ph D Thesis Titled "Changing Role Of Human Resources Departments, A Study of Selected I.T. Organisations Established in Pune Area 1995 to 2005" by Prof. Suvarna Deo under the guidance of Dr C N. Rawal.
- "Empowerment –A Perspective on Women of Today and Tomorrow" by Kathleen Patterson. H.R.M Review Oct 2009.
- Women Executives Glass Ceiling Myths and Realities by Yamini Reddy, Nirmala Daita, V Krishna Veni. H.R.M Review Aug 2009.
- Handbook on Women and Human Rights.
- Women Empowerment – Through Self Help Groups by B. K. Singh.

☆ ☆ ☆

4 A Study on Challenges Faced by Women Employed in the Corporate World

ABSTRACT

Women in the last decade have stepped out of their confines and kitchens and are exploring various avenues which include working in the corporate world. Women no longer sacrifice their career growth for taking care of their families, but to the contrary they have learnt to manage both with elegance and confidence. Indian women have changed a lot today.

But what has caused this change? Why are these women taking up employment and pursuing them even after having a family? Is it financial freedom/ increased strain on finances that has led to pursue their career? Are they as free as men when they opt to take up a job? What are the perils that these women face and what are the sacrifices that they make for pursuing a career in the corporate world?

This research paper focuses on the aspects to examine the above issues and also the social and economic and educational background of these women, the time these women could cater to children and for themselves by surveying fifty respondents in a suburb in Mumbai which is a busy metropolitan city in India. The study also suggests measures to improved their views and encourage their rights.

WOMEN AND THE CORPORATE ERA - A STUDY ON CHALLENGES FACED BY WOMEN EMPLOYED IN THE CORPORATE SECTOR

Status of Women in India Today: Women are the key inputs of household at first, then a partner in agriculture, industry and service sectors. Women are not only a reproductive agent of civilizations but also a strong living supporter of sustainable development of any society.

The status, freedom and respectability accorded to and enjoyed by women in society is a mark of wisdom and civilization of that particular society. We can conceive of a continuum wherein at one end of the continuum women enjoy equal rights, respectability and are equal partners in economic pursuits and social position and at the other end, one finds women treated inferior to man, deprived of freedom as enjoyed by men. The gender question is a perennial question. The world body may declare equal opportunities and rights for women and men but it is the nation states and the religious and ethnic groups that have to translate such a principle into reality. One is forced to come up with a statement that so long a man does not treat a women his equal he is not civilized. Looked at from any angle, political, economic, social, religious, spiritual or moral, the woman is an equal partner and should be an equal partner in all pursuits of life.

In a changing environment, the Government of India has made a significant move and declared the year 2001 as the year of "Empowerment of Women/" It may be mentioned here that four world conferences on women have been held over the past twenty–seven years. The first was held in Mexico City in 1975, the second in Copenhagen in 1980, the third in Nairobi in 1985 and the last was held in Beijing in 1995. These conferences have, in fact, strengthened the socio-economic, political and legal dimensions of the role of tribal women to a great extent. In the Mexico Conference, it was decided to celebrate the decade 1975-85 as the decade for women. During this period, the United Nations has adopted Conventions on Elimination of Discrimination Against Women (C.E.D.A.W) in 1979. Later on, this has been adopted by India in 1993. In Copenhagen (1980), the concentration has been made on poverty alleviation imparting education, enhancing avenues for professional advancement and addressing the problems of women in developing countries. By the end of the decade for women, the women of developing nations were successfully able to advocate, lobby and ensure full participation at the Nairobi Conference in 1985 wherein discussion had been held primarily on the issues of women in the third world countries.

The Beijing Declaration and Platform for Action is very comprehensive aiming for equality, development and peace, acknowledging the diversity of communities, religious and indigenous rights and the uneven progress in empowerment and increasing poverty. The meet has demanded equal participation of women in Government and decision making process. Some important commitments made in this conference are: to protect and promote the human rights of women and the female children as an integral part of universal human rights; to eradicate the persistent and increasing burden of poverty on women; to remove the obstacles to women's full participation in public life and decision making at all levels including the family; to eliminate all forms of violence against women; to ensure equal access for girl children and women to education and health services to promote economic autonomy for women, and ensure their access to productive resources; and to encourage equitable sharing of family responsibilities.

The country's concern in safeguarding the rights and privileges of women found its best expression in the constitution of India. While article 14 confers equal right and opportunities on men and women in political, economic and social spheres, Article 15 prohibits discrimination against any citizen on the grounds of sex, religion, race, caste etc, and article 15(3) empowers the state to make affirmative discrimination in favour of women. Similarly, the article provides for equality of opportunities in the matter of public appointments for all citizens; Article 39 stipulates that the state shall direct its policy towards providing men and women equal right to means of livelihood and equal pay for equal work; Article 42 directs the state to make provisions for ensuring just and humane conditions of work and maternity relief, and Article 51(A)(e) imposes a fundamental duty on citizens to renounce derogatory to the dignity of women. To make these de-jure equality into a de-facto one, many policies and programs were put into action from time to time, besides enacting/ enforcing special legislations, in favor of women.

WOMEN'S CONTRIBUTION TO ECONOMIC DEVELOPMENT

Today, a woman actively contributes to economic development in different capacities as mother, labourer, scientist, technocrat and executive officer. That is why the necessity for their equal treatment with men is stressed by many persons and institutions. Our late Prime Minister Mrs. Indira Gandhi has rightly said women's emancipation or equality is part of our general development plans but government actions can neither be effective nor adequate unless women themselves become more aware of their rights and corresponding responsibilities. The rise in her educational status had encouraged her to economic independence through gainful employment to look for material comforts and to express her individual status along the lines of democratic equality.

Against this background, a study was taken up to analyze certain select aspects of women workers employed in corporate sectors in Mumbai. The objectives of the study were, to examine the need for taking up employment, their social and, economic and educational background, health status, the time these women could cater to children and for themselves and further to suggest measures to unimproved their views and instill their rights.

The necessary data were collected with the help of an interview schedule administered to 50 women working with various corporate organizations based in Tilak Nagar, Chembur, (a suburb in Mumbai populated by the middle income group people).

RESULTS AND DISCUSSION

Personal and family details of the respondents: From among the 50 respondents, Eighty Eight per cent were married and the rest were single with regard to the number of children, forty per cent had two children, which is in consensus with the national family norm, however, forty six per cent had only one child and only two women had three children. The age composition of these women is depicted in the following table.

Table - 1
Age Composition

Age Classification (in Years)	Number Stating	Percentage.
20-30	8	16
31-40	20	40
41-50	19	38
51 and above	3	6
Total	50	100

Among the samples selected forty per cent of these women were in the age group of 30-40 years and thirty eight pre cent is the age group of 41-50 years. There were only three women (six per cent) who were above 50 years of age. However, eight respondents below the age of 30 were found to be working in some corporate sector.

EDUCATIONAL STATUS OF WOMEN IN INDIA TODAY

Education enhances the position or status of an individual. This is very true in case of women. Sen (1998) is of the view that education enhances decisional power within the family through its effect on her social standing, her ability to be independent, her power to articulate, her knowledge of the outside world, her skill in influencing group decision and so on. It is some of these factors coupled with economic independence that many women have realized the need to be educated. It is a common sight in our society that many mature women are pursuing higher education, many girls who get married during their college education, do continue their studies. It is believed that the mother is still the best teacher on life and health. The education imparted by her remains with children as long as they live. Women, if properly educated, can really help in the socio-economic development of the country. In the light of this, the educational status of the selected women were studied and it is given in table-2.

Table - 2
Educational background

Education level	Number of respondents	Percentage
School dropouts	2	4
Studied upto 12th	6	12
Graduates	32	64
Post Graduates	10	20
Total	50	100

The table reveals that majority of women (sixty four per cent) were graduates and around 10 women (twenty per cent) were not able to continue their studies for personal reasons. All of them were of the view that it is education which has helped them to get into some jobs and all in one accord stated that they would educate their children to attain great heights.

SOCIO-ECONOMIC AND HEALTH STATUS OF TODAY'S WORKING WOMEN

In the emerging social and economic scenario, women have taken up many new roles to create a meaning for themselves. In countries with economies in transition and in other countries undergoing fundamental political, economic and social transformations, these changes have led to an increase in women's employment opportunities and an enhancement of her economic and social position. With the education attained, the survey found out that a whopping percentage (eighty two per cent) of women was working in private sector and the rest were employed in government sector. A further classification revealed the firms in which they were working and the reasons for them taking up job is depicted in the following tables.

Table - 3
Job Classification

Type of organization	No of respondents	Percentage
Banks	12	24
Investment / Insurance	17	34
Corporate	21	42

Around 21 women were working in the corporate sector and most of them served as consultants. Twelve women were in banks and 17 of were in private insurance companies.

Table - 4
Reasons for taking up job

Reason	No of respondents	Percentage
Financial compulsion	16	32
Supplement family income	38	76
To make use of the education and skill acquired	12	24
To get rid of boredom	2	4
Other reasons (to get out of mental tension caused due to family problems)	1	2

Many of the respondents had more than one reason for having taken up employment. 38 of them said that they wanted to supplement their family income and 16 of them had taken it under financial compulsion. While 12 respondents opined that they had wanted to make use of the education and skill acquired by them.

Many of the respondents opted for financial compulsion and to supplement family income. Some of them even stated that in a costly city like Mumbai it is not sufficient if men alone work to lead a decent life and to cope with the household expenditure. It was found that they also supplemented their monthly pay received from the regular job by getting in to direct marketing.

On questioning the job satisfaction of the respondents, ninety per cent of the respondents were satisfied with their job, while the remaining was doing it under compulsion. Some of them also opined that in a city like Mumbai, only if both the parents work, can they afford to lead a decent and comfortable life.

It was learnt that fifty four per cent of women work for 8-10 hours per day and 8 per cent work more than 10 hours, only thirty eight per cent of the women reported to be working within 5-8 hours, which is the stipulated working hours set by the government. This shows that around sixty two per cent of the women are working, more than the required time. This is mainly because a private firms take an upper hand and the,employee are at their mercy. Since many had to spend a substantial time in the workplace, the hours they spend at home were limited. This is more so in the case of women who have to travel 1-2 hours. Ten women had to travel two hours while 32 women took 1-2 hours, to reach their workplace. They travel either by bus, auto rickshaws or train. The waiting, travel and other difficulties they face make them very tired and they stay away from attending any social activity or function or family obligation. In a sample, ninety six per cent said that they don't attend any social activity. This is cause of irritation to husbands and children. Gradually tension builts in the family causing chaos, confusion and quarrels.

Even after reaching home she has to do other household chores. Around eighty eight per cent of the women stated that they have to rush to the kitchen and take care of everything after coming home even late at night.

To our question whether there is work pressure, eighty eight per cent of the women replied in the affirmative. Forty eight per cent reported that the work is highly pressurizing. Twelve per cent seems to have had a relaxed approach towards work. More than the pressure, these women do skip meals due to lack of time. Twenty four per cent skip meals quite often. Work pressure coupled with lack of food would definitely affect the health of women and this situation is serious.

On questioning about their health status, it was learnt that many of the respondents had health problems. Twenty per cent (10 respondents) of them are found to be diabetic, forty per cent are found to have blood pressure problems, ten per cent respondents suffer from heart problems and forty respondents suffer from fatigue.

Some common problems faced by these respondents:- They are not able to take care of their family properly, not able to take care of them and their health, not able to spend quality time with the children.

It is also found that these women's children have started going for tuition classes in order to complete their homework right from the kindergarten level. This shows that they are not able to take proper care of their children's education.

CONCLUSION AND RECOMMENDATIONS

(1) Organizations can avoid loading women with extra work so that she is able to balance her work family and personal life.

(2) Organizations can implement the concept of "me time" for women so that they also get some time for themselves and get a break. This will make the employees feel very refreshed which will have a tremendous positive impact on their work (improved efficiency).

(3) To overcome transportation problems, women should be left at ease at the work spot. The mode of transport can be arranged by the company.

(4) Organizations can also arrange for stress-relieving programs more specially for their women employees.

To conclude, it can be said that these women have ignored their health as a result of which, they are not able to spend quality time both for themselves as well as with their family. They become totally stressed out.

In spite of all these, facts, today's women in the corporate era have to prove that they are more capable than the men folks as they are able to play their roles both at workplace and at home very efficiently.

BIBLIOGRAPHY

- Sen Amartya (1998) "development as freedom", Oxford University Press, New Delhi.
- Prasad B.K (2005) Human and social development: women and children in India's development Agenda, Anmol Publications, New Delhi.
- Chitrasen Pasayat (2006) Development of Tribal Women, Problems and Potentials, Anmol Publications, New Delhi.
- Websites referred
- http://www.unu.edu/unupress/unupbooks/uu37we/uu37we0i.html
- http://womentodaymagazine.com/career/dualwork.html
- http://pewsocialtrends.org/pubs/745/the-married-life-of-the-working-mother
- http://ohioline.osu.edu/hyg-fact/5000/pdf/Women_Balancing_Work_Family.pdf
- http://www.buzzle.com/articles/working-women

☆ ☆ ☆

5 The Glass Ceiling : A Truth in India

INTRODUCTION

On the occasion of Women's Day, March 2008, Chitra Sood, Staffing Director at Microsoft India Development Center, gave her view on the position of career women in today's India. She said that "India will find a lot of women accepted in lower and middle management role, but while you go up, you will find that there are not many women there. There is a glass ceiling and I have myself experienced it. To overcome such difficulties women have to be dogged and dedicated." She added that passion, dedication and attitude of a karmayogi are what makes her a successful career woman and capable to break the glass ceiling.

A Woman at the Work Place

The money world culture and institutions were inspired almost by men, male-dominated energies, support and employees. But the awakening is in part about female energies coming into force towards the creation of more balanced and integrated societies. This is reflected by the importance of female leadership in two critical areas, the e=Environmental Movement and New Business Formation. Today, women own 1.3 million SSI and 9.1 million SME's but only 14% women got success in their corporate world which is just 1/3rd of male numbers in the corporate world. Survey conducted by the National Foundations for Women Business owners reveal that women entrepreneurs are driven by a number of motives- some by an idea for a product or service, others by the desire to be their own boss and escape the frustrations of corporate life including rigidity, glass ceiling and a feeling that their contributions are not recognized or appreciated.

A Woman at Home

The Glass Ceiling for women started from her home. A woman should always be under a man, as a child she should be under her father, as a wife under her husband and as a mother under a son. A woman should easily carry the job. Family is her first concern which is the first step for her glass ceiling.

MEANING AND HISTORY OF GLASS CEILING

The term glass ceiling was first used to refer invisible barriers that impede the career advancement of women in the American workforce in an article by Carol Hymowitz and Timothy Schellhardt, in March 24,1986, edition of the Wall Street Journal. However, the term was used prior to that, in 1979, Hewlett-Packard, article by Katherine Lawrence and Marianne Schreiber and in 9th March, 1984, Adweek article by Gay Bryant, to describe that while on the surface, there seemed to be clear path of promotion, in actuality women seemed to hit a point which they seemed unable to progress beyond.

"Glass ceiling, is a discriminatory barrier to the advancement of women and minorities into upper echelon of business, the profession and the government."

In India, glass ceiling history is very old and prevalent even today. In the 19th century, position of women has been described as that of "Caged Bird" and girls who were educated were also said to become "Dustha". Our society is still male dominated: women are considered low in the country. Women are not treated as equal partners both inside and outside the four walls of the house. As such the Indian women have a disadvantageous status in the society such as low literacy rate 40%/60%, low work participation rate 28%/52% as compared to male counterparts. Glass ceiling is just run dramatically in India. No doubt there are various sectors captured by women but still they won't get the desirable post or appreciation like their male counterparts which we call glass ceiling of women at the corporate sector.

CAUSES OF GLASS CEILING

In a recent study, almost 3/4th of women and 2/3rd of men believed that an invisible barrier like glass ceiling prevented women from attaining top management position. The social status of women in India is comparatively lower. Though the constitution of India guarantees 'Equality of Status' to women, they do not enjoy full equality in the society. The majority of women are illiterate, underpaid, exploited and underprivileged. But in urban areas, with the spread of education the numbers of working women are increased and the situation is gradually changing: Despite these changes Indian society remains male-dominated and therefore, male employees feel humiliated is being ordered by a woman superior. But there are various reasons of glass ceiling which are classified into two groups-(a) By Herself (b) By Corporation.

(A) By Herself:

(1) Self-imposed: Women may choose to work in the corporation, for fewer hours than men to handle her two sides of positions i.e. the home front and the office front. She wants to justify both the places simultaneously. But she is inclined to spend more time with her family. Due to this attitude of hers she has to face glass ceiling in the corporate areas.

(2) College and Social Training: Her college training and work-experience taught her to make a living, not to bake a cake. Hence, she gets half the success as compared to man in a job.

(3) Motherhood: A lack of access to affordable childcare is one of the biggest reasons; women quit or take time-out from the work force. Balancing the need of children and career, she is exhausted and ignores her for before her child.

(4) Her common Beliefs: (a) Men are intellectually superior, more intelligent and more competent than her. (b) Men are emotionally stable than women. (c) Men value achievement, promotion and meaningful work more than her. (d) Men are inherently more assertive than women.

(5) Way of Measuring Success: Women measure success at the workplace differently than men. Men tend to measure success by salary and important job titles whereas women place a higher value on their relationships with colleagues and community services.

(6) Refusing Extensive Travel: Sometimes women employees are found to have refused promotion in order to avoid travel or transfer and they do not prefer to stay away from their family.

(7) Typical factor of Women: Maternity leaves are a serious interruption of work and many companies do not hire women employee for safety concern and avoid the losses due to maternity leaves.

(8) Mindset of Indian Women: It can be explained under three views- (1) The economically well to do Indian women often are at equal with male counterparts when going for MBA abroad. After marriage it is her personal choice to go for alternative courses like fashion industry or interior and jewellery designing. (2) The economically not so well off Indian women after marriage left their jobs or lose the drive to study and stay as a homemakers. (3) If such women continue their job, they want a typical 9-5 job and have a very less intention to go ahead in the job.

(b) By Corporation:

(1) Male Ego: Male representatives of private companies give various reasons for their appalling talks about hiring women in the companies. Actually, their male ego is hurt by a superior woman boss.

(2) 'Lady College 'as a Concept: In the Indian context men learn to see women as mother, sister, wife and daughter. The idea of 'Lady Colleague' is a new concept and quite intimidating to them.

(3) Less Approval and Recognition from Bosses: The women from business school were interviewed and shown that that inspite of them getting higher marks than the young men for better performance, yet they received less approval and recognition from bosses and were slower to be promoted.

(4) Role Played by Media: Many women achievers from corporate world believe that media is tilted towards glamour and thus the real women achievers often get neglected. The women achievers from the glamour world are negligible (just 2% only).

(5) Factories Act 1948: The Factory Act, 1948 provides restrictions of hours of work that women cannot be asked to work between 7pm-6am for safety protection of her. Such provisions severely restrict the employment of women in the management of factories and production facilities.

(6) Organizational Culture: A national daily recently ran a news story saying that at the turn of the century big name in India Inc. treasure an unwritten code "Do not employ women".

Surprised? Not really, as experts say that mere 3% women occupy senior positions in private companies across India and most of the companies only have 5-6% women employees. Such organizational culture is a cause for glass ceiling.

(7) Selection Procedure and Gender Stereotypes: Both employees and management staff recognize the persistence of masculine values and gender stereotype beliefs, so they don't want to employ women as managers. According to ILO, in India, the number of females holding managerial posts is 2:100 against men.

(8) Social Culture of India: In India, there is no place in sports, education and employment to the women. Till 1st March 1954, women were excluded from the prestigious IAS and IFS services. The justification for exclusion was that women were unsuitable to serve in far flung and remote places in the country and the world.

EFFECTS OF GLASS CEILING

There is glass ceiling for women and it is true for the world as a whole. Though women constitute 40% of the global workforce, their share in management position is mere 20%. The percentage of women in top positions is limited to 2-3% worldwide. The percentage of women in administrative and managerial jobs varies from country to country, 43% in the US and Australia, 33% in UK, 47% in Philippines, 42% in Russia, 33% in Thailand, 18% in France and Germany, 17% in Srilanka, 9% in Japan and 3% in India. Thus from the above facts following are the effects of glass ceiling:

(1) Increase in Stress Level: Due to glass ceiling, women are dissatisfied with the jobs and the corporations. Therefore, her concentration level is reduced and she feels more stressful. She de-stresses herself on her family members and makes them unhappy.

(2) Inferior Treatment: Most of the women managers face a differential treatment at the work which uploads the centrality and superiority of men and treat women as inferior and less important.

(3) Gets Less Challenging Job: Because of her stereotype attitude, women are offered less challenging jobs and are not involved in taking crucial organizational decisions.

(4) Disrupt their family life: Many of the managerial women have a fear that much determination towards their work will disrupt their family life. Indian Institute of Management, Ahmedabad showed that more than 70% of women do not pursue their career due to this reason.

(5) No Equality yet: In May 2003, Justice Leila Seth succeeded in breaking the glass ceiling by becoming the first woman judge in Delhi High Court. Soon she found that despite reaching the top there was no getting away from the old mind set and old rules which discriminate against women. Justice Seth discovered this when she was told that she was not entitled to the official reimbursement for her mother's medical bill. The reason given was that, the men who look after their mothers only should get the reimbursement. When she pressed the claim she was asked if she had no brother who could look after her.

HOW TO BREAK THE GLASS CEILING

No doubt there are so many problems in Indian Corporate sectors for women but there are women who always go ahead without looking behind what happened with their own sisters. Few corporate areas believe that "women are a lot more sincere and diligent workers". For instance, Indian Film Industry is more male dominant industry where having more talented women personalities like UTV's Co-Founder- Zarina Mehta, Balaji Telefilms- Ekta Kapoor, BAG Films MD- Anuradha Prasad and TV 18's Executive Director- Vandana Malik. These are the few achievers who have formed the milestone to prevent the glass ceiling of women's career.

Rebecca Shambaugh, the President and CEO of Shambaugh Leadership, present women with possibilities for their future at work. She said that, "It's not a glass ceiling but it's a sticky floor". She pointed out that more than 1/3rd of Fortune 500 companies managers are women but hold only 14.5% of the CEO's positions. The reason is that there is a glass ceiling preventing women from moving into executive positions. Shambaugh asks women to look at their own self defeating or self limiting actions, what she calls 'sticky floors'. It's true that women are their own enemies in their workplace. So she has given various preventive measures benefiting women in their workplace like-

(1) Women need to know what kind of changes they want to make in their lives.

(2) Self-evaluation and life planning are important to them.

(3) They should recognize their work style through some exercises.

(4) Women should learn to balance work and life.

Women in Indian Corporates may have had to face the glass ceiling at work. But the Indian Woman is finally getting her place in the sun with the number of women now going on to hold important positions in some of the world's biggest companies. The study organized by the UK India Business Council says that women's employment participation grew to 17% in 1980, 26% in 2000, 31% in 2005, and 48% in 2008. It will be a necessity to business and government in the 21st century, ensuring that the glass ceiling roof is shattered with the following assistance:

(1) Women Education: There is a clear preference for certain professions by men and women in India like there is high demand for teaching and nursing for women and electrical, mechanical, defence for men. Now the time has come for the women to enter area of male dominating industry.

(2) Increase in technical education: Figure from Nasscom reveal that female technicians are steadily narrowing the gap on their male rivals as the number one choice for new intermediate or senior-level expertise in IT. Male to female ratio was 76:24 up to 2007 but today, this ratio is 65:35. This also represents the increase in number of women enrolling in engineering colleges in India and the absence of a gender based glass ceiling.

(3) Good Performance: The performance of the women has been impressive; some have made it as project manager faster than their male batch mates. Women power prevails in Ahmadabad as maximum respondent in the city feel that women bosses have better administrative people management and target aggression.

(4) Through Organizational recruitment: In Infosys, women constitute 40% of staff. This is a huge number and senior management is pushing hard to bring this number to 50%.

(5) Change the Mindset: Women must change their mindset; rather accepting lighter work they should enter in hardcore decision areas. 'Focus only on work' is Pune's Mantra, with over 70% people saying that the boss gender does not make a difference to their work performance.

(6) Changes in common beliefs: Many common stereotypes hold that men are more intelligent and emotionally stable in general but research proved that number of women can do better than men.

(7) Diversity training: Most of the organizations today provides special training, called diversity training to help people identify their own cultural boundaries, prejudices, stereotypes and develop skills for managing and working in adverse workplace. About $80 billion has been invested in this programme which could be helpful for increasing more number of women managers.

(8) Building your list: What particular value women want to follow in their life are honesty and integrity, independence, personal responsibilities, equality, continuous personal growth, family, spirituality, creativity, philanthropy, personal wealth etc. Women have built a list of these values that are important for them.

(9) Forget boundaries and rules: Boundaries and rules are the enemies of creativity which restricts women mind's ability and creativity. For breaking glass ceiling they must forget boundaries and rules.

(10) Other ways: Identify winning skills and utilize them to climb the way to the top. Recognize the internal behaviors and attitude that sabotage your natural work style and learn to transfer them into supporters of success. Gain confidence to develop and implement new ideas and try to achieve true goals. Make yourself promotable, valuable and powerful through self tests, introspection and advice from women who have done it. For instance, the new speaker of India's House of Parliament, breaks the glass ceiling. India's lower house elected Meira Kumar, a former diplomat, the first woman chosen to run a male dominated chamber known for its rowdy debates and frequent walk-outs. Kiran Muzumdar- Shaw established Bicon, Rs. 5000 cr Company, at the age of 25, without experience, business contacts and a starting budget of Rs.10000. Naina Lal Kidwai, who was the first Indian woman to graduate from Harvard Business School, is the Vice-Chairman and MD of HSBC securities and capital market, has been listed amongst the world's 50 top corporate women.

CONCLUSION

The survey by Fortune Magazine listed only two powerful women from India, namely Naina Kidwal and Kiran Muzumdar, both aggressive and hard-charging women along with masculine traits. They are using their feminine based talents to nurture their company and fellow employees. They are extensive communicators and build relationships. They inject passion and emotions into long cold corporate environment to transfer the future of their company and break the hard glass ceiling which is built by the woman herself and orthodox corporates. So be pro-active, build relationships upward, build a network and find the solution within yourselves and try to break the glass ceiling.

BIBLIOGRAPHY

(a) Books:

- Exceptional Women: the career path of women managers——Ester Barbera and friends, 1996.
- The Post-corporate World: life after capitalism——David C Korten——Berrentt-Kochler Publisher, 1999.
- Women in Management——Sanghamitra Buddha Priya——A P H Publisher, 1999.
- Dancing on the Glass Ceiling: tap into your true strength——Candy Deemer, Nancy Freidericks—Library of Congress Publication, 2002.
- The Voyage to Exellence:the ascent of 21 women leaders of India——Nischinta Amarnath, Debashish Ghosh——Pustak Mahal Publisher, 2005.
- Women's Empowerment Issues, Challenges and Strategies—— Hajira Kumar, Jaimen Varghese——Regency Publication, 2005.
- Indian Women across Generation—Uma Narula-Atlantic Publisher, 2005.
- Women in India: retrospect and prospect—— K Shanthi——Anmol Publication, 2005.
- Management in India: trends and transition——H J Davis, Samir Chatterjee, Mark Hewer, 2006.
- Women in Asian Management——Yukongde, Vimolwan, John Benson——Routledge Publisher, 2006.
- It's not a Glass Ceiling: it's a Sticky Floor——Rebecca Shambaugh——McGraw Hill Publication, 2008.
- The New Era of Management—R L Daft—Thomson Publication, 2008.

(b) Articles:

- The Genuine Article——Jan Tucker,19th Aug, 2007.
- Employment Review——Ministry of Labour.
- Rediff.com News—7th Mar, 2008.
- Suite 101.com

(c) Newspapers:

- South Asia——21st April, 2004.
- The Times of India——Shveta Bhagat, 30th Oct, 2005.
- The AGE——8th Dec, 2006.
- The Economic Times——9th Oct, 2007.
- The Hindustan Times——Radhika Panchali, 20th Jan, 2008.

(d) Magazines:

- The Diplomat——Jan, 2009.
- Campaign India—13th Feb, 2009.

☆ ☆ ☆

6 Work Place Challenges for Women in the 21st Century

ABSTRACT

The status of the woman has undergone a vast change in the past two decades from a mere homemaker to a dynamic multi-tasker, by proving her mark in every sphere, which includes even the male-dominated professions. But in reality she still faces the challenges at the domestic and corporate fronts which make her to take career breaks. At a personal level, she faces the orthodox beliefs and rigid stereotype perceptions of the society. At the corporate level, she is a victim of the harsh effects of glass ceiling, pay inequity and discriminatory practices. The paper highlights such challenges at professional levels in the organization and explores initiatives to improve their status at the work place. It also provides insights into the exemplary practices introduced by some of the reputed organizations in safeguarding the interest of women professionals.

The role of women in the modern scenario has changed form just a homemaker to a dynamic multifaceted personality, capable of balancing work and family responsibilities successfully. The reasons for this change are improvement in the socio-economic trends, an increase in the female literacy rate, rapid industrialization and availability of lucrative jobs in the era of globalization.

Nowadays, a woman is successful in defining and shaping her own identity in the male chauvinistic society by making inroads into the corporate world. The Indian society has evolved from a traditional agrarian society to modern industrial society, which has also changed the culture, mindset and the attitude of the people towards women.

It is rightly said by Bernice Johnson Reagon:

> **"Life's challenges are not supposed to paralyze you;**
> **they're supposed to help you discover who you are."**

Thus, a woman has also discovered herself as a dynamic, modern and progressive personality. But, even though there has been an evidence of progressive transformation in the society and the status of women in workplace, still the trends in this direction are not satisfactory. A professional woman of today still struggles with the harsh realities of discrimination, exploitation and violence in organizations added by social, political and domestic challenges.

Barkha Singh, Chief of Delhi Commission for Women, opines, "Men are not very much advanced when it comes to treating women and they are not used to listening to women." In fact, rising crime cases such as rape and female violence are indicators of a woman's losing position in the Indian society and they appear to be on the defeatist front in the battle for improving their status by fighting against the traditional stereotypes and the age-old cultural practices.

Women and Men in India, 2006, a publication brought out by Central Statistical Organization reports an alarming rise in the incidences of crime against the women over the past two decades. A recent survey by the Hindustan Times, a leading newspaper, on 500 males reveals that around 60% males prefer housewives to working wives due to such problems. What will happen to us and our Nation then?

The paper highlights certain challenges at the workplace faced by the women including glass ceiling, derogatory attitude, hostile men's leagues, pay inequalities, flirtatious behavior, delayed promotions, direct request for sexual favors and impression management.

Surprisingly, in India, presently just only about 6% (CII, 2005) of the women are successful in reaching the senior positions of management. The reasons may be work timings, no support, lack of mentoring, problems in relocation etc. Though the women are efficient multitaskers and possess impressive soft skills, challenges of balancing work life and other issues compel her to lose her ability.

CHALLENGES FOR WOMEN AT WORK

(1) Glass Ceiling: Nowadays, the female workforce is subjected to the problem of 'Glass Walls'- a situation where women who manage to reach the senior managerial positions are deprived of accessing responsibilities into strategic areas. Also, they face the problem of 'Glass Elevator' in which the male counterparts are rapidly promoted to the senior managerial positions.

(2) Societal Perceptions: Society finds it difficult to accept women in the dual role of caretaker and provider. A working woman struggles physically, intellectually and emotionally for maintaining work-life balance and also she is unable to cope with her guilt feeling as she stays away from her kids and other relatives.

(3) Work-life Balance Issues: The poor childcare facilities pose a severe restraint for women in continuing their jobs stressing them to take a break. Due to nuclear family, she has to depend upon professional care taker, which is either unaffordable or unreliable. Coping with increasing family demands stresses her. Monisha Advani, CEO of EmmayHR, a recruitment firm, says, women lack operational commitment against males due to their personal obligations. This problem has also increased the number of divorces.

(4) Self-Imposed Restrictions: Many women lack proper confidence and underestimate their professional competencies.

(5) Cultural Challenges: Lack of female role models, lack of proper mentoring facilities, lack of proper awareness or communication opportunities, lack of clear career path, lack of skills or experience and gender stereotyping are some of the reasons which keep women away from leadership positions.

CERTAIN RESEARCH FINDINGS

The recent research evidence highlights the following problems:

(1) The Double-bind dilemma for Women in Leadership: Women believe that they are expected to achieve higher standards in the professional field and so they have to work harder than males.

(2) Glass-Cliff: Here women face the problem of high levels of burnout which occurs due to the excessive stress on reaching the top positions in management.

(3) Mini-me: Here the executives choose successors who are similar to themselves. The woman community faces this kind of challenge through the succession planning process in the organization due to which they are deprived of climbing up the ladders of success in the organizational hierarchy.

(4) Impression management: In flat organizations, managers get direct report for promotions. These managers believe that those who do not push themselves forward are not seeking promotion.

All the above challenges can be tackled by **designing and implementing a well-planned comprehensive program** for women professionals which would help them to improve their confidence and performance. Some of the initiatives already taken are:

(1) Providing forums for women to express their feelings with likeminded people and reduce their feeling of isolation.

(2) Providing a supportive culture which offers them an opportunity to share their experience and practice skills through individual or group mentoring, coaching or networking.

(3) Developing leadership to handle the professional matters successfully.

(4) Developing a transparent and fair system of succession planning to ensure promotion facilities.

(5) Providing flexible work arrangements including paid leaves, compensatory time off, extended maternity or parental leave, part time, adjusted hours, career leave, vacation borrowing, vacation sharing etc. Also it can be telecommuting at home, working at off site locations, shift swapping, job sharing etc.

(6) Providing child care facilities etc.

BEST PRACTICES IN CERTAIN TOP AND RENOWNED ORGANIZATIONS FOR WOMEN PROFESSIONALS

Pepsico: It is one of the famous companies preferred by women due to its employee friendly policies. The company has formulated several policies for women as under:

- Multi-year strategic plans for diversity with goals like diverse recruitment and for fostering an inclusive culture and improved retention.
- External Diversity Advisory Boards, consisting of achievers from different fields like education, politics etc. to render their advisory support on various issues.
- Annual employee performance reviews to find out the achievers for recognition.

- Biannual organizational health survey for females especially, mentoring and employee networking.
- Corporate sponsored multi-level program for training employees to adjust in diverse environment.

Tata Group: They have introduced a Second Career Internship Program (SCIP) for women professionals who preferred opting for a career break and wish to get back to their profession. Here, the company provides a live project to woman based on her domain expertise and interest for tenure of 5-6 months of a total duration of approx 500 hours. They can work as per their convenience and can earn around Rs. 4 lakhs.

William-Sonoma Inc : It gives a privilege of reduced work schedule after returning from maternity leave under their phased return program provisions. This program reduces the work schedule by 50% in the initial two months based on the mutual agreement.

Deloitte and Touche and LLC: These are the main champions of Alumni Networking and Consulting Programs and Mass Career Customization programs for the employees. Through networking they keep close contact with the employees leaving jobs for personal reasons. They are continuously kept in touch through communication and invitation to attend the corporate parties and events. Also, they are trained to keep their skills updated.

Through Mass Career Customization module, they are encouraged to work with the employees to understand their custom career goals and work out for themselves.

Best Buy: It championed the Result Oriented Work Environment program, where employees get ample freedom to handle their work requirement as per their wish. Due to this the employees get rid of their dissatisfaction.

CSC India: It offers utmost freedom and flexibility to its women professionals at work. This has increased their workforce to around 21% in 2006 from 13% in 2004. Also they have introduced an exclusive website for women called Planet W. The site works as a forum for exchanging ideas and sharing problems. Also they provide different courses on dieting and personal grooming for improving the lifestyle of the female workforce.

CONCLUSION

Women in the 21st century have tried their best to make their presence felt in all the fields in spite of many challenges faced at personal as well as corporate front. Organizations need to take an active part in attracting and retaining the talented women professionals as they may equally serve as genuine assets in the knowledge era.

BIBLIOGRAPHY

- Empowerment of Women in India – M. Koteswara Rao, Discovery Publishing House, New Delhi.
- Empowerment for women – M.L. Narasaiah, Discovery Publishing House, New Delhi.
- HRM Review, The Institute of Chartered Financial Analysts of India University Press, September 2008.
- HRM Review, The Institute of Chartered Financial Analysts of India University Press, October 2009.

☆ ☆ ☆

7 Women & Environmental Management

INTRODUCTION

Environmental management aims at the development of the environment for the human benefit; it is the process of balancing the socio-economic, technological and ecological forces in the development and allocation of resources in order to fulfill the needs and aspiration of present and future generations.

Environmental management is necessary because the resources are limited and if they are not used properly they will get exhausted shortly. For centuries women have gathered forest products. The time spent in forest gathering food, has taught women the many uses of trees including providing fiber for cloths, mat making and basketry. Many trees are used as a source of medical uses. For women, trees and forest are multifunctional. Trees offer "fuel, food and fodder". The three 'F' as women say. With so much pressure on the land, women have little choice to use forest. As there are no alternatives, women must gather wood and other biomass for fuel wherever they can.

The need of the time is that appropriate household technology be introduced to lessen women's drudgery. Women themselves need to be involved in such innovations because they have valuable suggestions and solutions to offer. Women are more disciplined in carrying out any movement says 'Gaitridevi.' Women can take it till the end, men change their mind. Women put a lot of time and energy and labour to perform various domestic activities like cooking, cleaning, washing, childbearing and rearing, dairy, poultry and other household chores. They are also engaged in collection of fuel, fodder, fruits, leaves, and other forest products from nearby jungles. Women have tremendous management skills of running the home. They are the chief managers of their home. Their managing skill can be utilized in managing the environment.

Most rural women are directly dependent on their immediate environment and their own skill in using it, for the daily necessities of life. Women, particularly those living in rural areas of the third world countries, play a major role in managing natural resourses-soil, water, forest and energy. Their task in agriculture and animal husbandry as well as in the household make them daily manager of the living environment. They have a profound knowledge of the plants animals and ecological process around them.

Women empowerment through participation has become reality and need of the society. Women's participation in development programme like forest management and watershed management has become the centre to Indian policy making process as well as society. Women's full participation is essential to achieve the goal of women's empowerment.

Women constitute half of the world's population, perform nearly two third of its work, have received one tenth of the world's income and own less than one hundredth of the world's property. Women constitute 48-49 percent of India's population. Their role is increasing day by day in each and every field of the society. In fact, women are establishing themselves in every field which was previously represented by only males. In the ninth plan draft, as it focuses, "To create an enabling environment where women can truly exercise their rights outside homes, as equal partners along with men". The draft directs both the centre and the states.

There is no doubt that women's development is directly related to national development. The development of women's resources i.e. their abilities, interest, skills and other potentialities are of paramount importance for the mobilization and development of human resources.

Women are repositories of the vast knowledge of indigenous farming methods, seeds, crop-rotation and terracing and water conservation. There is need to develop channels at the perfect time to absorb an indigenous native wisdom of women to supplement most of the mega polices of development in villages.

Women group should be consulted prior to deal over their usable items.

WOMEN AND LIVESTOCK MANAGEMENT

Women play a predominant role in livestock management and dairy production. They fetch the livestock, feed and graze them, clean cattle sheds, collect and process dung and milk the animals. Dung is also composted and carried out to the fields by women. In deforested parts of the country where trees and other sources of cooking fuel are scarce, women prepare cooking fuel by mixing dung with twigs and crop residues.

Like most other activities, women's role in livestock management varies across class. Women of landless and small peasants household perform all the activities. Women of medium farmer's household perform the work such as feeding and milking whereas, women of rich farmer's households perform mainly supervisory functions.

It needs to be pointed out however that women's role in animal husbandry is significant not merely as a consequence of the number of tasks they perform, but also because of their traditional role in integrating agriculture with animal husbandry.

Despite the significant role played by women in livestock management and production, the 1985 dairy India yearbook estimates women's employment 85% of the total employed in dairy production. Women's control over livestock or its products is negligible.

ROLE OF WOMEN IN WATERSHED MANAGEMENT

Although women have never been involved directly as a 'target group' in watershed management programs in general and soil and water conservation programs in particular yet these programs change the stage of natural resources especially that of soil, water and vegetation.

Even such an environmental friendly effort may result in an increased pressure on farm women. She is more efficient than a man. These operations are performed by farm women over and above the routine house hold chores.

Watershed management is now a widely accepted technology for resource management in totality. Women's participation in WSM is an important component of people's participation in water shed management.

MEANING OF WOMEN PARICIPATION IN WATERSHED MANAGEMENT

- How many women come forward and take part in the preparation of natural management special reference to WSM?
- Are the women coming forward and planning to have a management of w.s.?
- Are they convinced that they would like to do because it would be of help to them and they see watershed as being beneficial both monetarily and from the environment point of view?
- Are they taking decision on the rights of the watershed, on the issues related management of WSM?
- Does this experience give them the confidence to work on other development activities?
- Does it increase the confidence and capability in dealing with problem situation?

A diagnostic survey was conducted on the basis of sample survey in Sukhomajra wsm (Punjab), Relmajra WSM and FAKOT WSM of central soil water conservation Research and Training Institute, Chandrabadni and Danda WSM of Bhuvaneshwari Mahila Ashram (NGO), Chandrabhaga WSM of state govt. of Uttar Pradesh now is in Uttaranchal. The survey indicated that mostly women in every watershed feel that their participation can increase only after getting good education.

HILL RESOURCE MANAGEMENT (HRM) SOCIETY AND WOMEN

The villagers of Relmajra and Sukhmajra (Punjab)organized themselves in to a Hill Resources Management Society; under the Society Registration Act 1860. Since stored water is common property resource, its proper distribution and management is imperative. The head of every family, residing permanently in the village is eligible for membership of society he/she abides by rules and laws of the society.

Only in Relmajra and Sukhomajra H R M is existing. over all women participation in all activities is very low. Hardly 1.12 % women are aware about H R M.

ROLE OF WOMEN IN NARMADA BACHAO ANDOLAN

Narmada Bachao Andolan is a non-governmental organization. Medha Patkar established Narmada Bachao Andolan 1989: Many other groups joined this national coalition of environmental and human right activist scientist, academics, and project affected people with a non–violent approach.

Medha Patkar's campaign organized a 36 days long, solidarity among the neighbouring state of the Narmada valley from Madhya Pradesh to Sardar Sarover dam site. She said that the march was a path which symbolized the long path of struggle that the rally had.

Using right to fasting, Medha Patkar undertook 22 days fast. That almost took her life. She further undertook a similar fast in 1993 and resisted evacuation from the dam site.

WOMEN AND FOREST MANAGEMENT

Women's Participation in Chipco Movement: Women's active participation in Chipco agitation was a very novel idea of managing the forest by the women. The Chipco movement reached its climax when in 1974, women of Pen village in Uttranchal, under the leadership of 50 year old Gaura Devi barred contractors form entering the forest, singing "the forest is our mother's home, we will protect it with all our might".

The movement is well known for its Gandhian principles of non-violence was advocated by Chandi Prasad Bhatt through the Dasholi Grama Swaraj Mandal. The further development of the movement was greatly dominated by women who also demanded their election to forest panchayats. The Chipco movement is also the most important feminist movement in the world.

FOREST MANAGEMENT IN THANE DISTRICT BY TRIBAL WOMEN

Adivasi women from several talukas of Thane District, Dahanu, Palghar, Talasari, Mokhada, Wada, revealed a sense of alarm over the rapid depletion of the forest and the conversion of mixed forest into plantation of commercially valuable trees.

The collection of food and medicinal herbs require knowledge about plants, trees, roots etc. Most adivasi women do know something about the edible as well as medicinal plants. They often treat family members specially children for common ailments. Depletion and destruction on natural forest has meant the destruction of material basis for such knowledge.

In Thane district initiative was taken by adivasi men and women for protection of small part of the forest, a resource that is still important for their survival. In some villages women have emerged as leaders in the Jungle Bachao struggle. Groups of women patrol the forest, they are not only willing to protect just timber but the forest as whole.

Adivasi women have not only opposed the traders and the forest officials, who they hold responsible for the depletion of the forest, but also their own men and women who steal from the forest, they have opposed the illegal trade of timber, which is a thriving activity in Thane.

Most environmental training programmes on soil regeneration, affirmation, energy saving, water management – still discriminate against women but there are important exceptions to this practice.

The centre for human development and social change in Chennai, for example, annually conducts a highly successful ecodevelopment camp for young people, Especially for women for ten days in camp participation lectures, discussion, film shows, tree planting sessions. They visit other groups to see and learn about practical environment action. Good training can benefit women as well as environment.

STRATEGIES TO ENHANCE WOMEN VOICE IN ENVIRONMENTAL MANAGEMENT

(1) Formation of separate women groups from the grassroots level according to problems and social and economic structure with special attention to the weaker section of women and landless women.

(2) Formation of local institutions of women like Mahila Mandal and self help group and HRMS.

(3) Training programmes for women in water shed management by the women.

  (A) Specialized training for a group of women which will represent all the sections of society.

  (B) This group will give the training to all the women of the village with the help of development of agencies.

  (C) Increasing the women staff with in the development agency like ACAR for rural women training as it is very essential.

(4) The strategy of appointing women coordinators.

(5) Building alliances with other grass root institutions like committees of panchayat etc.

(6) Promoting federation of women's groups.

(7) Local knowledge of women to be utilized in the design and selection of place and project activities.

(8) Co-ordination between different government departments like education, family planning and health etc.

(9) For development of the capacity for achieving participatory permanence, the women staff must has technical skills.

It is the time to help restore the precarious balance between women and natural resources. While this can often be done by making simple changes in the development projects, it also requires high level policy support. It is increasingly obvious that the participation of women in natural resources management project is crucial for their success.

India is in the process of developing where the development projects should be taken the shape of a movement. Small and experimental projects are not able to change the socio-economic status of women. The policy maker should make a way to explore the gender issues through recognizing the need of men and women. The need of men and women may not be same and the impact of project on them, therefore, be different. They should try to investigate the customs, taboos and time constraints that women face. They should also promote the role that women can play in development activities at various levels and analyze her inclusion.

In 1985 a world conference was held in Nairobi to review and appraise the achievement of UN decade for women. Representatives of several UN agencies including UNEP, UNDP and WHO focused on the relationship between women and environment and problems of environmental degradation pose for them. The first time in the history of women decade, the issue of environment as it is related to women was taken up.

All sources of information and dissemination should be mobilized to increase the self help potential of women in conserving and improving their environment. National and International emphasis on eco system management and the control of environmental degradation should be strengthened and women should be recognized as active and equal participants in the process.

BIBLIOGRAPHY

- "Rural women, poverty and Natural Resources; Sustenance, Sustainability and struggle for change, Aggarwal B.
- Studies of educational working women in India, Trends and Issues – Ahmad, Karvin.
- Local needs and forest resources management in the Himalaya's - Bandho Prd.
- Women's contributions to agriculture economy in the Hill regions of North West India. Bhahi, J.B, and Dr. Singh.
- Forest Reserve, Management, pre-workshop volume Datta, Sam.
- Restoring the balance, women and forest Resources, - F.A.O (1995).
- Women and agro forestry - Fortman, pre-workshop volume Datta samgk (1999).
- Government of India (1998), national forest policy resolution, informal Shramshakti, report of the national commission on self employed women and women in the Government of India, (1988) New Delhi.
- Internet (www.google.com)

☆ ☆ ☆

8 Women & Environmental Management

ABSTRACT

The impact of economic development on environment, particularly in the growing economies results in environment degradation. In Developing Countries, mass poverty and rapid growth of population are worsening the environmental problems like depletion of resources and conservation of resources. Hence, women have to play a crucial role in environmental management; the Chipko movement, the Narmada Bachao movement etc were indeed a kind of feminist movement on macro level in India to protect nature. Women, even on grassroot level use local resources, traditional knowledge, indigenous technologies, skills and, experience in the environmental management.

Women are an integral and intimate part of the nature. The ecological knowledge, traditional storehouse made her to appreciate the generosity and diversity of natural ecosystem. Women are dependent on environment for their five 'F's – Food, Fuel, Fodder, Fibre, Fertilizers to feed their families.

Environment degradation and women development are closely related. Therefore, women have great stake in the concern for environment for their own development. Environment management aims at sustainable development which seeks to meet the present needs without compromising the ability to meet the needs of future.

Therefore, involving women in the protection, promotion and regeneration of natural resources is important for women empowerment and their families.

In this paper an effort has been made to outline the relation between environment and women. It will also focus on the need of environment conservation and attempt to emphasize role of women in environmental management. The paper will attempt to highlight the problems faced by women in environmental management and the urgent needs to empower women to equip in environmental management and for social equity.

BACKGROUND

The power of economic development leads to environmental degradation. Less Developed Countries (LDC) experience various environmental problems like over population, depletion of resources, lack of pollution control devices which further engraves the problems of environmental degradation. It is widely accepted that the development process in LDC has neglected women and environment for several years.

Generally, women constitute half the population of any country. In Less Developed Countries women are deprived of many opportunities, they lack proper education, lack access to the ownership of natural resources. Women are responsible for ensuring availability of basic daily necessities for their households. Hence women depend on nature to meet the basic needs of five 'F's – Food, Fuel, Fibre, Fodder, Fertilisers – and medicines.

Even in day to day life, ordinary women from India relate herself to nature by medicinal plants like *Tulsi*, Banyan tree, *Peepal* tree. They also worship animals like oxen (*bailpola*), snake (*nagpanchami*). *Vandana Shiva* states that she is nurtured by the feminine to produce life and provide substance. The nature (*prakriti*) is an expression of energy (*shakti*), which is the feminine expression of creative principles of the cosmos.

Nature is not only the feeder but also protector of women. In a desert, the trees guard them as a windbreaker and stop the gush of sand. It saves their settlements from slashing. This led the women in Rajasthan to take resort behind the shady and massive *khejri* trees. And for saving them, the villagers, led by women, challenged the wood-cutters by hugging the trees and carried successfully agitation against them.

Thus, women can easily relate themselves with nature and appreciate the generosity of Mother Nature, its diversity of natural ecosystem. When such nature is plundered and the Mother Earth is raped, it is no wonder that the Indian women rise to lead ecological struggles expressing their concerns about hardship being caused to them by scarcity of water, fuel, fodder and the fibre which the caring nature, otherwise bestows on their families.

ENVIRONMENTAL DEGRADATION AND DEVELOPMENT OF WOMEN

Along with the poor and landless, it is the women and female children who suffer the most due to environmental degradation. The women in rural area, hilly and semi arid regions usually have to spend longer hours for getting firewood, fodder and water to meet the need of their family.

A girl walks a long distance under the scorching sun in semi arid *Kutch* region to fetch water. Hence, they suffer from the ill health and low level of energy as well as loss of energy due to daily strenuous work of fetching water, firewood and fodder.

A woman in the *Tehri-Garhwal* hilly region walks in search of firewood for kilometres. They were first to notice that village commons are disappearing.

In both the cases, hardly any time is left for the girl child to go to school. Environmental degradation and women development are thus closely related. Therefore, women have great stake in the concern for environment for their own development.

WOMEN AND ENVIRONMENTAL MANAGEMENT

The sustainable management of natural resources means providing a security of livelihood for its people and the economy of the country. Women are basically the best planners. They can easily identify the needs of their families and accordingly satisfy them.

Women's consciousness of the environment and therefore their conservative approach is then not something inherent, arising out of their being women as is often propagated. It is rooted in their roles and work tasks which laid them to interact extensively with natural resources for survival.

Women can play a crucial role in detection of encroachers in the forest like the *thekedars* (contractors), who in league with the Forest Officer flout the rules and denude the forests. Women have been the eyes and ears of the village and forest communities and hands and hearts of the eco-struggle. Therefore, involving women in the protection, production and re-generation of natural resources is crucial for women empowerment, family wellbeing as well as for social forestry schemes. And their involvement in generation and monitoring of local natural resources through *Panchayati Raj* institutions (*Anil Agarwal).*

Sandhya Venkateshwaran has pointed out how women need to be perceived not merely as victims of environmental degradation, but as managers who have traditionally managed natural resources through informal management systems. However, they are now excluded from the formal systems of resource management.

Women continue to operate with inadequate mechanical aids and work with traditional techniques. In village *Betanda, Cuttack district*, women make dung sticks by applying cattle dung on special sticks. In village *Karatang, Bolangir district* of Orissa, women make fuel rolls out of tender *tendu* stems and *tendu* leaves wrapped with creepers. Thus women use combination of biomass to produce fuel and to save both conventional fuel and cooking time (*CPSW 1992*).

Women use many indigenous technologies based on their knowledge to manage safe drinking water for home, E.g. drumsticks seeds or *tulsi* is used as a water purifier, copper or brass pots, having antiseptic properties, are used to bring water from source and for storage unlike plastic which breeds bacteria. Such competitive technologies used by women for water purification are based on locally available natural resources products and knowledge (*Shiva 1988*).

Peasant women know the nutrition needs of their families and the nutrition content of the crops they grow. That is why women in *Garhwal* continue to cultivate *mandua* and women in Karnataka cultivate *ragi* in spite of all attempts of state policies to shift to cash crops. Because they said that they could not labour without this energy giving local food, which happens to be the source of their health and strength.

WATER MANAGEMENT

Women can successfully participate in and manage water related activities. E.g. in Pune, *Gram Gaurav Pratishthan* is initiating *Pani Panchayat* System, which consists of only women members. Similarly *Ralegain Sidhhi*, Maharashtra, has a very substantial involvement of women in *Pani Panchayat*. In the *Sree-ramsagar* project of Andhra Pradesh, women are sharing equal responsibilities relating to irrigation management along with men and also taking up certain responsibilities solely upon themselves (*Rao 1991*).

In the Water User's Association of Himachal Pradesh about 50% of the membership comprises of women. They take an active part in clearing channels and diverting water. They also share in the decision making process for water sharing and distribution system, the crops to be grown as per the availability of water. In many places hand pumps maintenance responsibilities are given to women and they are paid.

Despite women's traditional knowledge and role in water collection and management, they are perceived as beneficiaries of water and sanitation projects rather than as partners in planning or managing it. Studies have shown that it is essential to involve women, particularly when the project is at the conceptual stage or in the assessment phase. If it is not done, women continue to use the traditional systems of water despite the installation of hand pumps.

FOREST MANAGEMENT

Women depend upon forest mainly for fodder and fuel supply. There have been several instances of informal forest protection mostly around tribal areas. There women have played a significant role. *Pipar*, Orissa has organised local communities with significant women's involvement to protect forests from contractors. There have been instances of women stopping truckloads of timber being taken away by contractors. Similarly in *Singhlohoom* district in West Bengal with the support of the Rural Development Agency (RDA) a Forest Protection Committee (FRC) was formed with the initiative of women.

Over the years women have built up vast resources of technical knowledge on aspects of forestry livestock, water use and other activities. These pools of knowledge relate to optimal methods of performing tasks and to optimal use of management of resources as it has evolved over generations. As women frequent the forests more, they know more trees, species than men. Tribal women certainly feel close to trees and the forest around them. They have also shown more enthusiasm for the potential of social reform. Hence, when males could suggest a few varieties of trees of commercial importance under Social Forestry Programme, women insisted on a variety of plants catering different needs such as fuel, fodder, timber and so on.

The *Badlao Foundation* in *Dumka district*, Bihar, has been organising tribal women and training them in forest extension work. The Birsa Agricultural University has provided technical guidance.

The biogas technology failed because it did not take into account women's requirements. Males also lost their interest since they wanted energy for production and not for cooking. In household technology adoption where the problem of cash expenditure comes, it would depend on the priorities of men who handle the cash and other decisions. In this way, women continued to operate with inadequate mechanical aids and traditional techniques.

NEED OF WOMEN PARTICIPATION IN ENVIRONMENTAL MANAGEMENT

When entire households are victims of macro developments, men are able to find escape routes with greater ease than women either via migration to urban areas in search of employment or turning towards alcohol and domestic violence to give vent to their frustration. It increases women's vulnerability and work burden. Hence efforts are needed to alleviate women's hardship, involving them in land-related projects. This is one of the important ways of ensuring their interest and needs are assigned priorities. Such projects may facilitate providing them income and importantly grant access to local natural resources as well as enhance their knowledge and minimise hardship. *(Sarin 1991)*

The other reason to involve them comes from the vast traditional knowledge women carry. The knowledge about trees, species, forest produce and its uses, seeds, agricultural practices, water harvesting etc. The best way of making optimal use of this knowledge is to ensure women's participation in projects relating to the management of the local resources.

MOTIVATING FACTORS

Access to resources – Women's access to land resources is not merely a question of making land available to them. It is equally the question of their having a voice in its management. Many states of India have joint *pattas* (title deeds) in the names of husband and wife. But Andra Pradesh has issued instructions that it should be exclusively in the name of women. In Bihar, many land *pattas* have been transferred in the name of women as agricultural loans were conditioned to it.

The extent of women's involvement in a project largely depends on orientation of the NGOs and migration of males in search of employment. *Burra* points out that nature of women participation in project varies from wage labourers to decision making and management. NGOs having specific focus on women, show high involvement of women. Similarly, absence of male members in the society too shows high involvement of women.

Limited technical expertise and perception of the staff regarding women abilities. limit women participation of decision making and management. Hence women should be given training through workshops to upgrade their skills.

Institutional Support – Migrant women agricultural labourers at *Jhilmili, Bankura* district, West Bengal formed an organisation and created 'income' generation activities by wasteland management. The group of women received gift of plots from local poor households whose women migrated seasonally and males were not in position to fill the land. Women organisations received training in the aspects of management, enterprise and relationship with other political and bureaucratic bodies.

The workshops gave them a sense of solidarity and enabled them to form *Nari Bikas Sangh* (NBS) in 1986. The NBS initiated community based activities in cooperation with the *Panchayat Samiti*. The NBS acted as a catalyst in the formation of educational groups generated about 36,000 person days of direct employment through plantation activities (*Mazumdar* 1989).

GLOBAL PERSPECTIVE

An appreciation of women's role in environmental management, especially in developing countries where livelihoods are based around biomass economies and their simultaneous exclusions from decision making processes led to the adoption of "Global Treaty" of NGO Women in search of healthy and Just Planet". The treaty stated that the women's exclusion from leadership and decision making was one of the major causes of environmental degradation and demanded a balance of success in the analysis of public policies at the local national and international level. Population pressure is the major cause of environmental degradation hence the needs for women's reproductive freedom and knowledge to exercise that freedom was stressed in agenda 21.

CONCLUSION

Women being a minority group have limited scope to decide how to manage environment because in development ideology, it has been assumed that the environmental management is technical and scientific and have no capacity to make decisions. Environment Management measures of women have evolved through trial and errors, taking into account local needs and resources, indigenous technologies and skills, experience and knowledge. A woman's right to resources has to be recognised. Their environmental management practices have evolved through interaction with environment. Externally adopted management resources remain artificial and tend to disappear when external support dries up. Environmental Management by women is strongly connected with measures securing long term conditions.

Analysis has revealed that despite the prominent role women may have played in environmental movement like *Chipko*, translation of this into leadership or political role in their daily life, or even any significant change in their status has rarely taken place. Taking example of *Chipko*, Sharma (1984) observes how despite the dominant role played by women, their representation on local or regional political bodies is negligible.

To secure the contribution of marginalised sector like women is to empower them. Locally practiced management resources must be institutionalised locally, regionally and nationally with suitable policies to support them.

Following measures will empower and equip women for effective environmental management–

(1) Holding various conferences in provinces regarding women's role in environment and publishing and distribution of books

(2) Encouraging research and preparing scientific articles regarding the issues of women and environment

(3) Supporting knowledge and natural household technologies of women which traditionally exist in rural areas and among nomads such as *Ayurveda*

(4) Facilitating access of women involved in agriculture, fishing and husbandry by training

(5) Evaluating environmental impact of policies and programmes and access of women towards usage of natural resources

These findings could then be used as input in policy formulation to ensure that women's needs are being addressed.

BIBLIOGRAPHY

- Sandhya Venkateswaran, 1995, ISBN 0-8039-9212-2: Environment, Development and Gender Gap, Sage Publications.
- V. S. Mahajan (Edited), 1994, ISBN 81-7100-528-4: Environment Protection – Challenges and Issues, Deep and Deep Publication.
- Pravin Sheth (Edited), 1997, ISBN 81-7033-406-08: Environmentalism – Politics, Ecology and Development, Rawat Publication.
- Krishna Ghimire and Michel Pimbert, 2006, ISBN 01-85383-415-7: Social Change And Conservation, Earthscan Publication, UK..

☆ ☆ ☆

9 Women Entrepreneurs a Journey Ps to Es

This paper is directed to explore the status of women entrepreneurs, the problems they face and the challenges ahead in the light of the social perception as well as self perception towards women's position in general and as entrepreneurs in particular.

Woman entrepreneurship is a relatively new concept in many developing and transitional economies and is emerging worldwide. This is a fact as it has been expressed almost a decade ago thus in a global summit:

Global markets and women are often not used in the same sentence, but increasingly statistics show that women have economic clout – most visibly as entrepreneurs and most powerfully as consumers.[1] – Irene Natividad, 1998, Summit Director, The fifth Global Summit of Women & Chairwoman, U.S. National Commission on Working Women.

Woman entrepreneurship actually emerges from an individual's creative spirit into long-term business ownership, job creation and economic security. Therefore, women entrepreneurs are the ones who own and control any enterprise having a share capital of not less than 51% as partners / shareholders / directors of private limited company / members of co-operative society. They are the women who think of initiating, organizing and operating a business enterprise; combine the factors of production, undertake risks and handle the economic uncertainty involved in running a business.

Women are considered homemakers in most parts of the world. Hence, traditional schemes which don't require full-time attention like candle, agarbatti (incense), pickle, powder and paper making; tailoring and handicraft are suggested to enable them to attend to their household chores. But societal patterns have changed almost over the last 25 years, from a male bread winner model to duel earner families – and young women are increasingly presented with the challenges of reconciling family responsibilities with full-time employment. Therefore, from playground to boardroom, more women today are in power when it comes to business. Brendra C Barness of Saralee, Janet L Robinson of The New York Times, Anne Mulcahy of Xerox, Maragret C Whitman of eBay, Nayla Hayek of the Swatch Group, Nainalal Kidwai of HSBC India, Indra Nooyi of Pepsico, Smini Jindal of Jindal SAW Limited, the list goes on. It indicates that women entrepreneurs are active domestically, regionally and globally as well. In 1994, none of America's top 500 companies had a woman at the helm, this is an evidence of entrepreneurship presently being an extension of their kitchen activities.

Women all over the world enter in business for both pull and push factors. The pull factors encourage them to start an occupation with an urge to do something independently while push factors compel them to take up their own businesses to tide over their economic difficulties. Women entrepreneurial activity all over the world has spurred due to the startling pace of socio-political and economic transformations and demise of dictatorship in the last decade of the 20th century and later on, the support by women business associations which play a vital role in identifying appropriate emerging sectors where woman entrepreneurs can succeed.

According to 1995 survey, legal equality in economy, granting women equal access to education and training, and growing awareness about business prepared environment for abled and competent women who want to own and operate businesses in economy over the period. Therefore, they have started shifting from the 3Ps – viz. powder, papad and pickle to 3 modern Es, viz. -engineering, electronics and energy and excelled. Resultantly, women in advanced market economies own more than 25% of all businesses which are growing rapidly. The surveys conducted by NFWBO indicate that women owned firms involved in global market place have greater revenues, and are more optimistic about their business prospects and are more focused on business expansion than women owned firms that are domestically oriented. Obviously expanding into international trade can pay off for women owned firms. However, it is not clear whether smaller enterprises are benefiting from this potential as much as the larger firms. Women entrepreneurs are generally found in informal and marginalized sectors outside the formal and traditional mainstream sectors dominated by man because the difficulty is- to move from the acceptance of equal rights to the reality of equal opportunities. Therefore, setting up micro enterprises and SME's in both formal and informal sectors is proposed to them for sustainable development and alleviation of poverty. They tend to seek small personal loans but the banking world has thus far shown little interest in small loans or micro credits, given the relatively high handling costs. The result is that institutionalized banking practices remain for the most part opposed to micro credit concepts. Besides, banker's anti-feminist perspective also fosters a reluctance to grant credits.

A study by Peggy Clark and Amy Kays also asserts this fact as 41% of women entrepreneurs report that lack of money is the greatest obstacle to start a business and 47% cite lack of capital as the greatest barrier to business growth. They suffer on two counts – (i) they don't have property in their names to use as collateral for obtaining funds from external sources. (ii) Banks consider women borrowers less creditworthy and discourage them too in the belief that they can 'at any time' leave their businesses. Thus women setting up micro enterprises, SMEs, or formal large-scale businesses, all encounter varying degrees of difficulty in obtaining capital, collateral and fair lending terms. Subsequently many women owned businesses fail. To overcome this, various groups and financial institutions like SEWA (India), VOICE (Africa), FINCA (USA), Grameen Bank (Bangladesh), NGOS and as International Coalition Women & Credit, RESULTS education fund (USA), Women's World Bank and many others promoted the idea of micro credit micro enterprises in policy circles. In 1977, Micro credit summit launched its global campaign to reach 100 million of the world's poorest families, especially the women of these families by 2005.

Besides the said problem, the woman business owners face the general problems- pertaining to raw material, marketing, infrastructure, skilled manpower, delays in promotional procedures, difficulties in availability of govt. concessions and subsidies and (ii) specific problems- lack of need based achievements, absence of risk bearing capacity, lack of educational skill, male dominance, lack of business information, training and experience, heavy involvement in family problems, lack of viable concepts, social stigma attached to certain vocations etc. Added to this, are certain stereotypes regarding women's roles and abilities to limit their mobility in business.

"Catalysts have done research on the stereotyping of women business owners and found that women are likely to be perceived good at "taking care" and not good at "taking charge" ".[2]

Most of the women enterprises are plagued by the scarcity of raw materials and inputs due to the high price of and minimum discount available at the raw materials. Even they don't have organizational set up to pump in a lot of money for canvassing and advertisement. So they have to face stiff competition for marketing their products with both organized sectors and male counterparts which results in liquidation of women enterprises.

A single woman asking for room is still looked down upon with suspicion in various regions of the world. They are considered weaker and made to lead a protected life since time immemorial. It leads to less access to education and economic independency and thus reduce their potentiality to bear risk involved in running a business enterprise. Women doing international businesses face challenges common to all entrepreneurs besides limited international business experience, and lack of access to international networks, societal, cultural and religious attitudes. In revitalizing the economies, they may also face intractable infrastructure problems, legal hurdles, lack of political contacts, custom tariffs, bureaucracy, extortion in developing and transitional economies.

On reviewing the NFWBO 1998 surveys from Argentina, Mexico, Brazil, Ireland, Russia, Latin and Iber American Countries, it was found that the uppermost business concerns of the women are making profits, hiring and keeping qualified employees, acquiring state-of-the art technology, complying with govt. laws and policies, obtaining business management training, securing adequate credit and improving the overall state of the economy. These obstacles parallel concerns of women business owners in US, Canada and Britain. In developing and transitional economies the double shift syndrome, corruption, gender discrimination and patriarchal traditions are also serious concerns.

Despite these obstacles, women entrepreneurs, even now realize that they too can enter the race and somehow find a way to engage in as they are an emerging economic force, so government, policy makers and voluntary agencies cannot afford to ignore them and are making efforts to tap the hitherto unrecognized and unaccented for strength of women to integrate into the process of industrial development more especially small scale industries development. As they realize that "the question should not be a matter of "can she" or "why does she" but "how does she" and "where can she go for help" ".[3] The general consensus, therefore, is that promotion of women entrepreneurs should form an integral part of all development efforts by devising and diversifying vocational training facilities for women to suit their varied needs and to promote appropriate technologies to improve their efficiency and productivity, to provide assistance for marketing their products to involve women in decision making process. NGOs are organized to overcome isolation, promote one another's interests and expand businesses. WBO offers a venue, and resources for females seeking to set up a business. The NGOs are important to the health of budding entrepreneurs as they influence policy makers, role models, mentors and provide a collective voice to advocate for public policies that benefit these women members. Women are also seen seeking out and participating in business associations to mitigate the various barriers and to gain a sense of commitment.

Madeline Albright mentioned, "Focusing on women is not simply the right thing to do, it is the smart thing to do".[4]

Dr. Khotkina, trainer and consultant to entrepreneurs stated, "The . . . process of women setting up small enterprises, firms, foundations and associations, which began so recently is so dynamic that even information a month old is out of date".[5]

This statement shows that women entrepreneurship is catching on with great rapidity. Women are changing the face of business ownership internationally as between 1/4th and 1/8th of world's businesses are owned by them. As their numbers grow and their businesses prosper, they will change the way the world does business. These women contribute significantly to global economic health, national competitiveness and community commerce, as they bring many assets to the global market. They have demonstrated the ability to build and maintain long term relationships and networks, to communicate effectively, to organize efficiently, to be fiscally conservative, to be aware of the needs of their environment, and to promote sensitivity to cultural differences. They also share risk taking propensity, high energy level, personal motivation, social adroitness, intuitive people skills, consensus building competencies, and certain specific characteristics which promote their creativity and generate new ideas and ways of doing things. Therefore, women's enterprises are qualitatively different from men's. Studies indicate that women business owners create a culture of their own. Female enterprises tend to centre on delivery of services responding to traditionally unsatisfied needs. Author Sally Helgesen commented that women managers liberally seek information, exchange ideas with others, and let information crystallize before making a final decision. They also show tremendous willingness to seek business guidance and education to compensate for perceived weaknesses. The WBOs cite that their one quality, the key to their success, is the ability to focus intensely. Various studies and interviews suggest that women entrepreneurs tend to be self-directed and exhibit a high internal locus of control and achievements. As owners of SMEs, they also supply MNCs with ideas, inventions, technology, raw materials, supplies, components and services.

Women entrepreneurs are functioning as role models and mentors too. They, thus, carve out paths for other budding entrepreneurs. Resultantly, the gap between male business owners and female business owners has narrowed significantly from 26 in 1970 to 40 in 1990 for each 100 men. Although largely absent from the decision making positions in multinational corporations, women are advancing as major actors in entrepreneurial activities yet NFWBO, UN, OECD and other studies demonstrate apparently that women entrepreneurship has grown significantly in the past decades. OECD in 1998 estimated, 75 to 80% of new enterprises in the U.S. are created by women. Canadian Research shows a 172% increase in the number of self employed women between 1975 and 1990. The fact is that women are just as capable as men to make board room decisions and many a times their strategies have created business opportunities as it is not just the board room where women are succeeding. They are no longer seen as second class compared to their male counterparts. They have come a long way from the days when their opinions and voices were left unheard and unrepresented. They get to enjoy better life, more equality, better opportunities and power to make decisions as they have come together to make a difference. Not only NABW in Malawi, WEAN in Nepal etc. play a vital role in economic empowerment and training of women entrepreneurs but also provide moral and psychological advocacy, create safe and growth oriented atmosphere which is ideal for incubating new businesses. Typically, mutual support is the prime reason in their decision to join business associations despite resistance and opposition because they learn from each other and these networks expand. The women entrepreneurs also say that without WBOs they feel isolated which is most certainly a helping hand in making them skillful business women. They also recognize that they can't grow without right tools. The various surveys reflect that women business owners in various countries perceive training in finance, marketing, technical skills and other related business issues should be focused on for their growth and profitability potential.

Although women have started businesses and succeeded too, they are creating job opportunities for others and improving the economic standards of their families yet they are not getting expected corresponding respect, recognition and self esteem as prejudices prevail. There has been a long argument whether women should join a male dominated organization such as trade associations or chambers of commerce. Brian Lee asks, "Why splinter off, and declare that you are women first, business people second?"[6] She says that they should join mainstream chambers or business groups because they are most likely to meet those who can demonstrate and coach powerful business techniques only in male dominated organizations.

Even Naina Lal Kidwai said, "Women have to shed "self imposed" glass ceilings. It is not a man or woman thing, you are a leader because you do it right."[7]

Sheron Hardy, executive director of NFWBO asserts, ".... The bond of being a woman business owner supersedes the cultural differences."[8] Thus women need to overcome psychological, cross-cultural and gender related barriers to assume responsibility as women business owners. They also need to establish a strong level of credibility by having guts to handle and thrive on upcoming challenges and changes in the business world. As these entrepreneurs are always restlessly in search of newness, enjoy pushing their creative boundaries and experimenting with new ideas, the pressure acts as trigger. So they suffer from stress. Although they have shown strong work ethics, and worked doubly to justify people's (investor's) faith in them by showing 100% commitment, building new reliable trademarks, sustaining them and bringing ideas to corporate life; yet entrepreneurship is a highly personal and subjective process of encountering, assessing and reacting to a series of experiences produced by political, social and cultural changes. So these entrepreneurs must show continuously strategic and lateral thinking, self-motivation, positivity, patience, determination, good decision making and public relations skills, patience and hard-working nature to sustain themselves in this prejudiced society.

Erkki Liikanen, European Commission for Enterprise and Information Society says that we definitely need more women entrepreneurs. We know now that women in general create smaller but relatively more viable enterprises. Keeping this in mind, we need to promote continuously women entrepreneurship. For this, the UN International Trade Centre's Women in Trade Development Programme defined three areas where intervention is needed-

(i) at grass root level as an individual entrepreneur.

(ii) at operational level in co-operation with WBO and

(iii) at policy and institutional level to systematize governmental efforts because women are not only under control but they are not taken into account when public policies are formulated. Ducheneant at OECD remarked that women running SMEs are quite frequently handicapped by lack of management training.

Thus, there were also times when entrepreneurship was rare and looked at with circumspection and yet there are those who tried and failed and tried again till they hit upon an enduring idea that brought them distinction as entrepreneurs. These new age women entrepreneurs are radiant, confident and always leave behind an aura. They are, at the same time, multifaceted and love their freedom, for example:- IYDEY 2007 award winner Gunjan Gupta, Director of Wrap Art & Design and India's creative future 2007 winner Priya Patil, a talented fashion designer and stylist for Gratzia Magazine. Consequently, from kitchen to business, the world is shifting for women while it may not be still ideal. The fact is women have definitely come a long way as the women who are considered to be powerless, poor, passive and right for manufacturing powder, papad and pickles for their families only, have now emerged as empowered, enriched energetic and enigmatic entrepreneurs who have excelled in e-commerce too.

To conclude, the women need not stop here as sky is the limit for them. They need to strive at least till they get the titles of company like Jain Sisters and Mrs. Chand & Daughters Company. Thus, to progress further, these women have many promises to keep and miles to go before they sleep.

BIBLIOGRAPHY

- *http://www.cipe.org/pdf/programs/women/jalbert.pdf* [Susanne E. Jalbert, Women Entrepreneurs in World Economy, p.8]
- DNA, Mumbai, 28th September 2007, p.15
- Susanne E. Jalbert, Women Entrepreneurs in World Economy, p.23
- Op.cit, p.28
- Op.cit, p.11
- Op.cit, p.42
- DNA, Mumbai, 28th September 2007, p.15
- *http://www.cipe.org/pdf/programs/women/jalbert.pdf* [Susanne E. Jalbert, Women Entrepreneurs in World Economy, p.42]

☆ ☆ ☆

10 Law and Gender Sensitivity

INTRODUCTION

In recent years, the role of judiciary has extended beyond issuing directions on social issue concerns to ensuring effective and fair implementation of the same. As a judge this requires elimination of subtle ways in which the courtroom perpetuates discrimination and violation of women's right..... As judges we need to be proactive and take charge of our courtroom to ensure that the subtle ways of discrimination through spoken and unspoken words are eliminated[1] .

Former Chief Justice of India, AS Anand

GENDER SENSITIVITY

The ability to recognize gender issues and to recognize women's different perceptions and interests arising from their different social positions and gender roles. Gender sensitivity is often used to mean the same as gender awareness. But it is actually the beginning of gender awareness, which is more analytical and critical; a question of gender disparities, and motivates one toward actions to address gender issues.

The researcher's present study attempts to understand the justice delivery mechanisms from the perspective of women litigants. This research work empirically examines and explores the process of women's resistance to the gender insensitive dominion within the sphere of law. The study suggests that the justice delivery system does provide, a platform for a woman to raise her concerns and a space to negotiate for her rights, yet, at the same time, it also acts to disqualify her claims and often ends up in re – victimizing the victim.

Even if laws are fair and impartial, the implementation of laws is carried out in an unfair manner, it may act as barrier to achieve the goal of justice. For instance, lacunae in both content and procedural aspects of law dealing with rape have been pointed out through several studies or recently in the year 2004 where protests by women in Nagpur against the Criminal Justice system resulted in lynching of accused Akku Yadav within the Courtroom on August 13th 2004. August 16th several other similar incidents were also reported in a TV Channel Aaj Tak in its

1 A.S Anand, Bringing the Rights Home, Justice for Women: Concerns and Expressions, Universal Law, 2002 at p 12.

report JURM: dated 2.1.05. The present work focuses on similar contradictions existing in the justice delivery mechanisms. It examines the problems that exist at the level of framing of law as well as the impediments that continue to act as hurdles in the pathway of justice.

EXPERIENCE OF WOMEN VICTIMS WITH ENFORCEMENT AGENCIES OF THE STATE

(First Field Study): Resources: Availability, Accessibility and Utilization

To identify women for this study, the choice was women litigants approaching the Mahila Courts directly. Reason for choosing the direct method was to gain access to unmediated first hand experience of women as litigants and to obtain a glimpse of wider perspective of the situation. Informants were located within the premises of three Courts in Delhi. One at the Patiala House, the other at Tis Hazari Court premises and the third at Karkardooma Court Complex.[2]

Data reflect that major impediments in women's access to justice include availability of resources in terms of finance, knowledge and information about her rights and legal procedures. Majority of women (92%) claimed that initially they lack access to information about the procedure of filing the complaint. Legal content, legal jargon, concept and the context was alien to them and it is only after they had contacted lawyers and others and had experience in the Court over a period, they gradually became familiar with the system (held by 68% informants). The study reflects on lack of legal literacy and awareness among women. For majority of women, law is a 'mystique' and a complex subject which they failed to understand because it is 'too complicated'. 76% claim that they were not aware of their right to file a complaint against their husband though 20% said that they have heard of other cases where other women have taken action in such cases. A few of them said that they were aware of the fact that women's concerns are better heard these days. 76% respondents claimed that their natal family, neighbours (16%), friends or colleagues (23%) employers (2%), community leaders (2%) or NGOs (12%) were their source of information about filing a complaint. Perhaps education or employment has not made any impact in terms of enhancing legal knowledge or information. Ironically, programmes like victim assistance or witness assistance, which exists in the other parts of the world are not practised in India. Around 72% opined that filing complaint is a complex process therefore they felt that it was essential to consult lawyer before they initiated legal proceedings. Resources in terms of monetary capacity to pay lawyer's consultation fee, transport charges frequently appeared as a block to continue with the long drawn battles in the Court. Only one out of 50 respondents was aware of the provision of free legal aid. Yet another barrier relates to fear and stigma being associated with going to police station or the court (reported by 74% respondents). *"My parents did not want that I should go to police station or police officers coming to our house for investigation. For them it is the matter of 'family prestige'. Nobody in our parental family has ever been to police station or court"*, uttered a respondent. Reluctance to approach the state machinery hinders the women's way to justice. Often the common perception is that courts and police stations are meant only for a 'different' set of people and not for persons living in a familial situation.[3]

---

[2] Shalu Nigam, Understanding Justice Delivery System from the Perspective of Women Litigants as Victims of Domestic Violence in India, 2002 at pp 25 – 27.

[3] Ibid at p 27.

It was observed that the enforcement agencies, the Police, Advocates, and Courts share a great portion of the blame for the inefficient implementation of the protective laws.

(Second field study): The experience of women with enforcement machinery are not very happy. Most of them, 94% of the 87 persons were disappointed with the obstructive role of the police, the problems faced in hiring an efficient and knowledgeable lawyers and the tardy pace at which the case proceeded. Only 6% of the women who belonged to the upper strata of the society were satisfied. They could perhaps exert some influence and get speedier justice. Some women narrated in detail the difficulties in getting a good advocate and also told the researcher how the lawyers left no opportunity of fleecing them. These women expressed horror at the large number of adjournments of their cases and the courts bowing to the delaying tactics of the culprits.[4]

93% of the women victims felt let down by the system which promises so much yet gives so little. They say "the Judges just don't realise our plight and give adjournments even without giving us an opportunity to tell them about our plight or to prove that the culprit is not appearing just to harass us and to take advantage of our helplessness.[5]"

12 women who had won the court battle after years of fighting were interviewed. Seven of them were highly relieved mentally because the final verdict was in their favour but all of them dreaded to recall the torture of the years when their cases were inching towards culmination in the courts. "It is not worth all the harassment and the expenditure that we had to undergo. Laws should be simple and the remedies quick." Women, who had initiated the legal process but had left it half way through, confided that it is very difficult to prove charges in a court. The culprit blackmailed the witnesses and they turned hostile, so no crime can ever be proved, moreover the time consuming, legal process, harassment and expenditure involved is not worth. The lawyers charge a lot of money on each date but the case simply does not move. "Nothing can be gained even at the end of the legal marathon".[6]

Veena Mahajan, 43 a police constable with Mumbai Police, suffered domestic violence at the hands of her police inspector husband. Ten years on, she reflects on her experience. "One day there was a bad argument and he hit me and tried to push me off the roof, caring little that I was in the final stage of pregnancy. I rushed off to the police station. But the thane amaldar was my husband's friend. He refused to file a complaint against his own colleague. I insisted that my complaint be filed. My husband was called and suspended for six months. At last my complaint was taken. The case went on in the district court for a few months and then ultimately for ten years but my husband suggested that we patched up and assured the Magistrate. Still today it is a fragile peace. When you are thirty, you are all fired up and want justice. As you grow older compromises seem to be the only option.[7]

Experience with Police (Police Bias): 82% of the women were disappointed with the rude behaviour of the police force towards them. Complaints of wife beating were taken by the

---

4 Shobha Saxena, Crimes against Women and Protective Laws, Deep and Deep Publications, 2004 at p 332.

5 Ibid at p 333.

6 Ibid at p 334.

7 *Police officer, husband, thug. A constable recalls her 10 yr old fight for justice*, Indian Express, 2004.

police rather casually; they wanted to dismiss them as too trivial. Police took full advantage of the loopholes and the shortcomings of the law enforcement machinery to discourage them from lodging complaints. In most of the cases of cruelty and harassment, the police convince the victim that it is no point washing dirty linen in public because cruelty and torture can never be proved. They take it for granted that it is the woman's fault and ask 'what did you do to annoy your husband'. Thus the experience of women with the police at the thana level has not been very happy. In the month of May 1992, in South Delhi, Lajput Nagar, a sub-inspector was dismissed, after he tried to coerce a woman, who had gone to lodge a complaint against her husband, into flesh trade.[8]

Fortunately the experience of women with Women Cell is happy as far as listening to their complaints sympathetically and registering cases are concerned.

There are many cases being spoilt at the FIR stage by the police. Police treat dowry cases as a lottery. It gives them an opportunity to make contacts with influential persons. They avoid arresting the culprit. The corruption and indifference at the investigation level and at the stage of preparing the charge sheet is phenomenal. The time taken for investigation is too long and often evidence is destroyed by the time the investigation starts. Most of the policemen who investigate the cases have neither specialised skills in investigation nor do they have legal knowledge.[9]

With repeated complaints to Ghaziabad police falling on deaf ears, a 20 year old woman has now approached the National Women's Commission to seek justice in an alleged case of harassment over dowry.

Tanu Chaudhary says in her complaint that she married Ajay Katara in October 2005. They demanded Rs 10 lacs and a Maruti car as dowry and started torturing her when her parents could not comply. Then, when she was six- months pregnant she was thrown out of the house.

Chaudhary also alleged that she filed a complaint with the Ghaziabad SSP on November 10th. But the police took no action. So on January she approached the Chief Judicial Magistrate for helping in lodging an FIR against her husband and in laws. The Court ordered the police to file the said FIR. She was told that a case under sec 498A, 323, 504 of the IPC and the Dowry Prohibition Act had been registered. But the police had not taken from her a single statement. Even the copy of the FIR was kept away from her. In fact the police filed a final report within 24 hours and closed it immediately. Investigations revealed that the allegations were made without proof and hence the case was closed.[10]

This brief statement of the case adequately illustrates the police attitude to women:

A battered woman went to complain against her husband. She had dark bruises all over and a few cuts on her arms. The constable at the police station tried to shoo her away saying cases like her are not handled by the police. At this point the woman began to cry loudly. She was allowed to enter the duty room. The sub inspector on duty shouted at her to stop crying. He then told her that it is tradition that the husband beat his wife to discipline her. The woman was forced to return home without making any complaint.[11]

---

8 Shobha Saxena, Crimes against Women and Protective Laws, Deep and Deep Publications, 2004 at p 335.

9 Ibid at p 336.

10 *20 yr old tortured for dowry*, Hindustan Times, 26th February 2007.

11 Rinki Bhattacharya, "Behind Closed Doors; Domestic Violence in India", Sage Publications, New Delhi, 2004 at p 194.

The Chairperson of NCW Poornima Advani too feels that police have been shying away from lodging FIRs in order to hide the rising crime graph against women. In a recent statement she said that the complaints of women against police for not lodging FIRs had been pouring in at the commission's office in Delhi.

Even judges are critical of the police action. Reacting to the attitude of the Delhi Police in a case in February 1994, the Supreme Court observed: *"This Court is determined to show to the country what type of police force they are paying taxes for. If these police officers serve a sentence, then only they will learn lessons".*

A judge of the Allahabad Court a few years ago observed that *"the police was the most organized group of criminals"*[12]

In the present study majority (78%) of women seeking justice viewed the role of police as significant in their ordeal. However, only 28% respondents found them helpful. 78% opined that police did not respond efficiently and took a great deal of time to respond to their complaints. More specifically, the data illustrates that cases pertaining to domestic violence are treated as 'private' family matter by the police. The process of law, far from trying husbands as criminals, often normalizes the husband's violent actions as a reasonable behaviour. 64% opined that they were dissuaded by police officials to register their complaints. 66% respondents felt that police authorities used coercive powers and compel them to 'compromise' with their opponents. 2% reported to bribe or sought the interventions of local politicians or senior police officials to get their complaints registered.[13]

Getting a copy of the complaint report is a legal right of a complaint. This however has not happened in all cases as (claimed by 16%). Further, the foundation of the criminal justice system relies on the investigation done by the police. However, a majority of respondents said that the facts stated by them were not correctly recorded by the police. Often procedural lacunae during investigation make it easier for the accused to seek bail or even acquittal. A sizeable number of respondents felt that their opponents were not arrested promptly by the police. A large number of women (74%) reported that they were released on bail due to the inefficiency of police. 64% respondents opined that police did not accord fair and impartial treatment to them. Slightly more than half the respondents felt that they were treated with downright hostility and suspicion. 36% opined that their opponents have used political power to influence the police. Majority of them found police behaving rudely, indifferently and unsympathetically. 46% reported of harsh language used by police. Police stations are viewed as unfriendly places with hostile environment.[14]

Experience with Courts (Judicial Bias): Nearly 83% of the women complained of the impersonal attitude of the judges. 'The judges, whether a man or a woman, do not seem to be sympathetic to our plight,' told most of the victims. The delay in lodging the FIR is seen by the courts as a material to doubt our testimony'. The judges do not realise that it does take time for a woman to muster enough strength and support for the registration of the case which is socially stigmatized.[15]

---

[12] Preeti Mishra, Domestic Violence against Women: Legal Control and Judicial Response, Deep and Deep Publications, 2006 at pp 441-442.

[13] Ibid at p 35.

[14] Ibid at pp 35 – 37.

[15] Shobha Saxena, Crimes against Women and Protective Laws, Deep and Deep Publications at p 355.

The cases are adjourned and long dates are given which frustrates the victims. The release of the persons on bail or anticipatory bail has a very demoralising effect on the victim. The freedom after getting bail is normally used to circumvent the process of justice.[16]

The Judges and Magistrates are more interested in completing their quota of the cases on which their future and promotions depended. The number of cases to be tried ran in thousands so the question of concern for the victim did not arise. 'Why should we be the knights in the shining armour when the Apex court and the Government did nothing to alleviate the situation and to clear the back log?' 'Instead of appointing judges to fill vacancies they appoint committees to know the facts which are already known.' said one of the Sessions Judges. Mostly the judges select few simple cases that they intend to decide, for the rest of the cases, court peons and other officials are asked to give new dates; this is the common practice. Judges and Magistrates were not even concerned about urgent cases for which the time frame was given in the legal enactments or the rules framed thereunder. 'There are thousands of such urgent cases, what can we do? We are not super humans.' was the stock reply.[17]

Cases showing insensitivity of the judges to dowry victims was distressing.[18] If there is need to protect the victims by discriminating and judicial application of criminal law by the police, there is also the need to sentence the offenders and provide deterrent models of behaviour to people in society. Do judges always succeed in divesting themselves of all fear, anger, hatred, love and compassion? Do judges pay diligent attention to hearing what the victim's lawyers argue? Theoretically, the claim of judges having patience in hearing and reasoning may be true but in practice it may be difficult to stick to such thinking. Judges cannot be free from human frailties. They are human, subject to prejudices, hostilities, pressures and other human problems that might colour their opinion. As, such sentencing differentials do exist. In dowry death cases, one accused gets seven years imprisonment, another gets life imprisonment and yet another is discharged. It is not being maintained that all these differentials are arbitrary and wrong. They have to be there. What is being suggested is that in a good number of cases, the accused manages to escape punishment by getting the evidence manipulated through law enforcement officials. Consequently, the criminal procedure and penal sanctions are not correctly used and judges are not unbiased in selecting the type and severity of sentence. The victims are required to withstand lengthy cross-examinations in the court. They have to defend their character against the defence lawyer who attempts to discredit the victim and show that she invited the attack. The low rate of convictions by the courts reported in the press creates doubts for the victims and family members whether they will, at all, get justice.

Atmosphere prevalent in the courtrooms was found to be unfriendly and hostile by 82% informants. Small sizes of courtrooms as compared to large number of people they have to accommodate during the day's proceedings further complicate the situation. Most respondents reported that at times, they have to stand outside courtrooms waiting for their turn in the premise along with the perpetrators of violence. 64% reported to have heated argument outside the courtroom with their opponents. 72% women claimed that encountering with their violent husbands has lead to increase in hostility, anger and frustration in them.[19]

---

16 Ibid at p 356.

17 Ibid at p 357.

18 Ibid at p 358.

19 See foot note no 45 at p 36.

Further, the Court staff is found to be 'unfriendly or non helpful' (64%) and at times 'hostile' (28%). Respondents complained about the rude behaviour of staff. Most felt that their case was not being heard properly by the court. Moreover, the courts have their own procedures and practices to deal with the victims. A victim is often not allowed to participate in proceedings except when called as a witness to testify in her case. Though as the complainant she is entitled to attend the hearing and appear before the court on the given dates. 68% respondents felt totally alienated from the system because of this. A few reported that often they could not make out what is happening. It was also observed that during the time when courts make efforts for 'reconciliation' and lawyers prevent women to speak out.[20]

The adversarial system of justice delivery is thus based not on dispute resolution but is based on the assumption where 'solutions are dictated by an outsider, won by a victor and imposed on the loser'. The truth finding approach in adversarial system is based on competition, dialectic argumentation and binary outcomes. Perhaps, the process of fact interpretation in the adversarial process views 'reality' as multifaceted, confusing and subject to varying interpretations. Experience however, reveals that it is extremely difficult to prove violence by husbands and in laws 'beyond reasonable doubt' as required by criminal jurisprudence. 74% of respondents said that they could not produce evidence as frequently the episode of violence took place within the privacy of four walls of the house. Cross examination emerges out to be an abusive aspect of adversarial trail which traumatises women's experience in the courtroom. Treatment during cross examination is often describes as humiliating. This is frequently done by invading her private life, alleging her character, typical questioning techniques adopted by the defence lawyers. The study indicates that the complainants are compelled to give their evidence in 'fragmentary testamentary style' as strictly controlled responses to specific questions. Thus the improper and degrading way of cross - examination adds unnecessarily to the trauma of litigants, testifying in the court and affect their ability to give evidence.[21]

Besides above, several other barriers exist varying from indifference of family members to pursue the case to witnesses turning hostile as emerged out of the study. Further matrimonial litigation is considered as 'different' from other forms of litigation and often less seriousness is devoted to it. It is considered as a litigation in perilous conjugal tie within an emotive situation where 'parties often change their moods and minds frequently'. One of the lawyers during an informal discussion shared, "*Matrimonial litigations are fruitless. We, therefore, are less concerned about them and often see to it that they drag for a period. As the time lapse, clients do change their minds and without much effort we may reach an amicable solution. And, of course, it is paying too.*" Often the cases drag on for years and for victims this becomes a tiring and a frustrating ordeal. In courts, a victim has to sit for hours and wait for their turn. Sometimes, a Magistrate does not turn up or the defence lawyer seeks adjournment on some pretext or the other. Repeated adjournments dampen the faith of the victim in the legal system. And as time passes and initial shock of grief lessens and the daily routine of life reasserts itself and often less importance is accorded to pursue the case. State conducts the criminal case and an aggrieved party depends on State prosecutor, who is frequently not sympathetic to a woman's concern and is burdened with a pile of cases. They are not paid by the aggrieved party and their priorities are perhaps different. His or her sensitivity to gender concerns is yet another factor that may come

20 Ibid at p 36.

21 Ibid at p 38.

into play while arguing for a case. Criminal justice system is, therefore, weighed against the victims. At times, women (26%) complained of public prosecutor being bought over by their opponents. Mostly judges show a pro – male prejudice. Probably they import own 'valves of life', customs, manners, prejudices and beliefs. It was found that often Mahila Courts are considered as substandard forums where judges are least interested to work in. Also, assessment of their work in these forums is based on the success in the number of cases they have been able to get 'compromised' or 'settled'.[22]

Overall, it may be said that the Mahila Courts, though started with the motive to provide women a space to raise their concerns, in practice, ended up being an admixture of a criminal and family court where the proceedings are taken up in the manner as done in criminal courts but they operate on familial ideological underpinning. It may be said that these forums do provide a space for women to raise their voice and render them a platform to negotiate their claims as wives, but its biases, lacunae and pitfalls hardly allow them to negotiate on their own terms.[23]

Husbands are allowed to slap their wives if they spend lavishly, a Saudi Judge has said. He made the statement at a seminar on domestic violence recently, reported at CNN. "It is okay to slap Saudi women who spend too much. If a person gives 12,000 riyals to his wife and she spends 900 riyals to purchase an abaya (the black cover that women in Saudi Arabia must wear) from a branded shop and if her husband slaps her on the face as a reaction to her action, she deserves that punishment. Judge Hamad Al – Razine was reported as saying by Arab news, a Saudi English daily based in the Saudi Arabian capital of Riyadh. (Source: "Saudi Judge says its okay to slap spendthrift wives", Times of India, 12th May 2009.)[24]

Some scholars (Stuart Nagel, in Shubert, *Judicial Decision Making*, 43-44) have associated the socio economic background of magistrates, such as age, family background, class membership, occupation before appointment to the bench and training with decision making or judicial behaviour. Our view is that Magistrates have traditional and conservative in their judicial opinions. The numbers of years Magistrates have spent on the bench and the values they develop with experience and judicial scholarship also seem to influence the decisions of the magistrates. Even the kinds of Law College attended by the Magistrate or the nature of his practice before his judicial career are elements in judicial decision making. Thus, a Magistrate who had been engaged in the practice of dowry and divorce cases as a lawyer may have an entirely different decision pattern than one who had devoted much of his prior practice to criminal law. Sometimes, a Magistrate may be reacting against his past as a criminal lawyer and become less harsh and positive in dealing with rapists or molesters he used to defend.[25]

DISSATISFACTION WITH JUSTICE

Interviews with victims of offences against women and also with their relatives bring out one universal grievance, namely, dissatisfaction with the administration of justice. The social expectation is that since the law is found on reason, judicial pronouncements must not only punish the

22 Ibid at pp 39 - 41

23 Ibid at p 43

24 Source: *"Saudi Judge says its okay to slap spendthrift wives"*, Times of India, 12th May 2009.

25 Ram Ahuja, Violence against Women and Women against Violence, Rawat Publications, 1998, pp 252.

offenders but also look to the interests of victims, and that law should not discriminate between rich criminals and poor victims. But the experience of young victims with the law, lawyers, courts and magistrates has taught them that laws are merely arbitrary technicalities, lawyer's only interest is to knock out as much money as they can from the complainant or the accused, Magistrate are more concerned with the literal interpretation rather than liberal interpretation of the law, and police official's enthusiasm to protect rich and influential offenders is a great that they manipulate evidence which largely results in injustice. This inevitable discontent with the law results in lack of respect for the law and law enforcers and contempt for the doctrine of supremacy of the law. The dissatisfaction with the discretion enjoyed by Magistrates arises from the fact that they confine themselves to minute and detailed rules without giving importance to the trauma suffered by poor (female) victims and changed moral, social and political conditions.[26]

Inefficiency and Callousness of Judicial Officers: Inefficiency and indifferent attitude of Magistrates in lower courts and corruption among the lower staff in courts are perennial sources of dissatisfaction with the administration of justice. Some respondents felt the Magistrates lack detachment, honesty, dignity and wisdom. Lack of wisdom was explained in terms of lack of humility on the part of the Magistrate to see his own bias and discount it. The victims' relatives complained of the prevailing corrupt practice of paying bribes and getting hearing dates postponed through the lawyers of the accused persons or through the court clerks. All this leads to the prolonging of cases for years together.

Women who have been able to register a case of marital rape or domestic violence face additional hurdles from the criminal justice system. In many countries, trial procedures reflect societal biases against the successful prosecution of such cases. Too often, prejudiced judges doom a case from the outset and help impunity for the perpetrators.

Many judges view victims of violence sceptically and tend to hold them responsible for bringing violence upon themselves. Thus, at the trial stage, judges frequently consider the behaviour of the woman as a factor when weighing the evidence and if, there is a conviction, in determining the defendant's punishment.

Like others in the criminal justice system, judges seldom receive adequate training on the significance of the medical legal evidence and do not know how to interpret it at the trial. Thus crucial information that could convict the defendant may be disregarded or even used against the complainant. Despite such cases, magistrates at the Johannesburg court have resisted such training out of fear that it would prejudice them against defendants.[27]

In a Russian case, a domestic violence victim in court for a custody hearing was subjected to a harangue by a judge on the importance of staying with her husband, despite ten years of physical abuse.[28]

The delay in the courts has created a crucial problem for the speedy justice. A classic example of delay was the Sudha Goel's case where the accused husband married again and had two children from the personal marriage while the case dragged along. It is found that the longer a case is dragged, the more likely that the case will not result in guilty disposition. The rising rate

---

26 Ibid at p 256.

27 Ibid at p 257.

28 P.K. Goyal, Human Rights and Humanitarian Affairs, Vista International Publishing House, 2005 at p 156.

of inter-family violence indicates that the present criminal justice system is not as effective deterrent to break the cycle of violence.[29]

The horrifying judicial scenario on the Indian side is the majority of these cases ended in acquittals for want of clinching evidence. The courts failed in a regrettable way in taking into account the special circumstances that surround violence nor should the courts be able to look at the totality of the situation.

ROAD FROM MERE GENDER JUSTICE TO GENDER SENSITIVE JUSTICE

Trainings programmes for judicial personnel: The role of a Judge in trying to meet the challenge of growing incidence of crime against women assumes great significance and relevance. Judges are drawn essentially from Lawyers – hence the need for continuing education. The Courts are therefore, expected to deal with cases of crimes against women with utmost sensitivity, and that is where "Education of Judges" in issues relating to gender justice assumes great importance. A socially sensitized judge, in our opinion, is a better statutory armour in cases of crimes against women than long clauses, of penal provisions, containing complex exceptions and provisos.[30]

Thus one of the most important tasks a judge is expected to perform is to be responsive and responsible. He must be creative – and may create precedent, where no law exists for women but where it is actually needed. Judicial decisions can influence and under certain circumstances even compel the Government to enact appropriate provisions to cover up the deficiency in the existing law.[31]

It is in this context that we have to consider the necessity of Judicial Education for Judges. This education should not be treated as an affront to the independence of judges nor a threat to their deciding fairly, fearlessly and impartially according to their own judgment. The object is to change one's awareness, knowledge, skills and behavior in relation to gender issues and to provide an opportunity to evaluate and discuss the issue against existing understanding and social context.[32]

Gender sensitive judges can take a more proactive role in the proceedings rather than simply responding to the material presented by the lawyers. They can exercise their discretion to assist the processes wherever appropriate. They can recognize the need to obtain the best quality evidence from witnesses particularly women in criminal trials who have been subjected to violence and women litigants in civil cases. They can pay particular attention to the way in which this evidence is recorded. In their appreciation of the evidence they can be aware of the gender context and take care to avoid stereotyping. Deciding a case in the courtroom involves settlement of the dispute between the parties and a decision about the application of law. Judges have ultimate control over this process. They determine what evidence can be given under the rules of

---

29 Subhash Singh, *Protection of Battered Wives: A searching look for some alternate ways*, Criminal Law Journal, 1996 at p 130.

30 Chief Justice (Dr) A.S Anand, "Justice for Women", Universal Law Publishing, 2008 at pp 88, 89.

31 Ibid at 89.

32 Ibid at 89.

evidence. An important factor in this behalf is change in the outlook and perception of the judge. However, the exercise is a delicate one – there must be proper restraint and caution – lest the judges overstep the limits of their jurisdiction or create uncertainty in law.[33]

We expect a great deal from our judges – we expect them to be objective, knowledgeable, independent, discerning, practical, sensitive and above all we expect them to be fair and impartial. We expect this because judges have such an important and crucial role in society. They make decisions which affect people's lives, their livelihoods, their safety and their humanity. This huge task requires us to have complete knowledge and understanding of the substance and procedures of law. In recent years, the role of judiciary has extended beyond issuing directives on social issues and concerns to ensuring effective and fair implementation of the same. As a judge this requires elimination of subtle ways in which the courtroom perpetuates discrimination and violation of women's right to integrity. The judges need to be protective and take charge of our courtroom to ensure that the subtle play of discrimination through spoken and unspoken words are eliminated.[34]

Judges are obliged by the Constitution, the laws and oath of office to avoid gender bias not only in their own decision making but also in Court interactions. To encourage such judges and to sensitize other judges, regular training courses are required. No judicial officer can function effectively without proper training. Such courses should be set up with a view to evolve capacities, strategies and attitudes in presiding officers of courts to eliminate gender bias from judicial processes.[35]

Role of Non Governmental Organizations (NGO'S)/Self help groups: The Women's movement in India has had a chequered experience in its campaign against domestic violence. In fact, the various interventions by the State were in response to the concerted pressure exerted by the women's movement. Most NGO's and women's organizations have ended up in tackling this issue at an informal individual level. Inspite of the issues of concern have been raised in the spirit of an honest appraisal of NGO strategies for best practices, it doesn't however detract their noteworthy contribution in launching a variety of initiatives to help women victims of violence. Yet, by far the most important achievement of the NGO action has been in terms of its conscientisation agenda that has successfully elicited community support for the cause.

The services provided by the NGO'S include shelter. Medical assistance, conciliation, counsel, removal of property from spouse house and also help women in approaching lawyers, police and doctors etc.

Legal Aid Cells: In pursuance of Directive Principles of the Constitution, legal aid cells came to be established in various Indian States. They offer:

Legal advice

Pre-litigation counselling

---

33 Ibid at 90.

34 Ibid p 90.

35 Ibid.

Payment of court fees

Representation by a legal practitioner in the case of litigation

Drafting of legal documents.

Attempts for reconciliation in pre-litigation cases form a substantial part of the activities of the legal aid cells. Another sphere of activity is to promote legal literacy by holding Shibirs (camps), symposia and seminars in rural and urban areas.

Women cells in Police Department / All Women Police Stations in Urban and Rural Areas: The role of the police is to uncover law violations and bring to book those people who threaten the social order. If they choose not to identify an act as a crime, or if they choose not to label a person a suspect, or if they choose not to take official action even when they have sufficient evidence against the accused. It is indeed unfortunate that the image of the police has steadily deteriorated in our society on the ground that either they escape their responsibility through indifference and callousness or they do their jobs through a variety of corrupt and unlawful practices.[36]

Crimes (Women) Cell which was created in Delhi on an experimental basis, has proved successful in dealing with crimes committed against women and in getting the culprits prosecuted. A law should be passed to create similar Cells in all States to inspire greater confidence in women and ensure speedy help to victims. There is an urgent need to set up such cells in all urban areas.[37]

Comprising example of state action the All Women Police Stations (AWPS) in Bangalore and Ahmedabad are entirely staffed by women was to make the right to police protection accessible to women.

Similarly, the FCC's (Police), established by the Central Social Welfare Board (CSWB) undertake family counseling and conciliation in cases of divorce and separation. Managed by trained social workers, these cells provide preventive and referral services to women and children. Despite low wages and lack of job security, the social workers currently working in these FCC cells are committed to their jobs; they have tried to make their services more effective by liaisoning with the police and they are able to ensure that both the spouses come for counselling.[38]

Thus the police officers, prosecutors and judges at all levels of hierarchy need to be exposed to the gender equality education which would enlighten them on existing assumptions, myths and stereotypes about women and how these can interfere with fair and equitable administration of justice.

Community Policing : Youth Groups, women organization, proactive NGO's should launch community clubs to create awareness among women. This campaign will generate sensitization among the neighborhood so that they will swing into action against the abusive male.

---

[36] Ram Ahuja, Violence against Women, Rawat and Rawat Publications, 1998 at p 287.

[37] Sobha Saxena, Crimes against Women and Protective Laws, 2004, Deep and Deep Publications at p 403

[38] Veena Poonacha, Divya Pandey, *Responses to Domestic Violence: Government and Non-Government Action,* Economic and Political Weekly, 2000 at p 568.

The Mauritian law on domestic violence provides for the appointment of 'public guardians' trained in law and in gender sensitization.

GENDER SENSITIVE MEASURES IMPLEMENTED IN OTHER COUNTRIES

Russians made attempts to pass national legislation on domestic violence, the effort failed, and little was done to improve the state response to the abuse. The federal government did not make financial resources available for combating violence. Activists, expressing frustration with the lack of progress nationally, focused their attention on local level initiatives, establishing cooperative links with local law enforcement, city officials and journalists. The number of non – government crisis centers grew across the country. While the few existing government sponsored centers and shelters closed due to budget cuts, Crisis center leaders travelled throughout Russia, training judges, police and activists. The Russian Association of Crisis Centers for Women was officially registered in 1999 and held a national meeting to coordinate its activities. In this way the legislation was successfully implemented.[39]

Investigations and Prosecutions of Complaints: In most jurisdictions, it is the responsibility of the police to record complaints and undertake initial investigations. In addition, the police also have power to intervene, expel and arrest perpetrators of violence in the household. Police should keep official records of all complaints and undertake investigation and evidence. Evidence should be properly collected and safeguarded and no burden in this respect should be placed on the complainant. All female complainants should have the possibility of making complaints and being dealt with, by skilled and professional female staff.

Successful implementation of the law requires resources to build both effective institutions and skills and capacities of personnel. Specialised police units, prosecution departments, Courts and Alternative tribunals hold promise but their effectiveness depends on many factors, including quality staff, amount of funding and relationship to other legal institutions.

The role of judiciary in enforcing and interpreting laws is crucial. In some jurisdictions, the pro – active role played by the judiciary has contributed significantly towards establishing new norms and standards.

In the Unites States, the National Judicial Education Programme to promote Equality for Women and Men in the Courts has prepared a training curriculum for judges, other Court Personnel and Prosecutors. The Council of Europe produced a self training Manual for police officers called the VIP Guide. The United Nations Division for the Advancement of Women implements for judicial officers. [40]

Baseline studies and gender auditing of all laws are useful evaluation strategies. All States should conduct research and gather statistics. In particular, the number of reported cases, prosecutions and convictions should be collected and trends over time noted. Use of protective remedies and awards of compensation should be assessed. Internal monitoring and external evaluation of the legal and enforcement process including court observation is crucial. Police and

[39] B.B. Batra, Encyclopaedia of Human Rights, Reference Press, 2004 at p 43.

[40] Ibid at p 20.

Court records should be available for bona fide research projects assessing the implementation of laws, with appropriate ethical safeguards including protection of victim confidentiality. Assessment should also seek the views of those whom the law is supposed to protect.

In Honduras, a multi - sectoral commission, which included Government and Civil society, developed proposals to reform the law on Women Non – government organizations participated in the formulation of the Malaysian Domestic Violence Act, United States Federal Violence against Women Act, and United Kingdom Sexual Offences Act.[41]

Once laws have been enacted there is need for ongoing independent institutional mechanisms for oversight. These can take the form of an Ombudsperson, a National Rapporteur or Gender Equality Machinery.

The European network WAVE (Women against Violence Europe) has developed quality standards for women services, including for help lines and shelters. It also provides guidance on empowerment practices. The Council of Europe recommends that one place in women' shelter per 7,500 inhabitants should be provided and the minimum standard be one place per 10,000 inhabitants.[42] There are a number of models of SAC/SARCs, with many countries having hospital based provision. Some countries such as Canada have extensive networks, whilst others, such as Germany, Kenya, Switzerland and the United Kingdom have a number of centres where either women's groups or committed medical staff have campaigned to improve local provision. Still others Iceland, Ireland, Denmark and Sweden aim to provide a high standard of comprehensive care to anyone who has experienced recent sexual assault.[43]

An Inter – Agency project, ACT in Canberra, Australia in coordination with the Victims of Crime Office, has over three years increased both arrest and conviction rates for perpetrators of violence against women. These results are the outcome of an agreed protocol between involved agencies and a dynamic, solution oriented process. The use of new technologies such as digital cameras to photograph victims and crime scenes which are made available to the court immediately along with awareness that prosecutors will not drop cases, has increased guilty pleas. A research project has also been undertaken to investigate victim satisfaction team.[44]

Using the Media

Successful communication strategies can have wide ranging impacts and are especially effective in reaching large audiences. In developing the messages and the visual contents it is essential to know as much as possible about existing attitudes, opinions and behaviours. This enables better targeting of the material and a clearer sense of what change is intended. At the same time, women's groups need to find ways to use the media effectively for more short- term responses, including developing good relationships with sympathetic journalists and providing survivors who want to tell their stories with media training. All prevention programmes should attempt to use communication materials as programme tools to inform and enrich other prevention activities.

---

41 Ibid at p 21

42 Ibid p 25.

43 Ibid at p 26.

44 Ibid at p 27

Using popular culture: A music video made by women's human rights group, Breakthrough with support from UNIFEM, addressed domestic violence and empowerment of the survivor. The video reached more than 26 million households throughout India, and made it to the country's top 10.[45]

Community Activation: One form of campaign is directed not at government or national change but seeks to engage and mobilize the local community to challenge domestic violence. Here good practice clearly requires participatory process and is best if underpinned by local research, audits and round-tables. Establishing baseline data about community perceptions and indicators through which progress can be assessed is an important early activity.

Kivulini Women's Rights Organization is working with a cross section of community members in Mwanza, Tanzania. Linking individual women and men at the grassroots, traditional and religious leaders, local government officials and institutions, they move beyond awareness – raising into help stakeholders themselves make and sustain tangible changes in their communities, workplaces and institutions.[46]

Local Activism: One strong approach is building a sense that a whole community – not just the individual woman is responsible for protecting and preventing of violence. This enables women and children to live in their neighbourhood with more security. However, this approach should not degenerate into "vigilante justice". Rather networks of activists should be enabled to explore how to build sustainable anti – violence climate.

Engaging Men: One key alliance in prevention is the engagement of men and boys in the struggle to transform gender relations. Again, women's movements in the South are taking the lead in developing constructive dialogues and new practices with men in good faith. This requires building coalitions in which men respect women's leadership overall and which have clear policies and protocols.

Project Touch in New York, United States, reaches out to students through reflection on gender roles, non-violence, interaction with victims and survivors and creative expression of art.[47]

Thus campaigns to change laws and support new and emerging practices can take many years or take root astonishingly swiftly. Where change appears to happen very fast it may be that actions are being taken in order to comply with international obligations, or in response to an atrocity or a high profile case. Whilst all positive change is to be welcomed, it will be short lived if not accomplished by the activism and longer term commitments. Many governments have introduced police units specially trained for dealing with spousal assault. It is well known fact that states have tended to adopt a passive attitude when confronted by cases of violations of women's rights by private actors. States should ensure that national legislation, once adopted, does not go unenforced. Any approach designed to combat violence must be two-fold, addressing the root

---

45 Ibid at p 34

46 Ibid at p 34.

47 Ibid at p 37

causes of the problem and treating its manifestations. Society at large, including judges and police officers, must be educated to change the social attitudes and beliefs that encourage male violence.

CONCLUSION

There is a firm belief that all the efforts and idealism; the protective laws do not protect women. As an institution, laws reflect the power structure of our society and are subject to the same prejudices and bias against women as the society is. Law is basically a set of power resources; it is the tool in the hands of the stronger section of the society to have their way, with a semblance of being just and charitable to the weaker sections of the society. There are people who believe that a judge is a mere umpire and the two parties fighting out the game are the victim and the criminal or the two counsel representing prosecution and defence. Such a feeling is unfair. We hold that a conscientious judge is surely not there to decide the consent as the two counsels present it; rather, he has to look for truth and justice independently. It is not the law that is in the wrong; it is the interpreter that corrupts and abuses it. Uncertainly, delay and expense, and above all the injustice inherent in deciding cases upon mere points of technicalities creates contempt for the cases and failure of protective laws in providing gender sensitive mode of justice to the victims.

☆ ☆ ☆

PART - D

CASE STUDY

1 Women Entrepreneurship: A Case Study of Navi Mumbai

Women have a key role to play in overall development of society, thus one significant target is of developing entrepreneurship among women. This target group forms a small segment of total number of entrepreneur promoted in the country. The national scene indicates that women entrepreneurs constitute to 8% of total entrepreneur. Empowerment in the context of women's development is a way of defining, challenging and overcoming barriers in a woman's life through which she increases her ability to shape her life and environment. It is active multidimensional project which will help women to identify their full identity and power in all spheres of life.

The number of women entrepreneurs has increased, especially during the 1990's. Women entrepreneurship lit1erature has revealed generally two factors Push and Pull factor to start with. The Pull factor refers to situation that attract women to come in the entrepreneur profession. The Pull factor may be referred to as the "urge to do something purposeful", "demand for product", "profit made by friends in the similar industry", "opportunities due to globalization and modernization" etc.

The Push factors are the responses that arise due to compulsions mainly the economic compulsion of earning a living. While it is difficult to make a clear demarcation between push and pull factors in real life situation, the distinction between the two is, however, useful because it clearly indicates the positive and negative response, to the situation in which the entrepreneurial activity was started.

The principle of "Achievements Motivation" as given by McClelland-theory is also an important motive that leads to any entrepreneurial activity.

Significance of the study

- This study is highly efficient in areas of gender study.
- It studies women enterprises.
- Women make up 48% of population of which only 8% are active.
- It is also useful in demographic study. It studies the planned city and its migrant population, its development and infrastructure.

Objectives of the study

- To study the socio-economic background of women entrepreneurs in Navi Mumbai.
- To remove gender barrier and widen the scope of women entrepreneurs.
- To promote growth of women entrepreneurs in Navi Mumbai, through the efforts of local bodies and to suggest the establishment of trade association and professional bodies in Navi Mumbai.

Need for the study

- Navi Mumbai is a cosmopolitan city belonging to the educated and to middle income group. It is seen from the survey that majority of households are a single earning member.
- There is a need to a bring women in economic activity.
- Further, there is a tremendous scope for starting entrepreneurial activities, which are traditional as well as techno savvy.

Research methodology: the study is designed to be empirical one based on the survey method. The interview was semi structured. Most of the questions were close ended questions which were examined and classified.

The questionnaire was first administered to 100 women entrepreneurs and thereafter the sample size was increased to 200 for coming to a proper conclusion. The questionnaire was administered by interview method.

Sample of the study

The survey conducted for this research encompassed a sample size of 200 women entrepreneurs, which reflect more than 5 percent for the study in the city of Navi Mumbai. Navi Mumbai is divided zone wise. It comprises of twelve zones some of which are highly developed while some are less developed depending on number of years of zone existence. It is a well planned city having all infrastructure facilities.

This is a form of case study

Table : 1

	Nodes of Navi Mumbai	Percentage of sample collected
1	Vashi	27.5
2	Nerul	12
3	Sanpada	10.5
4	Koparkhairane	10.5
5	Belapur	8.5
6	Airoli	8
7	Ghansoli	8
8	Jui Nagar	4
9	Kharghar	4
10	New Panvel	1.5
11	Dronagiri	2
12	Kalamboli	1.5
		100

Major finding of the study

Profile of sample women entrepreneurs indicates that most of women (85%) fall between age group of 31-45 years. It further reveals that 88% of women entrepreneurs are married. This indicates women venture out into economic activity only after they have established their homes. This is due to "drive of doing something in life", a few women 29.5% start very young and in initial years of marriage, are separated or widowed women, enter into business due to push factor.

- Religion wise two thirds of the women entrepreneurs belong to the Hindu religion. However, a city comprising of migratory population, all religions contribute to women entrepreneurship.
- Linguistic portion of the respondent shows 42% are Marathi speaking, 37% are Hindi speaking. This indicates there is greater number of migratory population in the younger age group of 25-30 years.
- Almost two thirds of women entrepreneurs that is 71% belong to nuclear families. However 29% women belong to joint family.
- Educational qualification is the most important, vital information, which reveals the socio-economic background of the women. Evaluation of the formal educational levels gives an idea about career aspiration of the women. Entrepreneurial activity in most of the educated women is taken as a purposeful career i.e pull factors.
- In the age group (20-35) and (36-45) years illiterates are nil. Therefore, this age group is having all family members who are at least literate. In the age group 45+ there are yet 4 (100%) illiterates.

Table - 2
Year of establishment of women enterprise

Year of establishment						
Age group in years	**20-35**	**36-45**		**45+**		**Total**
1984-1990	0	16		2		18
1991-1995	4	44		12		82
1996-2000	33	41		0		74
2001-2006	31	17		0		48
Total	68	118		14		200

The data of table 2 reveals that women entrepreneurship though started in 1984; there were only two cases from the 45+ years categories. After that, there has been a long gap in women entrepreneurship activity in Navi Mumbai. Navi Mumbai, as a city though, started in 1972 with Vashi as a node. As other nodes were in initial stages of development there was hardly any activity in those nodes. In all the 118 cases, maximum entrepreneurship was in age group 36-45 years.

Motives for establishments of enterprise: "Main motive of women entrepreneurs (93%) to enter into entrepreuneurial activity is the "desire to do something in life". Which encouraged them to start their own business.

Table - 3
Women respondents according to the sector of activity

Age group in years	20-35		36-45		45+		Total
Manufacturing	5	(71.43%)	0	(0.00%)	2	(28.57%)	7(3.5%)
Trading	18	(33.33%)	36	(66.67%)	0	(0.00%)	54(27%)
Service	28	(40.00%)	30	(42.86%)	12	(17.14%)	70(35%)
M+T	6	(15.00)%	34	(85.00%)	0	(0.00%)	40(20%)
M+S	8	(100.00%)	0	(0.00%)	0	(0.00%)	8(4%)
T+S	2	(10.00%)	18	(90.00)%	0	(0.00%)	20(10%)

Table - 4
Organizational structure of business

Organizational structure of business							
Age group in years	20-35		36-45		45+		Total
Sole proprietorship	58	(38.41%)	79	(53.32%)	14	(9.27%)	151(75.5%)
Joint family	8	(27.59%)	21	(72.41%)	0	(0.00%)	29(14.5%)
Partnership	2	(100.00%)	0	(0.00%)	0	(0.00%)	2(1%)
Private limited	4	(22.22%)	14	(77.78%)	0	(0.00%)	18(9%)
Total							200

Sector of activity indicates in table 3 shows that nearly 36 percent of women are into service activity and 27 into trading activity, nearly 4 percent are into manufacturing activity. Very few women enter into manufacturing activity. The organization structure of women enterprises is generally sole proprietorship (75 percent), Table 4 show that 14 percent is Joint family businesses 9 percent are private Ltd. Companies and only 1 percent is partnership organizations. Therefore, women are more oriented into trading activity.

Table - 5
Size of enterprise

Size of enterprise							
Age group in years	20-35		36-45		45+		Total
Small	22	(27.5%)	48	(60.00%)	10	(12.50%)	80(40%)
Medium	24	(37.5%)	36	(56.25%)	4	(6.25%)	64(32%)
Large	22	(6.25%)	34	(60.71%)	0	(0.00%)	56(28%)
Total							200

The size of enterprise of women entrepreneurs was studied on various indicators and it revealed from table 5 that 39% of enterprises were small, 31% of it were medium and 28% were large.

Using employees as an indicator, it revealed that 42% had employed less than 5 persons, 15% employeed 5-10 person and 32% employed more than 10 persons.

Using amount invested as an indicator, it showed that 42% invested Rs. 1-10 lakh, 30% invested Rs. 10-50 lakh and 9% invested more than Rs. 50 lakhs and 7% invested less than Rs.

10,000. Using turnover as an indicator less than Rs. 5 lakh and 16% had a turnover of more than Rs. 50 lakh 13% had a turnover from Rs. 25-50 lakhs, 16% respondents did not reveal the turnover of their business. Therefore, maximum women enterprises had a turnover of either less than Rs. 5 lakhs or from Rs. 5-25 lakhs. They are yet either small/medium enterprises.

Table - 6

Nature of the product

Age group in years	20-35		36-45		45+		Total
Consumer product durable	15	(57.69%)	11	(42.31%)	0	(0.00%)	26
Consumer product non-durable	13	(23.21%)	43	(76.79%)	0	(0.00%)	56
Non-consumable Product	20	(44.44%)	25	(55.56%)	0	(0%)	45
Knowledge based product	7	(20.59%)	23	(67.65%)	4	(11.76%)	34
Service based product	13	(38.24%)	16	(47.71%)	5	(14.71%)	34
Total							

Table 6 shows that Most of women are dealing in consumer products – (39 percent), Non consumer products – (22 percent), knowledge/information related products – (25 percent) and consumer durable products were only (14 percent). Therefore, most of the women entrepreneurs were small entrepreneurs (sole proprietors) especially in consumer (non-durable) products i.e. food sector. The nature of market that women enterprises enjoy indicated was local market – 80 cases, state market – 28 cases, All-India market 27 cases and in 8 cases they had access to foreign markets 63 cases enjoy mix market. Therefore, again it is clear women that entrepreneurs are small, sole proprietors, dealing in consumer (non-durable) products and dealing in the local market only.

Factors influencing the location of the enterprise

Location of the enterprise is the most influential factor for women entrepreneurs. Women need to look after homes and contribute to their business. Therefore, most of their businesses start from their homes or nearby areas.

Table - 7

Factors that influence the location of the enterprise

Age group in years	20-35		36-45		45+		Total
Proximity to market / consumer	49	(30.83%)	102	(64.15%)	8	(5.03%)	159(26.36%)
Proximity to residence	58	(38.67%)	84	(57.50%)	8	(5.33%)	150(24.87%)
Proximity to raw materials	30	(37.50%)	46	(57.50%)	4	(5.00.%)	80(13.26%)
Easy availability of infrastructure facilities	6	(21.43%)	18	(64.29%)	4	(14.29%)	28(4.64%)
Easy availability of skilled manpower	8	(16.00%))	38	(76.00%)	4	(8.00%)	50(13.9)
To take advantage of government schemes	44	(52.38%)	36	(42.86%)	4	(4.76%)	84(13.9%)
Other factors	12	(23.08%)	30	(57.69%)	10	(19.23%)	52(8.62%)

In case of factors influencing the location of the enterprise, it was seen that proximity of markets (80 cases) and closeness to residence (75 cases) were the main reasons for setting up the enterprises. Further enquiry into accessibility to various modes of transport revealed that 77 percent women felt that rail services were good and 88 percent women felt that even road transport was easily accessible. Ninety three (93) percent of women have their own business premises and only 7 percent worked from rented premises. Excepting a very few who have their enterprises in industrial areas the others small ones work from their homes.

CONCLUSIONS

- Most of the women were in the informal sector.
- The emergence of women entrepreneurs and women owned firms and their significant contributions to economy is visible in India and these businesses are ready for continued growth in the future. There is also greater awareness among Indian women about entrepreneurship as a career. The growing is mainly due to the fact that the profile of Indian women has undergone perceptible change during the recent past.
- Surveys conducted demonstrate that women primary entrepreneurial activity is focused on the small and medium enterprise (SME) sector. However, the involvement of women entrepreneur in the production sector is minimal and the development of this sector is rather slow.
- The number of women entrepreneurs has increased especially during the 1990s. The new generation of women owned enterprise is activiely seeking capital for their business. It is essential to formulate strategies to invigorate, support and sustain their efforts in the right direction.

BIBLIOGRAPHY

- Dr. Sudhir Sharma, Balaraj Singh, Sandeep Singhal (2005), Entrepreneurship Development, Page No. 19, Chapter 1- Entrepreneur & Entrepreneurship: An Introduction, Published by Wisdom Publication, Delhi.
- (Sharma & Sita, 2001), Issues in Urban Development – A Case of Navi Mumbai, Rawat Publication New Delhi, 2001.
- Dr. Sudhir Sharma, Balraj Singh, Sandeep Singhal, Entrepreneurship Development, Page No. 21, Published by Wisdom Publications, Delhi, October 2005.
- (Sita & Ray, 2001) In the article Land use pattern Issues I Urban Development – A Case of Navi Mumbai, Rawat Publications New Delhi, 2001.
- (Sharma & Sita, 2001), Issues in Urban Development – A Case of Navi Mumbai, Rawat Publications New Delhi, 2001).
- Piyali Ghosh and R Cheruvalath, The ICFAI Journal of Entrepreneurship Development pp9.
- Anderson, Robert Lee and Dunkelbert, John D., Entrepreneurship, Harper and Row Publishers, New York, 1990).
- Dhameja S.K." Deep and Deep Publications, Delhi, 2002.

☆ ☆ ☆

2 Empowering Women: A Case Study of Kudumbashree in Kerala

ABSTRACT

Women have a distinct role to play in the development of the nation. She is a unit of human capital, and is therefore capable of making a contribution to the economy of the nation. A major cause of women's subordination is said to be her economic dependence. Under the trickledown theory in the planning process it was expected that women will equally benefit along with men.

Economic empowerment results in women's ability to influence or make decisions, increased self confidence, better status and role in household etc. Micro finance is necessary to overcome exploitation, create confidence for economic self reliance of the rural poor, particularly among rural women who are mostly invisible in the social structure.

Microfinance is emerging as a powerful instrument for poverty alleviation in the new economy. In India, Microfinance scene is dominated by Self Help Group (SHGs)-Bank Linkage Programme as a cost effective mechanism for providing financial services to the "Unreached Poor" which has been successful not only in meeting financial needs of the rural poor women but also strengthen collective self help capacities of the poor, leading to their empowerment. Rapid progress in SHG formation has now turned into an empowerment movement among women across the country.

Saga of Kudumbashree tells more about life than mere statistics. It has altered lives of poor women in the state of Kerala, changed their perception, rebuilt their confidence, boosted their morale, rediscovered their dignity and honor, and empowered them economically, socially and politically. Today 3.1 million poor women participate in the Kudumbashree movement in the state cutting across political ideologies and religious faiths.

EMPOWERING WOMEN: A Case Study of Kudumbashree in Kerala

INTRODUCTION

"There is no chance for the welfare of the world unless the conditions of the Women are improved. It is not possible for a bird to fly on one wing". - Swami Vivekananda

Women have a distinct role to play in the development of the nation. Women in the households are the cruelest victims of deprivation and destitution. A major cause of her subordination is said to be her economic dependence. In India, policies and programs of the government at different levels cover various dimensions and strategies of gender development. Over the years, efforts have been made to empower women socially, economically and politically.

Empowerment is a process by which individuals, groups and communities are able to take control of their circumstances and achieve their goals. They can be empowered only through creating livelihood opportunities for her. Economic empowerment is undoubtedly the key, and may lead to all other kinds of empowerment. Women empowerment is possible when women have full autonomy to spend their income and resources.

Experience in many countries demonstrates that poor women make investments wisely and earn returns (Human Resource Development, 1995). **Self Help Groups** are voluntary associations of women/men residing in a given area, formed democratically and without any political association. The concept gained significance especially after 1976 when Prof.Mohammed Yunus of Bangladesh began experimenting with micro credit and women. The group-based approach not only enables the poor to accumulate capital by way of small savings but also helps them to get access to formal credit facilities (Shylendra, 1998). SHGs are emerging as the one of the promising and prime sources of informal banking in Indian villages.

The government of Kerala state in India has introduced a novel scheme of poverty alleviation based on micro credit and self- help grouping. The scheme titled **Kudumbashree** aims at improving the living standard of the women in rural and urban areas.

Kudumbashree: Kudumbashree, which means prosperity of the family, is the name of the women oriented, Community based, State Poverty Eradication Mission of Government of Kerala. The mission aims at the empowerment of women, through forming self help groups and encouraging their entrepreneurial or other wide range of activities. The purpose of the mission is to ensure that the women should no longer remain as passive recipients of public assistance, but active leaders in women involved development initiatives. Kudumbashree project for poverty reduction was launched on 17th May 1998.

Kudumbashree, of Kerala, a community-based self-help organization of poor women, although started as a micro-finance agency soon became an active subsystem of local governments and embarked upon several activities that address the question of poverty reduction.

Kudumbashree believes that poverty is a multi-phased phenomenon. Hence, we have adopted a holistic approach to tackle the multiple manifestations of poverty and this approach is equivocally stated in the **Mission Statement** of the project, which goes like this:

"To eradicate absolute poverty in ten years through concerted community action under the leadership of Local Governments, by facilitating organisation of poor for combining self help with demand led convergence of available services and resources to tackle the multiple dimensions and manifestation of poverty holistically".

Identification of the poor is one of the prime requisites for the implementation of the projects. The following risk factors are considered for identifying the poor.

(1) No Land/Less than 5 cents of Land
(2) No house/Dilapidated House
(3) No Sanitary Latrine
(4) No access to safe drinking water within 150 meters
(5) Women headed house hold/Presence of a widow, divorcee/abandoned lady/unwed mother
(6) No regularly employed person in the family
(7) Socially disadvantaged groups (SC/ST)
(8) Presence of Mentally or physically challenged person / Chronically ill member in the family
(9) Families without colour TV

If four or more of the above risk factors are positive in a family, such a family is treated as a 'risk family'. If all the nine risk indices are in favour of a family that family may be in a most vulnerable situation.

The Structure: For effective convergence of the programme, a three tier Community Based Organisation (CBO) is in action. The lowest tier constitutes the Neighbourhood Group consisting of 20-40 women members selected from economically backward families. Meetings are convened on a weekly basis in the houses of NHG members. In the weekly meeting all members bring their thrift, which will be collected and recycled, to the system by way of sanctioning loans. Micro plans for addressing poverty issues are also prepared after taking stock of the situation. In each Neighborhood Group from among the poor women Five Volunteers are selected for undertaking various functional activities.

(1) Community Health Volunteer (2) Income generation activities volunteer (IGA) (3) Infrastructure Volunteer (4) Secretary (5) President.

The Neighbourhood groups (NHG) are coordinated at ward level through Area Development Society (ADS) by federating 8 to 10 NHGs. To coordinate the activities at the panchayat level there is the apex body called Community Development Society (CDS), which is heading the Area Development Societies.

Fig. 1

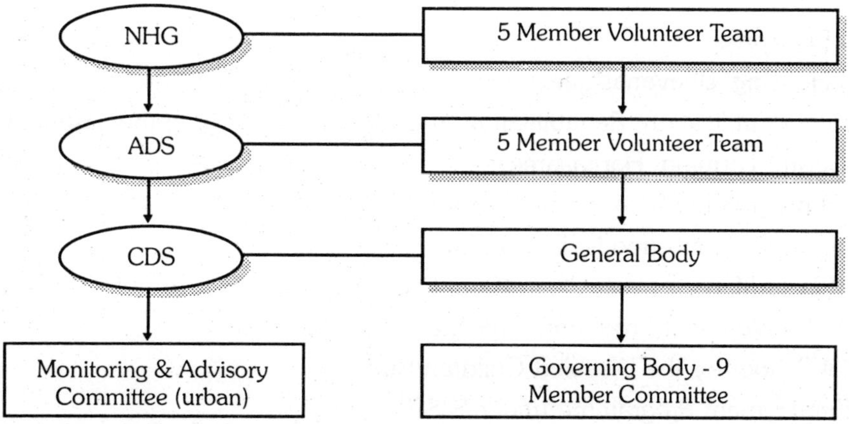

Source: www.kudumbasree.org

The CBOs are the lifeblood of Kudumbashree. The NHG members used to meet once in a week in one of the members house. The members who meet together discuss their problems and make joint efforts to find solutions to their grievances with the support of their functional volunteers. This would bring up interpersonal feelings among the members and would generate supportive attitude to build confidence in them. Apart from this, they practice small savings through thrift which should be used to create productive assets. The 'micro plans' are prepared at the NHG meetings and formulated plans would be sent to ADS for scrutiny and finalization to form the mini plan. After consolidating the mini plans by judicious prioritization at the CDS meeting a 'sub-plan is formed to become the anti poverty programme of the Local Self Government. The formulation of micro, mini, sub plans helps facilitate the poor women households to participate in planning process as a major stake holder.

The Strategies: Kudumbashree aims at empowerment of women to become the active leaders rather than passive recipients. The strategies are as follows :

(a) Formation of women collectives
(b) Information and training
(c) Skill up gradation
(d) Thrift-Credit operations
(e) Infrastructure development
(f) Micro enterprises development
(g) Power to the people, and
(h) Leadership

The ultimate objective, therefore, sets as **'reaching out family through women, and reaching out community through family.'**

THE PROGRAMMES UNDER OPERATIONS

The programmes conceived as a part of the strategy to reduce poverty are:

- Microfinance operations/Thrift and Credit Societies
- Micro Enterprises
- Micro Housing/ Bhavanashree
- Destitute Identification, Rehabilitation and Monitoring Programme /Ashraya
- Lease Land Farming/ Haritashree
- The S3 programme
- Children's Neighbourhoods /Balasabha
- Solid Waste Management /Clean Keral Business
- Special Employment Programme for the Educated Youth
- Special School for the Disabled Children/Buds
- Self Employment Programme under SJSRY
- GRQ Project

(1) Microfinance Operations: Thrift and Credit Societies are set up at Neighbourhood (NHG) level to facilitate the poor and to avail easy credits, which have now grown up to Informal Banks of the poor women at their doorsteps. The Thrift and Credit Societies are formed with the objective of encouraging the poor women to save their meagre means to widen the resource base of the NHGs. Women bring their little bit of savings when they come to attend the group meetings. This money is entrusted to the Community Volunteer, who in turn deposits it in the nearest bank. Each member is given an individual pass book. The Thrift and Credit Societies are considered as poor women's bank. Members can avail loans to meet their urgent needs like medical treatment, purchase of school books and uniforms for children, to pay off their old debts, etc. It is interesting to note that more than 90% of the savings in the thrift societies are given away as loans. It is observed that 100% repayments are ensured which are rare in banking history. The Thrift and Credit Societies becomes the largest informal bank in Asia. Most of the Thrift and Credit Societies are capable of providing financial assistance to income generating activities.

(2) Micro Enterprises: Micro Enterprises foster the economic status of women as an effective means to eradicate poverty. The income generating activities under individual and group initiatives to meet the livelihoods of the poor women are massively promoted. Canteens/ Catering units, IT units, Amrtum Food Supplement, Santwanam (home nurse training), Group farming units, Fruit Processing units, Footwear units, Condiments units, Umbrella units, Building materials units, Horticulture units, Electronics units, Readymade garments units, Soap powder units, Toys units, Grocery shops, are some of the examples of Micro Enterprises that are undertaken by poor women under Kudumbashree Mission. Women entrepreneurs are given training in entrepreneurship development, skill development, project management, and performance improvement by the Entrepreneurship Development Institute of India, Ahmedabad.

It is stated that empowerment of women is the prime motto of Kudumbashree. Therefore, the decision making power must rest solely in the hands of the poor women. In order to exercise this power, they need proper orientation and training. To achieve this objective a number of specially designed training programmes are being conducted with focus on community structures, leadership, roles and responsibilities, thrift and credit operation, community financial management and accounting. These training programmes are organized with the support of UNICEF, NABARD and other institutions. More than one lakh women have been trained so far.

Kudumbashree has started the extensive programme **"Samagra"** which looks at creating Local Production Marketing Networks, systematizing procurement mechanisms providing better technology and management options and improving product quality by establishing production protocols.

(3) Micro Housing/ Bhavanashree: Under this programme poor families, who are in dire need of constructing new houses are able to avail loans from banks and the repayment of which is ensured by tri-party agreement between the beneficiaries, the Community Development Societies and the Financial institutions/Banks. 19,922 houses were constructed by using credit amounting to Rs.6765.91 lakhs.

(4) The Destitute Identification, Rehabilitation and Monitoring Programme / Ashraya: This programme named as "Ashraya" in local language (meaning 'depending') aims at uplifting the poorest of the poor from their destitution. Poorest of the poor families, which lack adequate food, drinking water, shelter, educational facilities for children, sanitation facilities, and employment opportunities land for shelter, and worst sufferers of illness and chronic diseases are identified and rehabilitated under various schemes. The programme launched in 391 Village Panchayats and 6 Municipalities.

(5) Lease Land Farming/Haritashree: Lease Land Farming Programme, named 'Harithashree' in local language, lends helping hands to those cultivators who are having no land at all. So Kudumbashree pools uncultivated lands on rent and provide the willing cultivators for agricultural operations.

(6) The S3 Programme: The projects focus on self sufficiency, self reliance and sustainability (S3) of the village panchayats. The project envisages to address the problems of Child Development, Geriatric care, Mentally and Physically Challenged, Education, Adolescent care, women Empowerment, Enterprise development, Unemployment of the educated youth, Agriculture/Animal husbandry/ Dairy development, Revamping the traditional sectors Basic minimum Needs and Destitute Identification and Rehabilitation. Initially the programme was piloted in three panchayats viz., Venganoor in Trivandrum district, Kodakara in Trichur district and Munniyoor in Malappuram district. Later on, the programme extended to other panchayats.

(7) Children's Neighbourhoods /Balasabha: The children from poor families are organized to develop their intellectual faculties by performing cultural activities from time to time. Termed as Balasabhas in local language it functions as a platform of the children to help develop their overall capabilities that combine education, entertainment and empowerment.

(8) Solid Waste Management /Clean Kerala Business: Solid waste is serious menace for all the urban and semi urban areas of Kerala. Now Kudumbashree mission tries to tackle this problem by setting up 'Clean Kerala Business' units in an organized and planned manner entrusting to women entrepreneur groups to segregate, collect and transport solid waste from the households, commercial establishments, hotels, etc..

(9) Special School for the disabled children / Buds: Special Schools, called 'Buds', are set up aiming at providing for the developmental, social, and emotional needs of the disabled children. These children are being provided with the necessary medical attention, physical and mental therapy, mobility equipments, hearing aids, and vocational and educational training.

(10) Self Employment Programmes under SJSRY: Swarna Jayanthi Sahari Rozgar Yojana (SJSRY) is an anti poverty programme launched by the Government of India and is meant for the urban areas of the state. It covers the 53 Municipalities and 5 Corporations. Individual enterprises and Group enterprises with a minimum number of 10 persons can be set up. 1365 group and 15382 enterprises are undertaken under this programme.

(11) GRQ (Goat-Rabbit-Quail) Project: The Goat-Rabbit-Quail Project is a unique micro enterprises project for rearing the three species together to earn a steady income to the family entrepreneurs. The predominantly non-vegetarian population of Kerala necessarily ensures the potential market for the produce.

(12) Nutrimix- The Babyfood Products Production Project: The Nutrimix Babyfood Production Project is an ambitious project recently launched by the Kudumbashree mission. The Project envisaged to start 500 baby food production units in different parts of Kerala. 21 Nutrimix production units have already been started. It is estimated that 2500 women can find gainful employment through the programme, which targets the massive baby food market dominated by big brands. The expected turnover is Rs. 200 crore per annum.

ACHIEVEMENTS AT GLANCE

- Kudumbashree programme covers all the 999 gram panchayats, 53 muncipalities and 5 corporations.
- 180660 NHGs comprising of women from 37, 77,783 families have been formed.
- Thrift of Rs. 844.37 cr. and internal lending amounting Rs. 2139.07 Cr.
- Several awards from regional to international.
- 2552 Groups and 972 Individual enterprises started under Rural Micro enterprise 13.48 Cr. was as given.
- 845 Groups and 240 individual innovative enterprises started under Yuvashree (50K) programme for youth in 18-35 age group, grants worth Rs. 2.07 Cr.
- Poor women have become active participants in the planning and implementation process of various anti-poverty programmes.
- Started 118 Vidyashree units under IT @ School Programme.
- Cluster Development Programme with the support of Industries Department.
- Multipurpose job clubs formed with the financial support of SC Development Department.
- Loan linked Micro Housing scheme launched with the support of Banks.

THE CHALLENGES AND THREATS

The study raises certain issues.

- Indebtedness is very high.
- The severely poor have comparatively a lower repayment rate as compared with the moderate poor. This evidence shows that severity of poverty was not a significant factor to explain repayment behavior of households under kudumbashree programme.
- The repayment record of those households who attend group meetings regularly is better than those with irregular attendance.
- NHG members are often found to be members of other microfinance programs as well.
- A major threat is multiple memberships.
- Cross borrowing situation could lead to a high repayment of their borrowings with the kudumbashree programme. However, by availing cross financing, the financial indebtedness only worsens.
- Politicization of Micro Finance movement: - In Kerala, the banks are advised (i.e. directed) to provide credit linkage to Janasree SHGs supported by the ruling party at the centre. Janasree is a parallel programme to the widely known, decade-old Kudumbasree, involving women below the poverty line. Kudumbasree is supported by the Left. It is feared that Janasree will break the financial discipline of microfinance in the state.

CONCLUSION

In the early decades of planning problems of women were looked upon as problems of social welfare, rather than of development. The drawback of the welfare approach was that it did nothing to eliminate the social discrimination against and subordination of women. The empowerment approach is the most recent and is aimed at empowering women through greater self-reliance and internal strength.

The formation of 1,80,660 NHGs of the women from 37, 77,783 risk families and developing various enterprises is no doubt a commendable achievement within a span of 12 years.

Kudumbashree becomes lifeline to many poor women in the state of Kerala. Women who were regarded as voiceless and powerless started identifying their inner power, their strength, opportunities for growth, and their role in reshaping their own destiny. The process of empowerment becomes the beacon light to their children, their families and to society at large.

Kudumbashree presents a unique model of participatory development, which has gained national and international acclaim as an ideal and workable model. A new ray of hope to the women to identify herself as a part of economic development progrmmes is found emerging in God's own country.

BIBLIOGRAPHY

Books:

- Daniel Lazer, Professor P.Palanichamy (2008). Micro Finance and Poverty Eradication: Indian and Global Experiences, Pondicherry University, Pondicherry in association with New Century Publications, New Delhi. Pg: 594-606.
- Ganesh Murthy V.S. (2007), India: Economic Empowerment of Women, New Century Publications, New Delhi.
- Khatri D.S. (2009), Women Empowerment in India, Alp Books, New Delhi.
- Krishnamoorthy G.R., Singh Awadesh Kumar in association with Ananya Institute of Development Research and social Action, Lucknow (2007), serials Publications, New Delhi.
- Misra Kamal K., Janet Huber Lowry (2007), Recent studies on Indian Women- Empirical work of social scientists, Rawat Publications, New Delhi, pg. 302-323.
- M. Ravichandran, Revathy Bala (2008), Rural Credit; Access, Uses and Repayment, Abhijeet Publications, New Delhi, pg. 21.
- Narasaih M. Lakshmi (2008), Micro credit and women, Discovery Publishing House, New Delhi.
- Oommen, M. A. (1999), the community development society of Kerala. New Delhi: Institute of Social Sciences.
- Pandya Rameshwari (2008) Women Welfare and Empowerment in India- Vision for the 21st Centuary, New Centuary Publications, New Delhi.
- Pramanik Rabindra Nath (2006), Gender Inequality and Women's Empowerment, Abhijeet publications, New Delhi, pg. 170-180.
- Robinson, M. (2001). The microfinance revolution: Sustainable finance for the poor. World Bank.
- Satya Sundaram, Micro Finance in India (2007): B.R. Publishing House, New Delhi.

- Singh Ravishankar Kumar (2005) Poverty and Sustainable Development, Third world perspectives (vol.I), Abhijeet Publications, Delhi, Pg. 629-643.
- V. Girija Devi, Empowerment of women in Kerala: A Case study. Women Welfare and empowerment in India (2008), New Century Publications, New Delhi. Pg. 307-321.

Journals and Reports:

- Anand, Jaya S,(1999), "Self-Help Groups in Empowering Women: A Study of selected SHGs and NHGs in Kerala", KKRPLLD, Centre for Development Studies, Trivandrum, Kerala, India.
- D. Ajit. R. Sunil, K. Ravi Raman (2008), Micro Credit Repayment Rates: A Case study of Kudumbashree Micro enterprise programme in Kerala.
- Edward Manoj, Zakkariya K.A., Relavance of social marketing in Kudumabashree (2007), International Marketing conference on Marketing and Society, Research papers Part I.
- J. Devika, Binitha V Thampi (2007), Between Empowerment and Liberation: The Kudumbashree initiative in Kerala; Indian Journal of Gender Studies, Vol. 14, Pg. No. 1, 33-60.
- Kudumbashree. 2001. Annual report 1999-2000. Thiruvananthapuram, Kerala, India.
- Suneetha Kadiyala (2003) Scaling up Kudumbashree in Kerala, FCND Discussion Paper No. 180.s, **FCND,** Washington.
- Siwal B.R. A Case study of Kudumbashree Programme of Kerala, National Institute of Public Cooperation and Child Development, New Delhi.
- World Bank Reports (1995, 1998), World Bank Publications.

Web links:

- www.kudumbasree.org
- www.kudumbasree.sarovar.org

☆ ☆ ☆

3 Women Empowerment through SHG: A Case Study of Savitribai Phule Mahila Ekatma Samaj Mandal, Aurangabad

"A woman is the full circle.
Within her is the power to create, nurture and transform."
The most common way people give up their power is by thinking they don't have any.

Empowerment refers to increasing the spiritual, political, social or economic strength of individuals and communities. It often means the empowered developing confidence in their own capabilities.

Empowerment is probably the totality of the following or similar capabilities:

- having decision-making power of their own
- having access to information and resources for taking proper decision
- having a range of options from which you can make choices (not just yes/no, either/or)
- ability to exercise assertiveness in collective decision making
- having positive thinking on the ability to make change
- ability to learn skills for improving one's personal or group power
- ability to change others' perceptions by democratic means
- involving in the growth process and changes that is never ending and self initiated
- increasing one's positive self-image and overcoming stigma

One empowerment strategy is to assist marginalized people to create their own non-profit organization, using the rationale that only the marginalized people, themselves, can know what their own people need most.

A review of government's various programmes for women empowerment such as Swashakti, Swayamsidha, Streeshakti, Balika samrudhi yojana and other projects reveal that little has been done or achieved through these programmes. The discrepancy in the ideology and practice of the empowerment policy of women in India constitutes its continued economic and social backwardness.

Empowerment would become more relevant if women are educated, better informed and can take rational decisions. It is also necessary to sensitize the other sex towards women. It is important to usher in changes in societal attitudes and perceptions with regard to the role of women in different spheres of life. Adjustments have to be made in traditional gender specific performance of tasks. A woman needs to be physically healthy so that she is able to take challenges of equality.

OBJECTIVES OF THE STUDY

(1) To study the concept 'S.H.G', its functions and benefits

(2) To present a case study of 'Savitribai Phule Mahila Ekatma Samaj Mandal', Aurangabad, and its contribution in empowering the women of Aurangabad.

SOURCES OF DATA COLLECTION

The data has been collected from secondary sources such as reference books and journals, whereas primary data is collected through the interview method.

INITIATIVES FOR WOMEN EMPOWERMENT AT GOVERNMENT LEVEL

The Government of India had ushered in the new millennium by declaring the year 2001 as 'Women's Empowerment Year' to focus on a vision 'where women are equal partners with men'. The most common explanation of 'women's empowerment' is the ability to exercise full control over one's actions. The last decades have witnessed some basic changes in the status and role of women in our society. There has been a shift in policy approaches from the concept of 'welfare' in the seventies of the previous century, to 'development' in the eighties of the previous century, and now to 'empowerment' in the nineties of the previous century. This process has been further accelerated with some sections of women becoming increasingly self-conscious of their discrimination in several areas of family and public life. They are also in a position to mobilize themselves on issues that can affect their overall position.

Empowerment of women has been one of the primary objectives of the ninth five year plan. The National policy document on empowerment of women released in 2001 aims at creation of enabling environment for women through economic and social policies, active protection of women's rights, equal access to decision making and many more. The department of women and child development has initiated many programmes and schemes aimed at holistic empowerment of women through awareness generation and economic empowerment. Multi tiered institutional structure has been created to take care of the operational aspects of various schemes such as 'Swayam Siddha Yojana, Indira Mahila Yojana, Mahila Samruddhi Yojana etc. The S.H.G group is one such programme which contributes to the economic and social empowerment of women below the poverty line.

ORIGIN OF THE S.H.G

Professor Mohammed Yunus of Chittagong University, Bangladesh founded the Gramin Bank, Bangladesh in 1975 where he mobilized poor women, and through the formation of S. H. G. made them self reliant. This novel experiment won him several prestigious awards, including the Nobel Peace Prize. 100% success rate of this experiment in Bangladesh inspired many developing countries to replicate the same. India too adopted the concept for both, the urban and the rural poor.

WHAT IS S.H.G?

Self Help Groups—also called mutual help or mutual aid groups—are composed of peers who share a similar mental, emotional, or physical problem, or who are interested in a focal issue, such as education or parenting. Historically, people bonded together to improve their chances for survival, by pooling their social and economic resources; however, contemporary groups are more likely to organize around a theme or problem.

Most self-help groups are voluntary, non-profit associations open to anyone with a similar need or interest; however, spin-off groups also exist to meet the needs of particular types of people. For example, the elderly, women etc. Usually, groups are led by peers, have an informal structure, and are free (except for small donations to cover meeting expenses).

SHG is a group of rural poor who have volunteered to organize themselves into a group for eradication of poverty of the members. They agree to save regularly and pool their savings into a common fund known as the Group Corpus through a common management. Generally a self-help group consists of 10 to 20 persons.

Generally all members of the group belong to families below the poverty line. This may also include the families of occupational groups like agricultural laborers, farmers and artisans marginally above the poverty line, or who may have been excluded from the BPL list to become members of the Self Help Group.

The group devises a code of conduct (Group management norms) to bind itself. This is in the form of regular meetings (weekly or fortnightly), functioning in a democratic manner, allowing free exchange of views, participation by the members in the decision making process. The group needs to draw up an agenda for each meeting and take up discussions as per the agenda.

The members build their corpus through regular savings. The group collects the minimum voluntary saving amount from all the members regularly in the group meetings. The savings so collected will be the group corpus fund. The group corpus fund is then used to advance loans to the members. The group develops financial management norms covering the loan sanction procedure, repayment schedule and interest rates. The group operates a group account, preferably in their service area bank branch, so as to deposit the balance amounts left with the groups after disbursing loans to its members It also maintains simple basic records such as minutes book, attendance register, loan ledger, general ledger, cash book, bank passbook and individual passbooks.

INSTITUTIONAL SUPPORT FOR S.H.G

Efforts are also made to develop linkages between different self help groups and lending institutions to ensure continued access to credit facilities. District Rural Development Authority (DRDA) and National Agricultural And Rural Development Bank (NABARD) are designated as nodal agencies which monitor S.H.G programme under 'Swarna Jayanti Gram Swaraj Yojana' started in the beginning of the 21st century. A four tier structure is created as follows-

Fig. 1
Institutional Structure for financial help to SHG

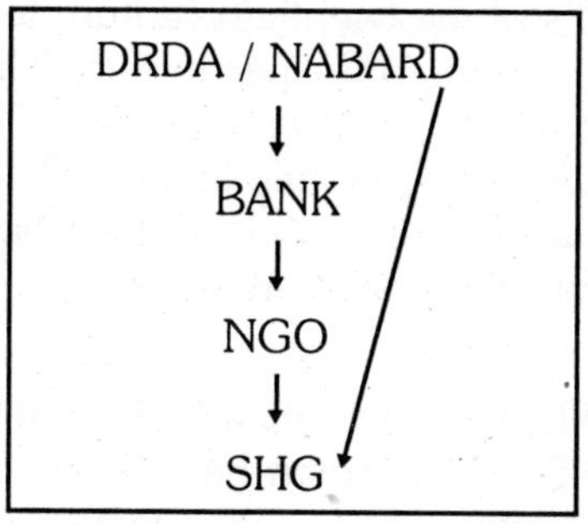

Collectively, S.H.G's can also approach banks through registered N.G.Os for availing additional loan facilities at very nominal rate of interest. They are also required to open cash credit account in the bank. The S.H.G has to go through first gradation after six months of opening the account where all documents are checked. This audit is done jointly by the bank and the N.G.O. After the gradation a proposal has to be sent to DRDA /NABARD for revolving fund facility which is released on the basis of balance in the Bank account (4 times bank balance). This fund may be utilized to meet the personal needs of the members. A second round of gradation is conducted after 6 months which qualifies the S.H.G for additional loan at nominal interest rate.

BENEFITS OF S.H.G

S.H.Gs in India have greatly benefited in terms of financial aid from banks. Easy accessibility to bank loans has helped rural people in their agricultural activities such as poultry, cattle rearing as well as in other small scale activities like tailoring, handicraft, grocery etc. Access to information, awareness about various government schemes etc. has led to the increased participation of the people in such programmes. Literacy training, health and nutrition, family planning and many such social programmes run by N.G.Os have helped to improve the quality of life of rural women. Regular meetings of S.H.G members have witnessed participation by rural women in local body governance which has made them politically aware. S.H.G also acts as a pressure group against social evils such as domestic violence, female infanticide, liquor etc.

A CASE STUDY OF SAVITRIBAI PHULE MAHILA EKATMA SAMAJ MANDAL, AURANGABAD

Aurangabad, a city in Maharashtra, is known for its rich cultural heritage as well as social engineering. A small group of doctors started Dr. Hedgewar Hospital in 1998 under Dr.Balasaheb Ambedkar Vaidyakiya Pratishthan. This was used as a 'nucleus' of social change by addressing the needs of both, the urban and the rural poor. Primary health care centers, with excellent health care facilities, too were started by these doctors at Milind Nagar, Mukund Nagar, Brijwadi urban Slums in the city and Khamkheda, Ambegaon, Pophala villages in the interior parts of Aurangabad. The outreach programme of primary health extended its ambit under the N.G.O trust 'Savitribai Phule Mahila Ekatma Samaj Mandal'. The trust has identified women and children as their core target because through them, they believe, they could make a difference to more people in society. Various social initiatives like adult education programme for women, training in vocational skills, Kishori Vikas Prakalpa for adolescent girls, family planning, and health camps were taken up, of which S.H.G is one successful programme.

S.H.G.s started in the late 90's of the twentieth century with a group of women who started saving anywhere between Rs 10/- to Rs. 100/- per month. The money is pooled and is lent to group members to start a business or to meet emergencies. The rate of interest is 5% which is nominal as compared to 10% charged by money lenders. The women themselves manage the group, write accounts, hold regular elections to elect office bearers and help in recovery. Many women have started their own business such as tailoring, making masala and chilli powder, selling crackers, fertilizers and grocery etc.

Till December 2008, 248 S.H.Gs were formed with total participation of 3600 women and a total turnover of Rs. 1,14,00,000. 453 women have started their own business in the last 10 years. Out of the 248 groups, 100 groups have taken loans from NABARD. These women meet every week to take stock and decide who should be given loan. The meetings also give a chance to discuss family as well as social issues, sing songs, read books and share stories they may have heard or read. The meetings are generally witnessed by social workers who speak on various socially relevant topics.

Successful implementation of S.H.G has given enormous amount of self confidence to these women and has made them self reliant. Since the money is contributed by all the members there is enormous moral pressure on the borrower to repay on time. As a result there are virtually zero defaulters.

Ratan Tata, Chairman, Tata Group, had visited the gathering of S H G women held in 2002. He was amazed with the magnitude of work of these groups with nearly 100% recovery rate and several success stories of self made women members of S H G.

CONCLUSION

The battle for gender justice has been a long drawn struggle. Throughout history, women have collectively struggled against direct and indirect barriers to their self development and their full social, political, economic and educational participation. To bring reforms in these fields, there is need for certain attitudinal changes that comprise change of contracts, change of relations and change of values. Government is making deliberate, planned and sustained efforts for women emancipation and empowerment. Steps taken so far are laudable, no doubt, but not sufficient. The creation of S.H.G. has given great impetus to this movement and the belief that when you empower a man, you empower an individual, but when you empower a woman, you empower a family and society, has been vindicated.

BIBLIOGRAPHY

- K. Shanti; "Empowerment of Women", New Delhi, Anmol Publication, 1998.
- C.Gnanapragasam; "Good Governance and Women Empowerment", New Delhi, Abhijeet Publications, 2009.
- Ganihar Noorjehan and Begum Shahtag; "Gender Issues and Women Empowerment", New Delhi, Discovery Publishing House, 2007.
- Internet Sources.

☆ ☆ ☆

4 The Women in the Agrarian Society as seen in the Agricultural Folksongs of Central Kerala

Folksongs are a fertile area of research and discussion since they reflect the social and cultural organization of the group which create them. These songs are handed down orally from generation to generation. Folksongs in general are expression of emotions that do not find an outlet in any other form either due to social restriction or due to personal inhibition. They articulate discontent with issues such as casteism, sexism, economic exploitation and so on. There is a dire need to preserve these songs as they are in danger of becoming extinct.

Central Kerala is a region where agriculture is the primary occupation. It is a highland- the top soil has rocky pebbles and the bottom soil is laterite. This is highly suitable for agriculture. The Kuttanad area of Central Kerala is known as the rice bowl of Kerala. Therefore it has a rich tradition of agricultural folksongs. My presentation aims to analyze the women in the agricultural folksongs of Central Kerala.

The agricultural labourers are drawn from the Pulayar and Parayar castes- the backward communities in Kerala. The word *Pulaya* etymologically has two meanings:*pulam* means the paddy field: *Pulaya,* therefore, means man of the field. (Vishnunamboodiri 35). The important tasks performed by the women were transplanting, field levelling, weeding and harvesting, while the men helped in bund construction and repairing, ploughing, sowing, applying fertilizers, pesticides, and tilling. However, these communities did not own the land they worked on. This was a privilege reserved for the upper castes the Namboothiris and the Nairs. Agricultural activity thus brought the upper castes and the lower castes into close contact. Power relations were played out while engaging in agricultural tasks and often these communities negotiated these relations with each other through agricultural folksongs.

The primary source of my presentation has been the songs collected from various agricultural workers, all women, both composers and performers.

Most often the composer herself sings the songs while a group of women, the performers join her in the refrain. The songs were recorded on audio and video either while they were being sung by the women in the field, on request, or from professionals who give performances. These songs were transcribed, translated and analysed from various perspectives. Through these songs the composer of these songs, the Pulayar and Parayar women gives expression to her experience of struggle and toil. These songs are not merely a genre, but a way of life.

Nowadays, these songs are sung in professional performances rather than in agricultural fields. Today, the women do not sing these songs while they are working because the worker's union prevent them from doing so. They believe that the labourers work more when they sing and do not approve of it.

As the Kerala society was principally and primarily agricultural, the peasant folks tended to be tied to agricultural work and were knotted to the agricultural situation. They evoked and reminded the specifics of their unsung past- their unmolested antiquity and their ancient, tranquil existence through these folksongs. These songs helped the singer to enjoy relaxation in work, as also respite, and while engaged in physical tasks have made for the diminution of strain.

Central Kerala has various categories of agricultural folksongs. In a society called upon to express its energies in the cultivation of field and fallow, these songs have become a pattern among the labouring folks who are oppressed, suppressed and repressed at every turn. The Pulayar and Parayar communities are the ones who have supplied physical labour for the landlords and these communities, by allowing themselves to be subjugated, have strengthened these system of oppression. These women in addition to working in the fields of their landlords also performed certain household chores such as washing the clothes and cleaning the utensils. Commenting on the grave injustice meted out to these women, Thangamma, one of the singers states that it was the custom that these women had to submit themselves to their husband's landlord and spend the first few days with him. Only then is she allowed to begin her connubial life with her husband. Sometimes beautiful women married to *Pulayar* or *Parayar* were taken away by their landlords and kept as mistresses. This view is also echoed by Pallath stating that the feudal system barred the *Pulayar* and *Parayar f*rom owning landed property or even venturing into any form of productive economic activity. The sole exception of a *Pulayan* being found in possession of property is when he receives in exchange for a beautiful woman:

...surprisingly a few *Pulayas* possess ancestral property. On inquiry, they said that it was the gift from landlord in exchange for beautiful *Pulaya* girls they had taken as their mistresses. (Pallath 40).

My paper attempts at a close study of the agricultural folksongs of Central Kerala to show that the Pulyar and Parayar women enjoyed more domestic and economic freedom than their upper caste counterparts, the Namboothiri and Nair women.

The folksong furnished below has reference to land and the women:

Flourish, flourish, flourish, flourish

Land must flourish, world must flourish

Thatched roofing flourish, threshold flourish

Just like the prime of sweet sixteen,

Thatched roofing flourish.

When thirty three trees were planted

Only three fruit yielding trees blossomed

Flowers of that tree is in my head.

"Turn away, turn away, Pulayan, make way

Thickets thither and thorns hither.

How am I to head the way?

I have children in my arms

And a toddy pitcher on my head

How am I to board the boat thither

Unless it come hither.

Didn't you break the coconut we gave?

Didn't you see the kernel and the contents?

When you are poked, it is the same blood

When we are poked, it is the same blood

Then why speak of caste superiority?

Why talk of caste and untouchability.

The burden of the above transplantation song is such that it evokes deep impressions of the oppressed past of the Pulayar women folk. This harks back to a time when the arrogant and adamant ruling class had more or less stifled the aspirations of the poor and the humble women folk of Central Kerala. The song is a reminder of the agonies palmed on the poor women folk by the demeaning, landlords. These dark women express the state of their day to day living by stating how they plod wearily forward with child in arm and a pot of toddy on the shoulder. The refrain in this song is how, despite molestation, the poor folks have necessarily lived a restrained life within the limits prescribed by the upper caste people. It is the upper most sentiment of the women folk that they must surge ahead towards a golden era of hope and fulfilled dreams, and that everything should be subordinated to a splendid future. The song attests to an elevated sense of happiness, when there will be no demarcation of the rich and the poor, the strong and the weak. The song hints strongly at the isolation and insulation of one community from others, and the social practice of untouchables is traceable to the mannerism of the puffed up landlords and upper-class representatives.

Thus the theme relates with poignant relevance the burning issue of caste discrimination and caste distinction. This song is a clarion call for change. The refrain of 'Flourish, flourish, flourish" is almost a catchword in the subject of discussion. It is a call for the flourish of the land and the world around. There is a prophetic hint that there should be a renewal and transformation of everything around in particularly radical charges in the thinking of all.

A woman labourer's life is brought into clear focus in the following agricultural folksong of Central Kerala. The stubborn difficulties of the neglected and socially downgraded Pulayar and Parayar and their difficult circumstances are highlighted and narrated. The song given below recaptures the precariousness of the existence of the Pulayar and Parayar as was found roughly a century ago :

O God, listen.

To this groan of agony

Cut forest to walk-made hut to make it a house

After six days of its birth the mother

Lay the baby under the tree

With the ox and the buffalo

Which is tied together for land ploughing

On return when she sees

The baby has been worn to death by the red ants

O God,Listen

To this groan of agony

The toiling masses are painted here as lacking even a protective roof or wall for the just born child who is bitten to death by ants for it was consigned to the inhospitable shade of a spreading tree. This unceremonious act of leaving the child to a natural berth under a tree shows the isolated situation of a mother who has brought forth a child and, with little respite after delivery, is seen toiling under the hot sun, with the child of a very tender age laid aside to rest. This is the groan of agony of a young mother who has lost her child. Thangamma, the agricultural folksong singer also recalls this degraded situation where she used to lay her children in the pits made in the field and work from dawn to dusk.

There were times when the mother had to abjure even feeding the baby as she would be reprimanded and denied adequate daily wages by the masters. The 'groan of agony' is evocative of various nuances of meaning such as a cry for protection, call for mercy, voice in protest against the ruthless exploitation and perhaps also the groan of a mother seeing her child dead.

When we review and critique themes of agricultural songs, composed by Pulayar and Parawar women, we are struck at once by what they reveal. The woman as pictured in them is a figure of resolute resistance against the fickle conduct of her master. She appears not only brave but also formidable in guarding her virginity. They are also characterized as being dutiful servants to their masters.

Incursions into the privacy and personal morality of the representative Nili girl is recorded in the following agricultural folksong as the burden of the song which is also the burden of her life:

"nîli girl nîli girl where are you going?"

"To reap the firstlings, young master"

"How thirsty I am due to the scorching sun"

"Give me some water that you had drawn from the well"

"The drawn water is not stored, young master"

"Receptacle and the rope have gone into the well"

"Give me a firebrand"

"Let me light my cigarette as a pass time"

"Even the firebrand has been extinguished, young master"

"Where has your father Pulayan gone?"

"To the hilly field to harvest young master"

"The young master sought a rupee currency from his pocket"

"The young master sought a rupee currency from his pocket"

"Slowly, slowly he stretched the currency note"

"Nîli girl being indignant thus said"

"The harvest sickle is in my hand, flee for your life"

This song records the sexual exploitation of the Pulayar and Parayar women by men of the upper castes. The young master is engaged in an exchange of words with the Nili girl. She is described as the possessor of strong moral values and also a high sense of honour. The young master makes sexual overtures to this young girl. Far from willing and withering under pressure, she adheres to a high sense of ethical conduct. She threatens the young master with dire consequences brandishing the harvest sickle.

The following folksong depicts the pleasant and joyous times that are dreamt of by the peasants:

Golden flower season

From your pretty lips

Why doesn't music rain down, O Cutie!

Golden flower season

When yonder eastern hills blossom from behind the horizon

Tears wiping hand in which first stocks dance

Bashful girl, I will sing rapturously about

Our land of birth

To the accompaniment of musical instruments

And rhythmic heartbeat

Sing beautifully, O you parrot

Day will dawn on the land

Why doesn't music rain down?

O, Cutie of the earth

What is striking about this agricultural song is its wealth of figurative expressions. It is noted that in most of the songs Land and Nature are closely related to women. The phrase 'golden flower season' is evocative of a rich and radiant comparison to a pretty maid.

The Pulayar and Parayar were not accustomed to the scriptural, civic forms of worship. The lower castes were denied entry into the temple porches and access to scriptures, and any well-meaning contact with their counterparts or compatriots. They, therefore, sought and obtained a tangible contact with the oldness and earthiness of the earth. They worshipped their ancestors, the Earth which mothered them and the Sky.

As the Pulayar and Parayar were engaged in agriculture, they were closely related to the soil and believed that the Earth was their mother (female) who paired with the Sky (male) and gave a rich abundance of crop. The evolution of this idea took the form of an all-embracing relationship with nature and its essential substance. They honoured the bounteous Mother Earth and invested it with sanctity and perennial meaning. The Pulayar and Parayar women came to be regarded by their men folk with an energy and fertility attaining higher nodes of consciousness. This investiture of a Mother is the one which has led to the exaltation in Hindu scriptures of Bhooma Devi and has also accounted for the Pulayar and Parayar communities clothing their women with filial and spiritual piety.

These songs highlight the fact that Pulayar and Parayar women work assiduously and untiringly as the bread-winners for their homes with their husbands. This entitles them to a greater sense of freedom than the upper class women.

In one of the folksongs the speaker is a young girl from the upper caste society. This girl is in love with a man from a lower caste and suggests that they elope. Though as an upper caste woman she enjoys property rights, in reality she has little or no control over it. She plans to steal money from her uncle's treasure-chest. This folksong narrates a true incident that occurred many years ago. The eloped couple was traced and brought back home by the girl's uncles, and she was married off to a boy from the upper caste society and her lover was beaten to death:

In the past, the Nayars lived in matrilineal joint families,known as taravads. The taravad comprised all the matrilineal descendents of a common ancestress and considering the suffocating conditions offered to the less fortunate members of the society, it will be seen, on closer scrutiny, that the poor though weighed down by cares, have nevertheless risen above the trammels of tradition. They exhibit a sense of moral and economic freedom. Though they are impoverished they are not stagnant, nor are they complacent. The woman in the agricultural folksongs of Central Kerala, worked alongside the men, and, as a result, had a reasonably free access to economic resources.As we see down the caste or class-scale, we find women enjoying a relatively higher degree of freedom,because women of lower strata are engaged in economically productive labour. (Vanamamalai 66-67)

Pursuing this line of argument we come at once to the conclusion that women of the lower stratum of society played a dominant role in social life by virtue of playing a greater part in economic activities. This higher degree of freedom is seen even in the Pulayar and Parayar women. An instructive example of these attitudinal differences of the peasant woman and higher caste woman is seen in one of the folk songs where it is interesting to review the situational basis of the attitudes of both the higher class woman and her counterpart, the peasant girl named Sita. The women belonging to the Nair community, it is widely believed, enjoy greater economic freedom because of the matrilineal inheritance system-are far from being economically independent. Praveena Kodoth cites studies, across the period between 1950 and 1994, which have discussed the inheritance practice and forms of property transfers. Studies have found that the *taravaad*, the ancestral house were inherited matrilineally, but sons and daughters inherited other property. She also records how though the taravaad was inherited matrilineally, the alienation of the house required the consent of all adult descendants of the land holder. She cites recent researches in Central Kerala which have shown that women continued to inherit a house but are less likely to receive agricultural land. (301)

Vanamamalai in his book Interpretation of *Tamil Folk Creations,* discusses the social stratification with special reference to the place of women :

The women of the lowest folk level, though economically poor, live a free life, because they have to work side by side with men and earn an independent income. They have the right of divorce and remarriage after dissolution of marriage or after the death of the husband. On the higher levels, the women are not so poor as their sisters in the last level, but are comparatively less free. Though chained by caste, sex, and caste-work rules, the women belonging to the last level of folk-life can challenge the restrictions to a limited extent.(72)

BIBLIOGRAPHY

- Altekar, A.S. The Position of Women in Hindu Civilizations. Delhi: Motilal Banarsidas, 1938.
- Eapen, Mridul and Kodoth, Praveena. 'Family Structure,Women's Education and Work'. New Delhi:Kali for Women, 2003.
- Pallath, JJ.Theyyam: An Analytical Study of the Folk Culture Wisdom and Personality. New Delhi:Indian Social Institute, 1995.
- Payyanad, Raghavan, Folklore. Calicut: Calicut Press, 1986.
- Vanamamalai, N. Interpretation of Tamil Folk Creation. Trivandrum: Dravidian Linguistics Association, 1981.

☆ ☆ ☆